Hello Professor

Hello
Professor

A Black Principal and

Professional Leadership

in the Segregated South

Vanessa Siddle Walker

with Ulysses Byas

THE UNIVERSITY OF NORTH CAROLINA PRESS

Chapel Hill

Set in Arnhem and The Sans
by Tseng Information Systems, Inc.
Manufactured in the United States of America

The paper in this book meets the guidelines for permanence
and durability of the Committee on Production Guidelines for
Book Longevity of the Council on Library Resources.

The University of North Carolina Press has been a member of
the Green Press Initiative since 2003.

Library of Congress Cataloging-in-Publication Data
Walker, Vanessa Siddle.
Hello professor : a black principal and professional leadership in the
segregated south / Vanessa Siddle Walker with Ulysses Byas.
    p. cm.
Includes bibliographical references and index.
ISBN 978-0-8078-3289-9 (cloth : alk. paper)
1. Byas, Ulysses. 2. African American school principals—
Georgia—Gainesville—Biography. 3. Public schools—Georgia—
Gainesville. 4. African American students—Georgia—Gainesville—Social
conditions. 5. Segregation in education—Georgia—Gainesville. 6. Racism
in education—Georgia—Gainesville. 7. Discrimination in education—
Georgia—Gainesville. 8. Gainesville (Ga.)—Race relations. 9. Gainesville
(Ga.)—Social conditions. 10. Gainesville (Ga.)—History—20th century.
I. Byas, Ulysses. II. Title.
LA2317.B795S57 2009
371.2′012092—dc22
[B]
2009006403

13 12 11 10 09   5 4 3 2 1

For all who would educate black children . . .

Contents

Table & Illustrations

Preface Me Speaks, Finally

Writing *Their Highest Potential: An African American School Community in the Segregated South* was one of the most tantalizing and rewarding activities of my professional life. The members of the school community who were constituents of Caswell County Training School (CCTS) in North Carolina invited me into a story of blacks in segregated schools that begged to be birthed. It challenged the dominant paradigm of black schools as defined solely by inequalities and unveiled a more resilient portrait of a school community crafting learning experiences for black children despite their segregated world. After the publication of *Their Highest Potential*, I imagined that no other story I would ever write would inspire my intellectual curiosity with the same drive to know.[1] And yet, I have found myself driven once more.

The voice of CCTS's respected principal, N. L. Dillard, whose early death deleted his perspective from the account of the school, has finally spoken. During data collection for *Their Highest Potential*, I wished for even one interview with him with such intensity that my subconscious mind would invoke his image and voice in my sleep. When I was subsequently introduced to another principal of a segregated school, one who appeared to have characteristics similar to those of the deceased N. L. Dillard of CCTS, I was captivated. Before me was the opportunity for the interview about which I had dreamed. Little did I realize the meeting would yield more than I could have imagined. Indeed, the conversation that followed precipitated the beginning of an unexpected journey.

On the day I first met this former principal, Dr. Ulysses Byas, we sat together on a wide front veranda and watched the shadows dance on his perfectly manicured lawn. I listened as he described the activities at the Fair Street High School, later rebuilt as E. E. Butler High School, where he had been principal in Gainesville, Georgia, and I mentally noted the ways these activities resonated with those of other segregated schools with which I was familiar. His students attended elaborate proms, received "Senior Class Advice" from their teachers, decorated homecoming floats, and experienced sweet victory and crushing defeat in athletic competitions. They worked on yearbook and newspaper staffs, attended regional press institutes, presented plays for fellow students and the community, and participated in a variety of clubs that reflected their interests and those of their faculty sponsors. As I later perused the yearbooks and school newspapers, the particular events of this school community were admittedly new, but the array of activities and the school climate were recognizable. Here was another school that nestled its students in a larger rubric where leadership, mission, teacher training, and parental involvement converged to support the development of black schools during segregation.[2] Although I did not know the actors in this particular school, descriptions of such schools were becoming increasingly familiar on the academic scene.[3]

However, some unnamed texture in the account, when chronicled by its leader, offered new perspectives, created intrigue, and compelled my repeated return to Macon. For many years I visited the home of Dr. Byas, always with a new set of questions. Each time, he talked, and I listened. Sometimes frowning, too often interrupting, I tried to make sense of the explanations he offered of school development and quizzed him repeatedly about his activities as a principal. I was searching for an explanation that would echo the story of segregated schools I knew. I was mistaken. The journey on which I was being taken rendered my understanding of black schools too simplistic. After repeated interviews, I finally realized I was not simply hearing an elaborated version of a story I knew. Rather, to my amazement, slowly surfacing from our conversations was a glimpse of an educational world heretofore veiled to me. Indeed, his story provided a comprehensive system of networked information dissemination that explained many of the events in this school but likely also explained the beliefs and activities of numerous black schools in disparate settings throughout the segregated South.

I continued to visit Dr. Byas's home in part because of his personality and stories but also because his personal library and document collection aroused my curiosity. With each visit, I was privy to a new stack of papers. Often during conversations he would swerve from his desk to retrieve additional records. The contrast between the ease with which he documented his descriptions and the difficulty I had encountered searching for materials for *Their Highest Potential* was striking. Unlike the methodological challenges confronted by myself and others who have sought to reconstruct the events of black segregated schools by triangulating multiple voices while relying on fragmentary archival sources, this principal had maintained an extensive document file that provided an insider view of his leadership activity. "Everything I say, I can back it up," he would unabashedly quip when my furrowed brow apparently invited the need for additional confirmation. As the years passed, I realized he was accurate in his description.

His collection includes, but is not limited to, school evaluation criteria, citywide school evaluation criteria, newspapers, yearbooks, teacher evaluation letters, student evaluation letters, and professional correspondence. In 2002, Randall Burkett, well-known Emory archivist specializing in black collections, visited Dr. Byas's home and assessed his collection. After reviewing the files, Burkett wrote in his summary memo: "He is EXTREMELY well-organized: Collection includes 10 filled 4-drawer file cabinets, 'Subject and General Files,' plus 2 four-drawer file cabinets, correspondence, as well as 15 thick notebooks of his correspondence. . . . He has every pamphlet, newsletter, other material about each of the black and integrated organizations he has been associated with. . . . This man is enormously well organized, saved everything."[4]

Savvy and well read, Byas exudes the segregated era fully capable of speaking for itself to another generation. "Me Speak for Me" is the title of one of his many community and academic presentations.[5] Telling the story of an unnamed elderly black man who refused to allow others to explain his whereabouts for him, Byas concludes the account by explaining that since he is the only one who knows where he has been and what he has been doing, "me [will] speak for me." Without ever studying postmodernist qualitative paradigms and the value of "informants" who do not merely "tell" their story to a researcher but participate in telling their stories to the world, Byas fully understands his place in his own story and appreciates the significance of his archival collection in validating his accounts.[6] Complemented by the records of the Horace Edward Tate collection of the Georgia Teachers and Education Association (GTEA), an organization in which Byas was a major participant, the resulting record provides an unusual glimpse into the internal workings of black school leadership and substantial confirmation of the oral report.

One final caveat also explains the intrigue that captured my interest in this story. The decades of the fifties and sixties, the period in which Byas worked as a principal, represent the nadir of black schools in the segregated South. In Byas's era, increasing funding for black schools, rising black teacher certification levels, and expanding employment opportunities were critical social and educational realities. Together, they directly influenced local leadership styles, community responses, and beliefs about black education during the years when blacks believed the *Brown v. Board of Education* decision would achieve an integrated world, but before *Green v. County School Board* would compel a disappointing deseg-regation.[7] In contrast, other studies of black schools during segregation have typically not focused on the changing activities and beliefs in those schools during this period, despite traditional historical chronologies establishing the presence of a different social and educational climate.

The resulting story of this school principal, the community in which he operated, and the broader system of schooling in which he participated has been incubating for a decade. I initially imagined that an article or a book chapter would suffice. The unveiling data, however, refused to be confined to fifty pages or less. Like a prism when held to the light, the data repeatedly lured me into new caveats of exploration and explanation. Every document linked to another, and another. Eventually, I was forced to abandon the idea that Byas's world was an addendum to an earlier story and embrace with enthusiasm the realization that this story of a school principal and the system in which he exercised leadership was a full-length account in its own right.[8]

As always, the number of people to whom I owe a debt in the comple-tion of anything I generate of publishable value far exceeds the space I can devote to enumerating each by name. I learn immeasurably from my pro-fessional colleagues, students, friends, and family. In my office, in coffee shops, on e-mail, and through extended phone conversations, I am gifted with intellectual exchange and motivation. All placate me with engage-ment and humor my distractions. In particular, two senior colleagues have been deeply influential. Friend and mentor Jackie Irvine has alternately clapped for, and offered critiques on, multiple manuscripts throughout my foray into segregated school life. I am a better scholar because of her. Likewise, James Anderson has consistently validated my interpretations and, in so doing, given me the courage to believe I could write history. I ex-tend thanks as well to my editor at the University of North Carolina Press, David Perry, who has been unfailingly encouraging while I imagined, dismissed, and then reconstructed a story of the black principalship; to Grace Carino, whose careful copyediting produced a more readable text; and to the Spencer Foundation, whose generous support of the Horace Tate project on black teacher advocacy provided the time and resources to uncover the structure of the black teachers' association in Georgia. On the last leg of this journey, two Emory graduate student assistants, Michelle Purdy and Tirza White, provided refreshingly frank editorial and collegial critique. I appreciate their willingness to listen to so many stories about "Dr. Byas" as I struggled to connect the many strands of his life. Among family and friends, no two people have walked this journey more closely than my husband, Melford, and our daughter, Sarah Elizabeth. My husband asks the critical questions that propel me back into the data source and patiently listens as I construct interpretations. Without his ear and investigative capacity to locate obscure books, newspaper accounts, and obituaries, I would have missed significant links. Meanwhile, Sarah is my jewel of inspiration. She patiently tolerates my distractions, shares me with people she does not know, cooks encouragement meals, and makes my life rich with love and laughter. I also thank Ashley Walker for typing, and I am grateful for the unconditional support always offered by Auntie Plum and Cousins Brenda and Shelton Davis. Each of these persons and so many more unnamed have unfailingly inspired my faith that community stories are important to tell. In my own ledger and in private conversations, I thank each one by name.

The important debt I must acknowledge, of course, is to the principal whose meticulous collection of documents and sharp memory have uncovered a hidden dimension of the segregated school story. For many years, I listened to him consistently greet me with an encouraging smile and an inviting "Hello Professor." Initially, I was befuddled, as I knew he was the professor (as black communities typically called their school principals during segregation), and I was, well, a college teacher and researcher.[9] Years of interviewing passed before I understood that his salutation invited me into a world that went far beyond the university descriptions of a professor that I had been trained to understand as a graduate student at Harvard or even lived as a teacher and researcher at Emory. Indeed, I was being invited into a sacred historical and cultural space where scholarship, mission, and responsibility merged. It was not a world I understood, and without Dr. Byas's patient collaboration and encouragement, this emic story of the "professor" who led a black segregated school and the systemic structure that undergirded his activities would have been impossible to discern, even with the extensive archival collection he graciously offered. I am grateful for his trust, for his model of leadership, and for his meticulous evaluations of the final manuscript. I am also grateful to his daughter, Laverne, for providing the entrée that allowed me to begin a relationship with her father.

The account that follows reconstructs the professional leadership of a professor in a segregated school community. In the community's usage, the term "professor" far exceeds the negative connotations sometimes associated with it that spawn images of subordination and accommodation to a white agenda for black education. To the contrary, in the community appropriation of the term, the title "professor" is accorded with respect and admiration. Far from being reduced to a leader who maintained the status quo as whites expected, the "professor" was an empowering leader who was the lever elevating racial progress in black schools and communities. In this book, although sometimes used interchangeably with principal, "professor" captures this community definition of an educational agent who used his influence to motivate the educational aspirations of black children.

Viewed through the lens of the professional beliefs and activity of Professor Byas during his years as principal of Fair Street and Butler High School in Gainesville, Georgia, *Hello Professor* introduces the leadership of the professor and the network of a black segregated system of schooling to a new generation of scholars and community members interested in amplifying their understanding of the segregated schooling of black children. Though the individual activity within his particular school is Byas's story alone, the system in which he operated captures the world of many unnamed professors who used schools to elevate black school communities throughout the South during de jure segregation. And, with the same sense of reward that accompanied the writing of *Their Highest Potential*, I have greatly enjoyed the telling.

Hello Professor

Introduction

Once upon a Time in a Forgotten World

A leader is best
When people barely know he exists

. . . .

But of a good leader, who talks little,
When his work is done, his aim fulfilled,
They will all say, "We did this ourselves."[1]

In recent decades, scholarly articles, books, newspaper stories, films, and local community narratives describing the segregated schooling of black children in the South have proliferated, inviting new dimensions into the traditional story that reduced all black schools to unilateral inferiority because of inadequate facilities. These accounts document the inequalities created as a result of the discriminatory policies of local school boards and superintendents but extend the portrait to explore the educational climate that emerged in segregated schools despite oppressive external circumstances.[2] Their collective rendering of the educational experiences of black children within southern segregated schools is strikingly consistent. Black schools are almost uniformly represented as both externally oppressed and internally resilient. Every account documents the external oppression black schools experienced as a result of school board neglect, thus confirming traditional historical accounts of poor black schools resulting from unequal funding. However, the same portraits are also replete with descriptions of the schools as having a cadre of committed and increasingly well-trained teachers and principals, or professors; a culture of teaching that blended professional training with local needs; a curricular and extracurricular program that reinforced the values of the school and community; and a strong base of parental support. Although these attributes may not be generalizable to every black segregated school, the increasing number of accounts, spanning more than nine southern states and reaching consistent similarity in conclusions, document a cohesion of ideas and practice. Indeed, the literature on segregated schools is more striking for its consistency than inconsistency.[3]

Vexingly, however, the very similarity of the schools invites a new level of complexity in efforts to build a comprehensive portrait of black southern schools during de jure segregation. Consider, for example, the ways each narrative has elevated parental involvement and school support. Among the activities of the parents are financial sacrifice and formal petitions to school boards as ways to gain increased funding for local schools. Yet why is it that so many black parents bought buses or used formal petitions as a strategy to acquire facilities in such similar time periods? How did black parents across the South consistently know how to petition, and to whom, in order to receive facilities for their children? Given the low literacy levels in most black communities during this era, the similarity of behaviors across time and region is perplexing. Or, consider the consistency of beliefs about how black children should be educated. Phrases such as "educate the whole child" or every child reaching his or her "highest potential" have become staple characterizations in the literature. How does one explain the similarity of values and activities evident in the research on segregated schools, expressed often using the same language, across multiple states and time, especially when the communities provide no evidence of familiarity with the activities occurring in other communities?

Unfortunately, the extant literature on segregated schools does not address questions such as these. Because the methodology is typically that of a case study, the results focus specifically upon particular schools as independent, individual educational units. This case methodology is important in that it provides detailed characterizations of activities within the school and includes salient context that explains community limitations and possibilities. However, the case study approach does little to make more lucid the rationale and motivation that explain the similar activities across the case studies. Even when the cases elevate the professor as an explanation for individual school success and describe the professor as "attending meetings" outside the school community, few informants are able to explain the types of meetings the professor attended, the agendas of those meetings, or the relationship of the meetings to their school activities. Moreover, the studies rarely provide a professor's first-person narrative that might clarify the community's remembered activities. The result is a case study record of segregated schools that provides compelling descriptions of individual schools but whose actors demonstrate little or no awareness of, and are unable to provide any explanation for, the ways their activities are paralleled in other sites. Instead, each community lauds the activities of its own school and the behaviors of its school leader. The result is a compelling portrait of *what* happened in segregated schools but little information that explains *why* or *how*.

To be sure, the activity of the black professor has been unearthed in some other scholarship. The most compelling up-close examples may be accessed in the unpublished dissertations completed by black professors of southern segregated black schools who were graduate students at elite universities. These dissertations typically explore the professional activities of selected black professors within a particular state using surveys as the primary method of data collection. They provide carefully researched insider accounts, most often from the 1950s and 1960s, of the professional activity of professors. Because the authors are usually professors in the states where data are collected, these unpublished and generally uncited dissertations constitute an important data source that can facilitate understanding of black leadership roles.[4] Generally, however, these dissertations and their findings are little known, and they have not been incorporated in the extant scholarship.[5]

Unlike the dissertations, the published scholarly research has been slower to explore the leadership of the black professor, with only some exceptions. Rodgers's compilation of survey data from black professors in North Carolina in 1964 provides one of the earliest published examinations and the one most closely linked in characterization to the unpublished literature. In Rodgers's description, professors fulfill a variety of roles in the school community, including counselor, financial assistant, role model, chief instructional leader, superintendent, supervisor, employer, politician, and liaison with the white community. These findings are consistent with the 1983 publication of Russell and Jackie Irvine, which analyzes the influence of the loss of the black professor after desegregation. Both findings are echoed in more recent historiography of the black professor by Linda Tillman and C. Calvin Smith. Each captures the professor in roles consistent with the descriptions elucidated by Rodgers.[6] In compelling ongoing work, scholars such as Adah Randolph-Ward, Judy Gibson, and Marcia Owens are also uncovering accounts of individual stellar leaders in communities in Delaware, Ohio, Virginia, and Mississippi. Their work affirms the consistency of the behaviors of multiple professors but simultaneously confirms the need to explore the networks and activity of leaders that might help explain the similarities in behaviors across settings.[7]

Some of the omission of an in-depth focus on the black professor as leader in the black school community may be linked to the perspective of traditional historical scholarship on black leadership. In classic accounts, historians omit professors as agents in developing black communities. As justification, these classic narratives centralize context and describe the limitation of environment as a way to explain the reported inactivity on the part of black professors. For example, renowned scholars on black leadership John Hope Franklin and August Meier assert that "principals and presidents of southern Negro schools, because of their vulnerable positions, tended to be among the most conservative elements in the community (as indeed they are today). They never ruffled white sensibilities, for they hoped to survive on state funds." Implicit in these characterizations is the confirmation of Eric Foner's assertion that black leaders at the grassroots level had to be independent of whites in order to lead.[8] These observations on the importance of context are accurate in explaining the public, easily observable behavior of the black professor. However, the elevation of context as a singular causation agent reduces the black professor to a leader defined solely by his or her limited circumstances. Moreover, it implies that the public face of accommodation represented the range of the response of black professors to inequality. By writing in ways that look no deeper than the public face school leaders have displayed, historians have often failed to search for and identify behaviors that might better illuminate the full range of the professor's activities. This search beneath the visible portrait is essential, especially since the conclusion that they were reduced to inactivity because of context contradicts available self-reports.

The research on black segregated schools offers little help in reconciling the disparate views reflected in traditional historical accounts and dissertation self-reports. Even when behaviors of professors are explored across settings, these behaviors are typically governed by narrowly framed research questions that apply to a particular setting. Like the segregated school literature in general, the scholarship on the black principalship fails to explore the activities and beliefs of the professor in the school in the context of the professional development and school community advocacy. More important, although the studies establish the consistency of certain activities of professors as leaders, they have not sought to explain the similarity of leadership styles across settings or to uncover the challenges of developing a black school in a context of racial oppression. The result is a historical portrait of black school leadership that elevates great figures while dismissing the forms of leadership within and beyond the community that explain the activities of the leaders.

Professors as Leaders in a System of Black Schooling

Hello Professor uses an individual biography as it intersected with a systemic structure to make more explicit the similarity of black educational activity and mission evident in the individual case studies. The book posits that the visible agency of one professor, Ulysses Byas, at Fair Street High School, later E. E. Butler, in Gainesville, Georgia, was inextricably related to the network of professional activity and community influences that grounded his work. Embedded in this argument is the proposition that a network of people and organizations throughout the South created a system of black schooling that focused specifically upon addressing the educational needs peculiar to students in the black community.

At the core of this system was the professional development of the professor and the ways that development was extended into local school communities. In the system, the black professor participated in professional activities at the national level and at the state level. The national meetings created spaces where the challenges confronting black education could be comprehensively discussed in settings that connected higher education personnel and local public school professors. In these national meetings, professors representing states across the South heard speeches, participated in conversations about cutting-edge educational ideas, and consulted with respected peers from other states. When they returned to their individual states, the professors also participated in the activities of the black teachers' associations, the black counterpart of the segregated white teachers' associations. These segregated state gatherings offered a platform for the same people, ideas, and educational beliefs that permeated the national conversation. Additionally, as is typical of the general structure of other teachers' associations, the black teachers' associations hosted regional meetings and some local county meetings, including some meetings specifically for the local professors. In these local settings, the same ideas were voiced. Indeed, embedded in the structure of the black teachers' organization was a method of information transmission that allowed perspectives about salient topics in black education to be disseminated throughout the South. Even professors who were not participants in national meetings had recurring opportunities to become familiar with the ideology for black education because of the repetition of the ideology in state venues.

The professor touched individual schools through his or her local leadership. Using the knowledge available in the professional network, the professor returned to his or her school, where national and state ideas were revised so that they could be practically applied. Professors used weekly teachers' meetings to involve teachers in school planning. Because many teachers themselves had also participated in the state and regional meetings, the ideas were familiar. However, in the intimate setting of their own school, the professor and teachers crafted plans suitable for local educational needs. Additionally, the professor used formal and informal interactions with parents to interpret for them the importance of local school practices and, thereby, disseminate the ideas being championed by the black educational network. Although not captured in either current professional development literature or the historiography of black schools, this system of professional development at the core of black schools, all of which hinged on the activity of the professor, is the single best explanation for the consistency in development of these schools across time and geography.

Some points are important to preview about the system of professional development that permeated black school communities. These may be best explained by defining its three interrelated forms. First, the system overtly embraced the goal of education as a mechanism to attain full democratic participation for black citizens. The goal is not a new one in the history of education, as education for democracy and citizenship has permeated the curriculum of schools and the production of textbooks since the founding of the United States. However, as James Anderson has argued, blacks existed in a dual system in which full citizenship and democratic participation were not the educational goals for those who controlled their education. Rather, blacks were expected to accept a lower status educationally and economically, despite their residence in a democratic nation.[9] Consistent with individual black scholars who have resisted the inequality imposed on blacks, the black system of schooling also resisted this assumption of second-class citizenship by fundamentally challenging its premise of exclusion. For many black educators, the goal of education was to resist the expectation that black schools would produce a pliable group of menial workers and to imagine a formula that might allow their students, practically and ideologically, to emerge as full participants in American democracy. Although the focus on democratic education was influenced by the early rhetoric of social studies educators, its roots emanate from a long-standing black communal belief that education was the means to attain participation in the democracy, and the incorporation of "civic education" became one means through which to advance a black educational and social agenda. This agenda was profoundly political and was pursued during a time when social studies educators and civic educators were generally silent about larger political movements such as civil rights.[10]

Second, the system of black schooling was also covertly engaged in a practical battle to eliminate the unequal distribution of resources in black schools. In this battle, the professor was the first agent to challenge inequality in local settings. Appropriating a larger educational ideology that superintendents could be expected to respect, black professors used the language of education to lure local school boards to attend to the needs of black schools. In the decades from the depression to Sputnik, when neither organizations, marches, nor federal mandates were successfully achieving needed resources in local school settings, the actions of black professors were significant, covert mechanisms used to raise the educational standards within a community. Their methods were rarely confrontational, and they never netted full equality in the distribution of funds between black and white schools, since significant strides in financial support of black schools are typically correlated with national or regional self-interest. Nonetheless, their efforts prompted funding for facilities, curriculum, and teachers that exceeded the resources that would otherwise have been available for local black schools.

A final description of the black system of schooling is also significant for understanding its influence. The black system of schooling crafted an agenda for black education that focused specifically upon meeting the perceived educational needs of black children. This agenda was formulated primarily by blending the knowledge base of two sources. Black educators embraced with enthusiasm both the best practices from schools of education and the best thinking of the black intellectual elite on issues related to black advancement. The presence of the language from white northern schools of education in the agenda of black educators is unsurprising. Historian James Anderson, in "The Black Education Professoriate," details the rise in doctorate production for black scholars between 1920 and 1951, particularly in education, at eighteen elite white graduate schools. Concurrently, blacks attended these institutions to gain master's degrees. As graduate students, black scholars' presence at white institutions placed them within the flow of conversations about education, particularly when they studied with some of the more well-known educators of the period such as John Dewey or William Kilpatrick or Harold Rugg.[11]

Black educators' understanding of best practice was also mediated by their access to, and interaction with, the intellectual elite of the black race. These elite scholars included academics such as Horace Mann Bond, Allison Davis, and W. E. B. DuBois, who are much better known for their scholarly contributions to race development than for their interaction with black public school professors.[12] However, rather than being disconnected to black communities, as some historians have supposed, the black intellectual elite, as their activities reveal, were connected in ways that expand traditional conceptualizations of involvement. That is, for the black intellectual elite, community connections occurred through their influence on beliefs and practices in local communities rather than their physical presence. Although typically they were not actually present in local communities to share ideas publicly, they lived in a segregated world with representatives of many of these communities and, through the structures of the black organizational networks, engaged in problem-solving on issues of mutual interest. In this little-understood interaction, black intellectuals were involved with black communities in that they helped craft an educational agenda for black schools that was designed to lift a people up into full democratic citizenship. The resulting vision addressed directly the limitations of their segregated education and envisioned new possibilities.

On its surface, this systemic plan for educating black children may be assumed to parallel the mission of white educators and schools. That is, the black plan utilized the language of education, and it imitated the organizational structure of white educational associations throughout the country. However, the black system diverged in norms, values, mission, and accountability. Rather than seeking to affirm a Euro-centric schooling definition that elevated competitive values and individual students, the black system embraced a deeply communal and political agenda that sought to elevate the needs of the race through education.[13] Historically difficult to distinguish because it operated embedded in the white educational system, it was nonetheless a separate system with an agenda for education that flourished parallel to the white system but evolved as a result of exclusion from it.

As the Byas story reveals, the central conduit through which the ideology dominating this system was disseminated into local communities was the black professor.[14] Themselves victims of the segregated system they sought to eradicate and compelled into education by the values of black families and the historically black colleges and institutions they attended, black professors linked the larger vision for black education to individual school communities. In these local settings, the professor worked in tandem with the black community and in covert opposition to the white superintendent's agenda of continued inferiority for black children. Moreover, the professor assumed responsibility for spurring professional development among teachers that would accomplish in individual classrooms the larger systemic plan for black education. Perhaps as Paulette Dilworth has postulated, local professors were "motivated by the moral imperative to respond" in their own settings, particularly since they had themselves been rescued by the very system in which they now participated.[15]

By unveiling the portrait of one professor as he interacted at various levels in his professional world and extended the ideas to a local school community, this book seeks to expand the dimensions of black schools beyond descriptions of compelling activities, committed educators, and resourceful parents in individual settings and, instead, peer into a world of professional development and community support whose web interconnects national, regional, and local activity. Together with his own courage, creativity, and resourcefulness, Byas's story is a microcosm of the ways the professional system could help spur a consistent vision for elevating schools and communities. Although the individual activities described are his personal biography alone, the focus on his leadership is an apt way of unveiling the black system of schooling and the leadership of professors within it.

Without an understanding of the role of the professor as a school leader coexisting in a broader professional world of black schooling, the stories of multiple similarities among individual schools, including the similarity in mission, defy explanation. In some biographical portraits, incipient hints of a complex narrative can be gleaned. For example, in the biography of black school professor Charlotte Hawkins Brown, who led a private school in North Carolina with characteristics similar to those documented in other black schools, the esteemed scholar and president of Howard University Mordecai Johnson is reported to have delivered the eulogy at her funeral. The biographer does not explain the relationship between a local professor and a college president that would make him sufficiently acquainted with her personally or professionally to deliver her eulogy. In a comparable example, John Hope, president of Morehouse College in Atlanta, is reported to have been part of a teachers' meeting in Oklahoma.[16] Similarly, no speculation is offered in this otherwise comprehensive biography that might explain how a college president in Atlanta came to be involved with teachers in the Midwest. While an examination of the series of first-person narratives of black teachers' associations composed in the late 1960s and early 1970s could help establish the intersection of people on the state level, these little-referenced accounts lack the expansive view that could explain the connection of educators across states. Perhaps because black education has more typically been relegated to a poor imitation of white schools, the queries that would demand a systemic exploration of the ways varied black educational actors lead, intersect, and transmit educational ideas have remained mute.

This omission is ironic, since the activities of the local professor provide a model of school leadership more expansive than mere school management. In black settings, leadership was accomplished by blending a professional educational world with a local community's world. It involved inviting parents to become co-participants in the language of black uplift that dominated the agenda of the black intellectual elite. To be sure, the professor was responsible for the management and administration of the school, including such challenging tasks as getting children to school and evaluating teachers. However, despite the lack of resources in their schools and the unique challenges created by the needs of their constituencies, these leaders refused to limit their roles to managing schools. Rather than being limited by circumstances, they used the confining circumstances to redefine a vision of leadership. It was a redefinition crafted of necessity.

To Tell the Story

This story of the professional development that undergirded black schools dusts the windows of individual schools to expose the dimly understood activity of a systemic educational world that has been almost uniformly forgotten or, at minimum, fragmented in its reconstruction. In its description of that educational world, this portrait focuses most specifically upon Byas's school and community activities from 1957 to 1968, the years in which he was a high school professor in Gainesville, Georgia. However, because both he and the professional development structure in which he participated cannot be fully understood without recounting events in earlier decades, the narrative also includes as context events from the mid-1920s through the early 1950s in sections where this context helps explain organizational missions.

To tell the story, the book presents the account of Ulysses Byas's professional development and the transfer of that development into his local setting in six segments. These segments intentionally deemphasize the activity of students within the school and elevate the professional development activities of its leader. Thus the book's goal is to illuminate three aspects of the professorship. First, the work depicts the professor as the creative agent foiling the superintendent's limited agenda for black schools. In the representation, the supposition of limitations is unmasked, and the professor is shown, in real time, coordinating teachers and parents to create a plan that would provide needed resources to the school. Second, the book elevates Byas's personal biography and his professional world, both nationally and within the state, and uses these components to unmask a professor at work. Finally, the book details interactions with, and beliefs about, teachers and parents to demonstrate the ways Byas's daily activity was buttressed by their cooperation. The narrative presents the ideas in a loosely chronological format with an underlying thematic style. However, this style of presentation creates a bifucation of the professor's world that did not exist in practice.

In Chapter 1, "Playing Dr. Jekyll and Mr. Hyde," the professional activity of Professor Byas is introduced. Casting its focus specifically upon the 1957–58 school year, the first year of Byas's arrival in Gainesville, it addresses directly the dual persona a professor was required to adopt if a recalcitrant superintendent was to be convinced to expand the educational opportunities for black children. This chapter sets the stage for understanding the activity of the black professor by chronicling the strategies Byas utilized in local settings to challenge inequality. Specifically appropriating the language of education, he concealed his real purposes for school initiatives, skillfully maneuvering to accomplish ends consistent with his professional world. Using an episode during his first year in Gainesville and revisiting the ways he had played a similar episode the year before in another school where he had also been the professor, the chapter explores in detail the dynamics of this persona, the educational expertise required, and the rationale for the adoption of a "game" in order to achieve education for black children.

After setting the stage of the professor's behavior in the late 1950s, the book goes on to explore in detail, in the next three chapters, the myriad events that combined to create the professor, with each chapter seeking to explain some facet of the personal and professional context that shaped Professor Byas's capacity to implement the Dr. Jekyll and Mr. Hyde game. Chapter 2, "From High School Dropout to Classroom Teacher," focuses directly on his personal and educational experiences prior to his becoming a professor in Gainesville in 1957. Black professors during the era were often the product of poor black communities and were placed in circumstances in which they were challenged, in Lisa Delpit's words, to create for "other people's children" the opportunities that were given to them.[17] Spanning the period from 1924 to 1953, the chapter seeks to capture the critical incidents in Byas's biographical narrative by exploring his evolution from childhood to the completion of his unofficial internship as a practicing professor and seventh-grade teacher. In particular, the chronology examines his beliefs and behaviors as an "at-risk" student and explores the convergence of World War II opportunities and a historically black college that reset his educational course. The chapter concludes by reviewing his experiences as a graduate student at Columbia and overviewing his experiences as a teacher/professor-in-training. Together, these events explain the unfolding saga of a rebellious student who transformed into a successful teacher and professor-in-training within the system. This background is central, as it is representative of the backgrounds of some professors, many perhaps, whose educational trajectory is transformed by the black professors and institutions dominating the landscape of the black educational system during their own childhoods. In real ways, the professor was created by the professional development networks in which he would later participate.

Chapters 3 and 4 deconstruct the professional educational network in which Byas was a participant. Less about his personal journey, these chapters seek to illustrate the professional world he inhabited by focusing more directly on the system in which he operated. Some reference is provided to his activities in the system and his perspective on the importance of the system. Chapter 3, "In Spite of This Old Devil Segregation," utilizes the terminology of Horace Mann Bond to demonstrate the resilience of the black professional community that worked across states to upgrade the quality of black schools. The chapter captures the network of black educators as it had unfolded by 1957 and demonstrates the ways the local professor could be enmeshed in a national dialogue saturated with discussions of educational ideas most significant to implement to develop black children. These included ensuring full democratic participation, responding to testing pressures, and recognizing their own roles in overturning a system of oppression. The chapter explains the ways in which, in contrast to national organizations headed by whites, the national conversation among black educators created a medium through which the professor could be informed about issues specifically devoted to black children and be given opportunities to discuss how to translate theory into practice. This national professional world was singularly focused, and it provides the intersection of the black elite and the local professor that demonstrates one reason the ideology of the elite can be identifiable in local school settings.

Chapter 4, "In Georgia, Where I Am Free to Express Myself," extends the national professional talk by depicting the way black national ideas were imported to Georgia and then disseminated throughout the state. Although not all professors could attend national meetings, the states utilized specific strategies to generate a comprehensive vision for black children. Thus, the black professors in the 1950s and 1960s were privy to a world that reinforced national ideology about best teaching practice and, through its network of professional activities, transformed those ideas into usable strategies for black children. The chapter explores the activity of the School Masters Club as one specific way the national network extended its influence locally and provides detail on the ways professional ideas were disseminated through the state network of black teachers, the Georgia Teachers and Education Association (GTEA). Although the activities of GTEA are much broader than those captured in this chapter, an overview of its professional development opportunities is provided, focusing specifically upon its structure and ideas and the role of the professor in this structure. By detailing these activities, the chapter captures the other facet of the educational world that shaped Byas's professional development.

The final two chapters of the book deconstruct the activity of teachers and parents captured in the Dr. Jekyll and Mr. Hyde game by exploring the role of the professor as the professional leader of school and community development. Echoing the national and state rhetoric central in the network of black schooling, the professor intentionally assumed the lead in bridging rhetoric and practice by crafting a united agenda at the school level on the plan for educating black children. Chapter 5, "Whatever Is in the Best Interests of Kids," unveils the faculty meeting at the local school as a scene for the professional development of teachers. Examining Byas's practices in the high school in the early to mid-1960s, this chapter shows the ways in which Byas functions as the professional developer in his own school community, drawing specifically upon a larger vision for black education prevalent in his professional development world. Since black educators believed teachers were the key to student acquisition of learning, the chapter demonstrates the ways Professor Byas implemented this ideology by converting his school into a site of ongoing professional development. In this setting, the national ideology about educating black children became part of local values and beliefs. Long hours, professional talk, and "no nonsense" when it came to educating black children characterized this environment. This chapter demonstrates the ways national concerns about raising the capacity of black teachers assumed shape and direction under Byas's leadership.

The sixth chapter, "Not without Partnering with the Community," examines the strategies the black professor utilized to develop the local community. The development of black communities—critical actors in the education of black children—could not be eliminated in the local job of the professor. The chapter examines the centrality of the black community in implementing a vision for black children by exploring the traditional ways the professor sought the support of the community and by examining the changing roles of the professor in the community in the late 1960s. It demonstrates the ways in which a professor who understood the community's norms and explicitly utilized these norms to craft a shared vision for educating children could motivate innovative ideas within the school. To get their cooperation, black parents had to be deliberately and intentionally pursued, and the professor was forced to craft interactions that necessarily both expanded and facilitated the community vision as it currently existed. In this chapter, Byas explains the multiple ways the professor sought the support of the community and explains how the school rewarded the trust of the community by generating activities believed to be in the best interests of the children. However, the chapter also reveals the ways traditional forms of leadership were re-created in the turbulent era of the civil rights movement. In particular, Byas contrasts his perception of the norms of black parents with those of parents in the white educational communities as he experienced those differences while administrating a summer school that included white parents.

The book ends with a conclusion, titled "The Price for Running Twice as Fast." This ending material recounts the story of Byas's abrupt departure from the world of the professor and synthesizes the meaning of his loss in the context of black schooling. Indeed, his departure provides an apt metaphor for the extensive work of black professors who operated black schools with little salary incentive but who (in the end) were removed from their jobs. Their dismissal was personally costly but professionally devastating, as it unhooked the structures that best explain the similar activities in black segregated schools. With the professor went the forms of professional development, leading to the dismantling of a system of black education.

The behind-the-scenes maneuvering of black professors captured in these chapters has generally escaped attention in contemporary conversations of segregated black education. Its omission is also implicated in the memories of local communities, where former teachers, parents, and students continue to be at a loss to explain the reasons for the success of their fondly remembered schools, despite the personal accolades for their own professor. Perhaps the elusion of the activity of the black professor and the system of black education in which this leader operated is best explained by black professors' characterization of themselves. Apparently, as captured in the quotation that begins this introduction, the best professor would be so good that people would barely know he or she existed. In this collective humility, if the leader did his or her job well, the people would all say, "We did this ourselves." As communities have believed and as historians have written, grassroots leaders and professional groups are the primary agents to whom the documented progress of the black community might be attributed. Their accolades are well deserved and respectfully applauded. However, another angle on the "we did it ourselves" story unmasks the black professor as the central agent whose professional network and commitment to extending the ideas in his local settings were essential in elevating local communities through schools. *Hello Professor* demonstrates that, far from individual communities having merely done it themselves, the black professor was the hidden dimension of help that produced the black leaders, activities, and beliefs communities remember.

For some scholars, attorneys, and community leaders nervous about a current repressive federal climate increasingly returning ethnic groups to segregated settings, the attention to deconstructing this educational era generates concern that the story itself will minimize the importance of continuing a legal strategy to maintain desegregated school settings today. Such concerns fail to consider the differing social and federal contexts that make the two worlds incomparable. Indeed, the activity and vision of the black professor during the earlier period could not be implemented in the current climate, in which all the structures that undergirded the professional activity of black schools in the previous era have been dismantled. In truth, the loss of these structures and the firing of the professors who led them make a "return" to this remembered world not a viable option in a contemporary climate.

Yet failing to recount the story handicaps the vision for future endeavors. Timothy Tyson addresses the dilemma of history and future well. Elevating the importance of truth, he suggests that the future cannot address the complicated matters of schooling in this century unless the historical record crafts a shared story of the past. His observations are echoed in the West African term "Sankofa," which literally interpreted means, "it is not taboo to go back and fetch what you forgot." The Sankofa term teaches the importance of threshing in the past to achieve full potential for people who wish to move forward. It posits that the past can be reclaimed and that it should be preserved.[18]

In that spirit of contributing to the shared record, *Hello Professor* reintroduces the activities of a neglected and little-recorded black educational network of professional development. Here the professor's educational and experiential world are reexamined and the professional network reconstructed. As communities have revisited the activities of individual black segregated schools and applauded their success in dismal circumstances, so the influence of the black professor and the hidden power of the professional world is a story worth resurrecting.

1 Playing Dr. Jekyll and Mr. Hyde

I've done so much with so little for so long, I think I can do anything with nothing at all.
— *Ulysses Byas*

On July 1, 1957, the possibilities that lay ahead for Ulysses Byas were as new and fresh as the recently completely Buford Dam he passed on his drive fifty-three miles north of Atlanta. His destination was Gainesville, where he and his family would join the thirty thousand residents in a city that dubbed itself the "Queen City of the Mountains." The setting was idyllic. Nestled in the shadows of the 750,000-acre mountainous terrain of the Chattachoochee National Forest, Gainesville offered to the north and west the crispness of the cooler mountain air and, slightly south, the arid heat of Lake Lanier, a newly created lake already touted as the new vacation spot for locals and vacationers. Among the nine surrounding counties, Gainesville was the prosperous center for retail sales. It imagined its future as being guided by "intelligent, determined people, with solid plans for constructive, prosperous and continued growth."[1]

Byas entered Gainesville having accepted the position as the new professor at the newly renovated, self-contained Fair Street High School for black children. He believed the city and the new position held promise. The salary was better than the salary he had received the previous four years as principal of the Hutchenson Elementary and High School for black children in rural Douglas County, just west of Atlanta. Moreover, his new school was considered by many blacks to be among the best high schools for blacks in the state of Georgia. In the 1930s, when many blacks were without high school education across the state, Gainesville supported a high school for blacks through grade eleven, which was then the final grade of a high school education in Georgia. By 1958, the total value of the school property was $878,467.87, and the school had been featured in the Georgia journal for black teachers, the *Herald*, as an exemplar of educational activity. Compared with some black schools in adjacent counties and other geographic regions in Georgia, particularly

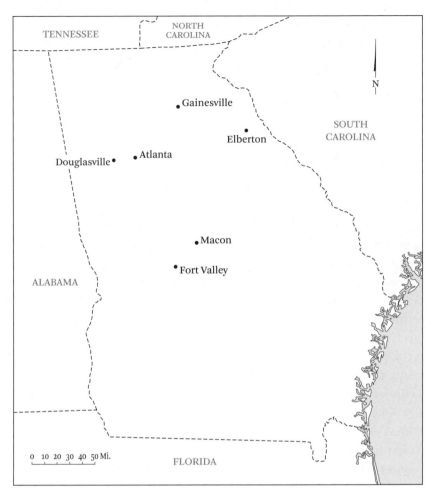

Georgia

rural areas in the southern part of the state, Gainesville did appear to be a setting where intelligent, determined people sustained constructive and prosperous growth.[2]

Still, amid the joy of a new school and the anticipation of a new principalship were the ongoing dictates of segregation. Although the town of Gainesville boasted a more open racial climate than many areas farther south, the reality of separation of the races was not one that could be escaped. Like other cities in the South, Gainesville in 1957 was a city where the cultural, professional, and fraternal organizations, religious activities, and varied recreation facilities were all divided by the same racial lines. White women and children passed the stately Victorian houses of Green

Street to lounge around the Green Street Pool during the lazy, hot days of summer; black children and black mothers went to the Fair Street pool for blacks. The Miss Georgia Chick Beauty Pageant, held in the Civic Center for contestants across the state, included no black participants. Fox hunting for men and soap box car driving for boys were popular sports in the town, but photos of the era show no blacks.[3]

The schooling for black children likewise suffered from the unequal funding that characterized the division of the races. Although Gainesville had provided for its black students in fiscal ways that exceeded the expenditures in some other areas of the state, equality within the system was not a point that could be boasted in the fall of 1957.[4] As Byas entered his new building and office for the first time to prepare for the beginning of a new school year, the manifestations of a poorly maintained school, despite its public accolades, surfaced immediately. Although Fair Street High School had a certified teaching staff and numerous extracurricular activities, its curriculum suffered the repercussions of fiscal limitations. Only four academic courses in each grade level were offered to Fair Street students, and all students were required to take these courses. The school had no chemistry, physics, foreign languages, or specialized math courses.

The reality of the constraints of the new school contradicted Byas's expectations. Given its reputation across the state, he imagined a more advanced curriculum and was dismayed to discover the sparse educational offerings and the lack of equipment needed to sustain even the present effort. As far as he could tell, no consistency existed across the curriculum in the content requirements that defined, for example, tenth-grade math versus eleventh-grade math. The brand-new facilities were also insufficient. According to Byas, the science lab could be identified only by a sink in the corner. Byas maintains that "the only reason you knew it was a science lab was that we told you: This is a science lab." Moreover, Byas was concerned with the lack of commercial courses in the curriculum, meaning that students had no access to business or typing classes.[5] Overall, Fair Street's curriculum was a disappointment to its new principal, who silently wondered how the school had maintained its approved status in the elite Association of Colleges and Secondary Schools, an organization charged with the approval process for black schools. Some additions were within his power, and he made them immediately by introducing a new chemistry course and French course in the first year of his arrival.[6] Other additions would require a skillful negotiation of external constraints.

Like most black schools, Fair Street was constrained because of limited funding, and its deficiencies merely mirrored the handicaps black students faced throughout the state. In Georgia, the story of school inequality would shortly be published by the Georgia Conference on Educational Opportunities, *Georgia's Divided Education*. Despite the passage of *Brown*, five years later this publication reported that black children in Georgia received thirty-seven dollars per pupil less than white children and one-fifth the money spent for maintenance of school buildings. In percentages, this disparity equated to 79 percent of the distribution of maintenance of operations supporting white schools and 31 percent Negro schools. To illuminate these differences, the authors sampled the eight most heavily populated counties in the state, thirty counties representing varied population levels, and nineteen counties with heavy black populations. After analyzing average daily attendance for black and white schools so that the comparative size of population could be accounted for in assessing differentials, the authors compared expenditures in areas such as instruction, maintenance, transportation, library books, teacher salaries, and so forth and concluded that "Negro youth are still being discriminated against in Georgia."[7]

Georgia was not the only culprit. The same inequalities existed across the southern states. Historians have repeatedly documented the inequalities that confronted educators teaching in segregated settings. These disparities have been identified across nine of the states in expenditures per pupil, capital outlays per pupil, training of teachers, salaries of teachers, length of school year, and school library books. Although gains were made in each category between 1940 and 1952 as litigation by the National Association for the Advancement of Colored People (NAACP) challenged inequity in educational provisions based on race and school boards responded with capital expenditures for black schools, the period of the late 1950s was not one in which local school administrators capitulated and provided equality of funding.[8]

Of course, the students at Fair Street saw few of these needs. As they entered a renovated school building in the fall of 1957, they embraced the youthful excitement of a new setting that boasted so many more facilities and resources than had been available in their school of the previous year. According to student writer Agnes Stephens, students made their way to school that first day on a "clear, crisp morning." Of their delight in the new facilities, Stephens writes:

As we approached our new building, we stopped suddenly, for before us stood the new Fair Street High School, which for years had been talked about and hoped for. Upon entering the building, we were forced to catch our breath, for the cheerfully decorated walls gave us the feeling that we were in a luxurious home rather than a school. . . . Peeping into the principal's office, we saw, among other things, an intercommunication system, which makes it possible for our principal to contact individually or all at one time the various class-rooms in the building. . . . As we continued our tour of the building, we saw several rooms which puzzled us because we couldn't decide for what purpose they were to be used. We were later informed that these rooms included a teachers' workshop, two lounges for teachers, a first-aid room, and conference rooms. They were all decorated in colors that seem to relax. The attractiveness of the library also caught our eye, for instead of the drab, dark room to which we had grown accustomed, was a light and airy room with lots of space. We knew immediately that using this library would be a pleasure."

Stephens's essay continues with a description of the lunchroom, where students had an "enjoyable social hour with soft, relaxing music and interesting chit-chat"; the homemaking and industrial arts departments, which they found inspiring and motivated a desire to retake previously taken classes; and the science lab, which "fascinated" them, despite its lack of equipment. For students, the school was "what we had dreamed about and prayed for," and they operated with the full expectation that the equipment lacking would be "added soon."[9]

The new professor was not nearly as enthralled by the renovation and expansion of the building. Had he stayed at his previous school in Douglasville, he would have been moving into a new building also. Rather, the looming concern Byas felt compelled to address was the inadequacy of the curriculum at Fair Street and the need for additional money to support an expanded curriculum. Added to the professor's dilemma about raising the educational standards was a black community sparring with the superintendent over a truancy officer.

To Byas's utter amazement, the energy of the black community upon his arrival was not mobilized around any of the curricular issues that disturbed him as a new professor. No one in the community was talking about the missing science equipment or the lack of curricular offerings.

Silence likewise existed on the overcrowding that was predicted to occur in the new school within a few years. School analysts expected that the school, with seventeen classrooms, would exceed its 510-student capacity by more than 300 students in fewer than six years. Eleven new classrooms would have to be added to the new Fair Street to accommodate these needs, according to a local report. Yet no talk floated about these concerns.[10] Byas was dumbfounded.

Black parents wanted a truancy officer, and they were in a gridlock with the superintendent about getting one. To be sure, Byas understood the parental concern that black students stay in school. At Fair Street, though student enrollment was increasing, average daily attendance was a problem.[11] The local difficulties echoed state norms. In a 1960 survey of Georgia schools, the state average revealed a 31 percent attendance rate for blacks, compared with a 69 percent attendance rate for whites. Additionally, in 1958, only one-sixth of black students in Georgia were in high school. According to Winfred Pitts, more students dropped out of school in Gainesville after ninth grade. In fact, the enrollment decreased by 46 percent between ninth and tenth grade. Although, according to Pitts, black students who were enrolled in school actually attended school at a slightly higher percentage than their white peers, with 96.66 average daily attendance for blacks and 94.50 attendance for whites, black parents would have little reason to know about attendance comparability in 1957.[12] Rather, the larger concern that black children be in school was the most formidable difficulty black parents believed they confronted.

Keeping black children in school was not new to Byas. At his previous job in Hutchenson, he had been sufficiently concerned about school attendance that he had ridden daily behind a white farmer's truck when the farmer went into the black community to pick up children for a day's work in his fields. The sight of the professor's car behind the truck had so intimidated many children that they refused to board. Their action, or lack thereof, reduced the farmer's capacity to harvest his crop and ultimately led to the creation of a work-study program at the school. In Gainesville, the problem was not that Byas was unsympathetic to the need to keep children in school. Personally and professionally, Byas understood that children needed to be spurred to attend school, especially when employment was available to them; although the jobs were low-wage ones, the desire to make money could usurp the desire for a high school diploma. Thus, his problem was not that he disapproved of an attendance officer. Rather, he was convinced the parents' request was too limited. How could they ignore the substantial curricular and resource needs of the school and expend all their energy demanding from the superintendent a truancy officer? Byas believed their demands would address only one of many problems the school faced, and he was committed to using this opportunity to address broader needs.

Further complicating the dilemma, the superintendent was entrenched in his refusal to address the requests of the black parents. The superintendent, J. R. Callison, was reportedly a former high school principal who had been demoted to a junior high school principal the year before he was elected superintendent. His actions regarding the education of black children were not ones that encouraged Byas to believe that he had the personal or professional disposition to address the fiscal and curricular needs of the school. The superintendent's primary concern was that the black parents not be given a truancy officer and that they be willing to accept his failure to honor their request. In other words, the superintendent wanted the community to keep quiet about its needs. To make needed changes at the school, the superintendent would have to be circumvented.

As Byas perceived it, the position taken by the superintendent was not unusual. One of the major obstacles to success in many black school communities was the white superintendent. According to De Lars Funches, great variance could exist in the perspectives of black professors and white superintendents about the professor's role.[13] In their actions, white superintendents often made decisions in ways that reflected their beliefs that the black school would be the recipient of either paternalistic benevolence or benign neglect but did not deserve equality. Many of the superintendents were also victims of the complex attitudes about race that dominated the South. Sometimes descendants of former Confederate soldiers, they embraced the virtue of the South and owed their employment to peers who frequently were unrepentant for the "sins" committed against the blacks in previous or present generations. The textbooks they studied minimized inequality, and the scholarly climate was one in which academics used social science and historical revisionism to buffer obvious disparity by elevating blacks' supposed natural inferiority. In the southern education system, the white superintendent was often a figure who served to maintain traditional southern values in local settings.[14]

The major constraint of an overtly benign but covertly anti–racial equality superintendent was no small matter. Superintendents and school boards were still 99 percent white across the state as late as 1970.[15] Although Gainesville was unique in 1957 in that it boasted two black school board members, their voices were insufficient to shift the position of an entrenched superintendent. In addition, the late 1950s was a period when educational turmoil existed in the state of Georgia because of the passage of *Brown*, and it, like other southern states, openly debated whether public schools should be maintained.[16] Thus, as Byas assumed leadership at Fair Street, he was confronted with the formidable task of garnering community support for demanding an expanded educational agenda and hoodwinking a superintendent who had no easily discernible agenda for black children other than maintaining the status quo. In attempting to accomplish any change in the school, Byas could not circumvent the superintendent because the superintendent was his employer. Simultaneously, however, Byas had to be politically savvy enough to work with someone in a climate in which black professors who overtly challenged inequality could be dismissed.

There was "one thing you had to do," Byas explains of the maneuvering the professor had to adeptly master in order to build the quality of black schools. "If you thought you had more sense than he [the superintendent] had, you had to hide part of it." Byas's summation directly addresses the interpersonal professional antics necessary for a professor engaged to be successful in an environment where whites manipulated the system to serve the needs of white children but demonstrated little regard for the development of black children. "You couldn't go around with all your sense on your shoulder because if you did, that was a good way not to have your job."[17]

Segregation norms required black professors to utilize strategies that would make them appear to be following the accepted social mores of the time while covertly crafting an outcome that would be in the best interests of black children. Moreover, this style needed to be sufficiently believable that the superintendent would not be aware of the ways he was being deceived. It was a masterful game of Dr. Jekyll and Mr. Hyde, or so black professors of the era called it. In this iteration of a familiar allusion, winning required the player professor to find creative ways to address the limitations imposed by segregation by assuming an external persona that would appeal to his or her nonsuspecting superintendent. The goal of the game was to utilize intellectual wit rather than direct confrontation to challenge limitations, with the result being increased facilities and resources or services for the black school. Clemmont Vontress, a black director of guidance in Indiana, captured the dilemma eloquently in an issue of *Phi Delta Kappan*. He wrote that the "Negro principal must respond to the expectations of the superintendent, who is generally white, and to his teachers, who are usually Negro. This dual responsibility creates an ethnic dilemma for him." Vontress correctly identifies the tension between the expectations of black personnel and white superintendents; however, he incorrectly assumes that black professors were often more "interested in presenting a good front than in ascertaining the real capabilities of their students and teachers."[18] The facade Vontress identified, and which superintendents accepted, was only the public face the black professor deliberately and connivingly displayed.

In the setting of the segregated South, as Professors Bobby Huff and Henry Brown, colleagues of Byas's, affirm, the game of Dr. Jekyll and Mr. Hyde had to be played so skillfully, with such a believable persona, that the superintendent would not realize that his employee was a master at deception. To the contrary, professors intentionally adopted a raceless persona and overtly engaged in behaviors and conversation that implied they were upholding the agenda for black schooling as outlined by the superintendent. The game could be as simple as blithely mentioning to the superintendent that it "wouldn't look good" to have a black basketball team go to a neighboring town in an old dilapidated bus. In the aftermath of the *Brown* case and the need for equality, to point out to the superintendent that he should not allow his black school to be seen as having insufficient resources would appear to represent interests similar to those of the superintendents, many of whom were unabashedly involved in efforts to resist integration of schools. However, the professor's real intent in making the statement would have be to provide better transportation to the black students. Thus, language often masked intent. The "key" in these interactions, Huff explains, was "to be smarter than your boss [in order] to get things done. People had to do it," he concludes.[19] His conclusion affirms the truth of historian Leon Litwack's assertion that teachers, school principals, and domestics all "had to practice deceit to keep their jobs."[20]

As Byas confronted the dilemma in Gainesville and began to imagine how he could indirectly force his superintendent to support an expanded program for his school, he had in his repertoire one episode of having successfully played, and won, a major game of Dr. Jekyll and Mr. Hyde. The episode had occurred the previous school year, just before he left Hutchenson in Douglasville to accept the position at Gainesville. The actors in the smaller town had been different, and the scripted activity had been different. But the intellectual creativity required, disguised with the accommodating demeanor that characterized the game, remained the same.

Round One: The Dr. Jekyll and Mr. Hyde Game at Hutchenson Elementary and High School in Douglasville

The situation confronting Byas at Hutchenson that had required him to play his first serious round of Dr. Jekyll and Mr. Hyde had been generated not by parents but by the expected moneys being made available from the state for black schools and the clash with the local school representatives over how these moneys should be disbursed. In the years before and after the *Brown* decision, the Minimum Foundation Education Program (MFEP) in Georgia would be used to upgrade and rebuild 511 black schools in the state. The MFEP was first suggested in the 1940s as a way of addressing the need for higher teacher standards and increased facilities for white children throughout the state, all of whom had also been handicapped by Georgia's historical lack of attention to education. However, it had become viable politically in Georgia, and moneys had been made available to black schools, only when rural whites and others realized in the next decade that passage of the MFEP was the only way the state might be able to preserve its segregated schools.[21]

As principal of Hutchenson, Byas was aware of the availability of the MFEP money. The teachers' association he had joined when he first entered the profession, the Georgia Teachers and Education Association (GTEA), was a well-organized collective that delivered a variety of information to its members through its state, regional, and local meetings and through its state publication, the *Herald*. In the *Herald*, for example, a writer had noted that "for the first time the state has become a partner with county and independent school systems in providing school buildings and initial equipment on a minimum basis for all school children." Moreover, during the first annual meeting of the GTEA that Byas had attended, a panel discussion had centered on implementing the MFEP.[22]

The problem for Byas in this first round of Dr. Jekyll and Mr. Hyde was that the local school board had accepted MFEP moneys from state coffers to build a new school for black children but was now was refusing to appropriate sufficient funds to equip the new school. This dilution of responsibility at the local level meant that a new building might be constructed for blacks with state money while the educational program could be sabotaged in individual districts because of insufficient allocations.[23] In the case of the new building at Hutchenson, Byas had been informed by his superintendent that he had $6,500 to spend for equipment for the whole school. Neither the teachers nor the community had this information. Instead, all believed the public press about the resources to be provided in the new building soon to be under construction. The new professor was silently incredulous. "I had more than that in furniture in my house that I was renting," he recalls, "and we [the school] had so many deficits that $6,500 was an insult to me. But I could not tell the superintendent that I was insulted by that." Echoing his colleagues, he concludes: "You've got to keep your job."[24]

For the new professor confronted with the vexing dilemma of limited school funds, the logical point of intervention should have been the director of the Division of Negro Education in the state, R. L. Cousins. Expecting the director of Negro Education to use the persuasive power of his office to intercede on behalf of the black community, Byas drove to Atlanta to meet with Cousins. The professor's decision to enlist Cousins's assistance was based on several factors. Both Byas and Cousins had master's degrees from Columbia University, and Cousins had reportedly been favorably impressed by Byas during previous encounters. Byas knew Cousins could be a "slick rascal," having seen how he had outmaneuvered a local superintendent to help Byas get the job at Hutchenson, and he expected similar creative energy to be applied in Cousins's response to the problem at Hutchenson. Moreover, in the world of black education, Cousins appeared consistently at professional meetings to report on the state of black education, and he used philanthropic money to support professional development activities for blacks across the state. Given the information Byas had in the days before historian James Anderson would expose the ways directors of Divisions of Negro Education, such as Cousins, were actually fulfilling the lower educational expectations of northern philanthropists, Byas's initial expectation that Cousins would intercede on the school's behalf was not an unreasonable one.[25]

Byas learned early, however, the truth of Anderson's assertion. His meeting with Cousins merely taught him that the black professor did not have a real advocate in Cousins. While Cousins was interested in promoting an acceptable program for black children, he was not, Byas believed, interested in promoting a good program. "I went to try to see whether or not he could assist me in getting more money," Byas recalls.

However, Cousins used the interview to explain the variety of ways the $6,500 Byas had been allotted might be spent. With this implicit suggestion that he accept the status quo of inequality, Byas reports that he was "insulted again." Although the planned school at Hutchenson was to be named the R. L. Cousins School, Cousins was not sufficiently invested in the education that would occur in the school bearing his name to lobby for needed expenditures.[26]

Byas is realistic in his assessment of the position Cousins was in. "He couldn't have much guts being the head of Negro Education—his job was to have a peaceable relationship with superintendents throughout the state. He couldn't have been a strong advocate for the black folk because the white folk employed him." Byas is convinced that Cousins did not want him to return to the school community "and raise sand" in ways that would implicate Cousins as a participant in the confusion because the men who headed these Divisions of Negro Education across the states wanted to be perceived as trying to promote good programs. Disappointed, Byas returned to his desk at Hutchenson with the same problem but with a new understanding that the responsibility was his "to devise something that would cause the superintendent and the Board to give us more money."[27]

Despite being told he had only $6,500 to equip a school, Byas firmly believed that he could accomplish whatever he set out to do. "You just find a way," he says. "The way is out there for you to get the job done, you just have to find it." The plan he hatched leveraged the federal and local climate of the era with an understanding of the constraints and possibilities he faced in this particular situation. He would need to create an imminently logical argument that made it impossible for the superintendent and the school to turn down his request. The plan could not include a frontal attack; rather, it had to be a calculated trap that would publicly place the superintendent and board in a position of needing to respond. His solution was to entangle the superintendent and school board in the contradiction between their public statements and private actions and to make them publicly accountable for the contradiction.

Byas decided to implement a strategy that would cause him to appear to be utilizing the $6,500 the school board had allocated to move his faculty and staff into the new building but that would deliver the students and faculty into the new building without any of the amenities the school board had publicly boasted would be available. These amenities included a lunchroom, kitchen, industrial arts shop, teachers' lounge, and library, none of which were available in the old building. To make the plan viable, Byas needed first to create a proposal for the expenditure of funds that would appear to be educationally sound. This requirement could be defended only if he garnered input from his staff.

Without revealing the financial constraints under which they were operating, the professor instructed each faculty member to "write down what they thought we ought to buy" to provide a strong program in the new building. Byas did not tell the teachers of the board's approved allotment because he was concerned that supplying this information would limit their vision. Moreover, his definition of school leadership required him to be responsible for solving school fiscal problems, and thus he "did not want to burden them" with the difficulty the school was facing. The faculty complied, and Byas compiled the submitted lists. Afterward, he made copies of the complete list and gave them to the teachers. On the new list, he asked teachers to note those things that "we absolutely must have." The faculty responded, and Byas now had a composite description of needs he believed he could justify to the superintendent as items that would be the "bare minimum" of what was needed to operate a school. He believed that the list was sufficiently streamlined that "if educators looked at [it], they [wouldn't] see anything frivolous."[28]

Using the revised list, Byas crafted a letter that created an ordering of school priorities, carefully ranking almost all the items the school board had publicly named as being in the building near the bottom of the list of school priorities. He then sent his proposal to the school board with the subject heading "Requisition for Equipment for R. L. Cousins School." Byas maintains that his purpose at the time was to get more money from the board at the same time that he had to "sympathize with the fact that the district had no money."[29] In its entirety, his letter read:

Dear Sirs:
    Because of certain limitations, namely, (1) the amount of money available, and (2) the uncertainty of the [an area] elementary school being consolidated, we find ourselves severely handicapped in making a requisition for equipping the new school.
    We were hoping that an expanded school program for the Negro pupils could be offered next year; however, the $6,500.00 available will not permit such.
    Our guiding light in submitting this requisition is first, to maintain

our present program in its very limited form; and, secondly, as more money is made available, to add the desired courses and activities to our offering.

To follow this procedure means that three major departments would not be in operation upon the opening of our new school: namely, the woodworking shop, the school lunch program and the commercial Department. Because we feel that it is better to do a little job well than a large job haphazardly, and in the light of events this is the best course educationally to follow.

In keeping with the guiding light, as mentioned here in, we have established the following order of preferences for areas to be equipped. (1) Library; (2) Home Economics; (3) Science; (4) Classrooms; (5) Assembly; (6) Commercial; (7) Lunch Room and Kitchen; (8) Shop; (9) clinic; (10) Secretary Office, Principal's and Teachers' Lounge.

This order is made assuring there will be no consolidation of the two school[s]. Our student seating equipment is geared to 550 students.

Accompanying the letter was a sixteen-page supplement outlining the inventory of furniture that could be transferred from the old building to the new building and a "partial order for equipment" that listed basic needs, such as teachers' desks and student desks. Byas also outlined in minute detail, including the specific color and exact cost of each item, the equipment that would be required to equip the school fully in the ten areas outlined in the letter.[30]

With this proposed list of expenditures, Byas demonstrated conclusively that the movement of students from one building to another and the purchase of sufficient furniture would consume the $6,500 allocated by the board. His letter set a tone implying his understanding of the financial limitations under which the school board was operating; however, his use of terms such as "partial order" also established the clear message that the school would be insufficiently equipped. Because of the meticulous specificity of detail in outlining school needs for a sound educational program, his proposal documented the seriousness with which he and his staff approached the task. Moreover, because the proposal contained a prioritized list that maintained current practices before expanding to include the anticipated new practices, he created a dilemma in which the new school could not even open the lunchroom and kitchen until the school board had reached item seven in funding the list. Although its language never challenges the inequality, the proposal provides explicit documentation of the lack of facilities for blacks in the county. In a post-*Brown* climate, public documentation of inequality, as the school board no doubt realized, could bring legal repercussions. In neighboring Irwin County, the school board was being sued by black parents for failing to provide equality in resources.[31]

Reflecting on the proposal, Byas explains that he simply could not give the superintendent an order for $6,500 worth of materials. If he supplied a request that totaled $6,500 and the superintendent filled the order, when the black community protested the sparse furnishings in the building, the superintendent would be able to rightly argue that he had supplied the school with everything requested by the professor. This strategy would allow the superintendent to publicly shift the blame for poor funding to the black principal. So, Byas says, "I wanted to take, number one, that argument from him." However, Byas realized that he had to present some kind of plan that would be educationally sound if he desired to gain support. He notes that by establishing the requests in order of priority, he was able to place at the bottom of the list the items that were not available in the current school, such as a commercial department and kitchen. This strategy created a dilemma whereby, if the board followed his list, the money would be expended before the amenities being publicly touted as available for black students in the new school would even be reached on the list.[32]

For the board to challenge his priority list, Byas knew that board members would have to agree with one another on a new set of priorities. Byas "reasoned that they wouldn't—because they were talking about this new school and what it was going to be . . . and what it would have. And here we are going into the school [without the things they promised]." By putting basic equipment first, such as chairs and teachers' desks, Byas created a scenario in which the board was caught between its rhetoric about the school and the reality of its failure to fund the school.

Upon receipt of the memo, not unexpectedly, Byas was summoned by the school board. The board and the superintendent were "upset" that he had established a priority list that had a kitchen near the bottom, and Byas was asked to justify the order he had presented. Byas appeared as requested, presenting a public aura of understanding the monetary constraints the school board faced while being simultaneously unflappable in his explanations. Because of his affiliation with the black teachers' association, Byas knew that $1 million was available for new buildings but that it was up to individual school boards to equip these buildings beyond the $6,500 state allotment. The local school board was apparently not planning to provide any additional funds from its own resources to upgrade a black school.

During the exchange with the board about his list of priorities, Byas patiently explained the rationale for his proposal. "What I am recommending is that you start with the first item—go as far as your money will let you, and then when you get more money, pick up where you left off."

"Professor, why did you put the lunchroom as number seven?" Byas remembers one board member asking.

"Well," the principal explained, "all these years we never had one. We've got classrooms and home economics. That's why they have a higher priority." His answer was unquestionably logical. Yet if the board failed to fund the lunchroom and shop, "a whole lot of the school" would be simply empty.

Along with one white principal sitting in on the meeting, Byas was one of only two people in the room to hold a master's degree. Even the superintendent did not have graduate training. Although to an observer Byas's language and manner appeared to be conciliatory and understanding, he was using his intellect and training to outthink both the school board and the superintendent and accomplish his own agenda for the school. No one among them, according to Byas, could reasonably say that his plan was frivolous. And no one did. At the end of the discussion, Byas's strategy prevailed. By the time he left the board meeting that evening, its members had "found" more than $30,000 for the new black school.[33]

Byas did not remain at Hutchenson long enough to occupy the new building. The year these events occurred was the year he was offered the job in Gainesville. However, Byas had played the black professor's game of Dr. Jekyll and Mr. Hyde so skillfully that the superintendent in Douglas County, upon hearing of Gainesville's interest in hiring Byas, reportedly said, "Professor, I sure hate to lose you." While that interest had not immediately translated into tangible efforts to keep him, the superintendent did finally offer to raise his salary so that it would be comparable with that of the white principal if he stayed. Although Byas was unfazed by the offer and continued with his plans to relocate to Gainesville, the superintendent's reported concession reveals the respect the board and superintendent had for him, suggesting strongly that they were unaware of the ways Byas had subverted their intent to limit financial expenditures for black education.

When Byas left Hutchenson for Gainesville and Fair Street, he left in the files all the orders for materials for one of the "best equipped schools in that area."[34] As he now confronted the delicate dilemma that surfaced almost as soon as he arrived at his new school and adopted town, he at least brought the victory he had netted just the previous year in his first round of the Dr. Jekyll and Mr. Hyde game. In Gainesville, Byas had new players and different concerns, but he would have to repeat the same old strategies of illusive confrontation with the superintendent in order to get the black school the resources it needed.[35]

Round Two: The Dr. Jekyll and Mr. Hyde Game at Fair Street in Gainesville

The replay of the game in Gainesville began with Byas meeting with some of the black citizens in the community to discuss school needs.[36] Before other plans could be made, obtaining permission from the community to exercise leadership in its contest with the superintendent was critical. His action reflected the suggestions offered in an article published the fall of that year in the black teachers' professional journal, the *Herald*. In this article, the writer noted that one of the five characteristics of an exemplary principal is the ability to stimulate the community to recognize its needs and organize it in ways that would help it meet its needs.[37] For Byas, implementing such a strategy meant he would need to steer black parents to embrace a larger vision of the difficulties confronted by their school, rather than merely rallying behind one facet of the problem.

Within weeks, Byas reports he was able "to convince some of the people who were hollering for a truancy officer [that they] may need a truancy officer, but [that they] needed some things even more than a truancy officer." As an example, he talked specifically with community members about the need for guidance counselors. In black schools historically, all teachers intentionally served as guidance counselors for the school, a fact that is documented in the literature on segregated schools and addressed directly in the Fair Street School Evaluation, which had been completed for Fair Street's approval as an accredited school. The utilization of teachers as guidance counselors was a necessary solution in segregated settings where money was not available for trained counselors. Byas explained to the community that having a full-time counselor would be significant for the delivery of services to students. In 1958, 51 percent of the seniors (juniors at the time of Byas's arrival) would note their intention of entering professional, technical, and managerial work. However, only 10 percent of recent graduates had actually been able to enroll in college.[38] A trained counselor would be one way to address this differential between aspirations and actualizations.

Byas's goal in providing examples of school needs was to convince community members to allow him to take the lead in negotiating with the superintendent to obtain the variety of materials and services that he believed would be in the best interests of the student body. He could not approach the superintendent without having the support of his parents because being sure parents were happy was a rubric by which many superintendents judged the effectiveness of a professor. However, he could not capitulate to the requests of the community either, especially when he believed the community's requests were too narrowly framed to be an effective solution to the myriad problems the school faced.

Having attained some modicum of support from his preliminary conversations with community leaders, Byas approached the superintendent. His strategy was to position himself between the real needs of the community, which extended beyond its request for a truancy officer, and the superintendent, who merely wanted to placate the parents until their attention might be diverted to something else. His strategy in this new iteration of the Dr. Jekyll and Mr. Hyde game was to request permission from the superintendent to conduct a "Curriculum Survey." Byas explained to the superintendent that the survey would be a way of assessing the school needs and would be a critical step in making decisions about distribution of resources and personnel for the school. Although Byas makes no connection between the two, his strategy also reflects the black professional ideology of the period. In the Public Relations Committee report at the annual meeting of black teachers in Georgia in April 1957, delegates were admonished that "each school should conduct a self-study to determine the direction it seeks to take." The report, furthermore, encouraged the cooperation of parents, teachers, and pupils to effectuate a "unity of purpose." Moreover, from the perspective of sound educational philosophy, as exemplified by the National Association of Secondary School Principals (NASSP) endorsement of surveys, Byas's proposal of a school survey was a cutting-edge idea for all schools, and not merely black schools. Apparently intrigued with Byas's request, the superintendent reportedly raised a query about the length of time conducting a survey would take. To the superintendent's pleasure, Byas explained that to complete the survey adequately would require the rest of the school year.[39]

For the superintendent, Byas's proposal of a survey was an ingenuous way to delay, perhaps postpone indefinitely, the parents' request. The school year was just beginning, and the superintendent reportedly wanted to stifle the black parents' complaints. "What about these people screaming for a truancy officer?" he reportedly asked when confronted with Byas's plan. "Can you hold them back?"

Without telling the superintendent he already had the support of key members of the community or challenging the intent embedded in the superintendent's language, Byas respectfully acknowledged that he thought he could hold the community back. As required by the unwritten rules of the game, this response allowed Byas to appear to be empathetically upholding the superintendent's concerns. Byas then left the office of the superintendent, having obtained permission to conduct a curriculum survey. As far as the superintendent was concerned, the idea was a good one. With the new professor requesting a curriculum survey instead of a truancy officer, the superintendent could report to the black community that he was not ignoring their demands. Instead, he could report that a different request had been made by the professor and that he was merely adhering to the professor's proposal.

The curriculum survey was begun immediately. It was a Herculean effort, the fruits of which would not be immediately apparent to participants. However, the time involved and the devotion to completing the task would unite the vision of the principal and community in advocating for school needs. Before it was over, 325 student questionnaires would be distributed and 285 returns analyzed; a stratified random sample of students would be selected for standardized testing, and the city would be divided into eleven areas to "make personal interviews" with 25 to 60 adults in each area for a total of 500 attempted interviews. As the faculty, students, and community entered the process, no one could have imagined how long it would take or what the results would be.

The project had several stages: coordinating committees, conducting inquiries and synthesizing results, and publishing findings. In the first stage, begun shortly after he had the superintendent's permission for the curriculum survey, Byas convened a series of faculty meetings with teachers to examine and evaluate the current program at Fair Street. In these meetings, the faculty members agreed that they wished to establish among themselves a clear purpose for the inquiry prior to soliciting the support of community members and students. After five faculty conversations, they invited thirty-eight students, grades seven through twelve, to join the self-evaluation process. These students also met on four occasions with the professor to discuss materials available to support the curriculum at the school. Faculty and staff, having reached a "general understanding" of the curricular needs in the school, announced a general meeting at the school, inviting members of the community to attend and become part of the conversation.

Rather than only one, two mass meetings with the community were held. Both of these, according to the published curriculum survey, were "very well attended by parents, faculty, and students." Descriptions of the second meeting provide the following glimpse of activity:

> We decided in our last mass meeting that in order to bring about a better understanding of the whole situation and to move toward the betterment thereof that a three-fold study would be made, namely:
> 1. a. To make an examination of as many graduates and dropouts as possible during the past five years.
> b. To conduct a study and administer selected standardized tests, on a survey basis of our present school population.
> c. To conduct a survey to determine the wishes and desires of parents and other interested adults relative to the school curriculum.
> 2. To draw conclusions and make recommendations as to course offerings and or activities.
> 3. To chart a course for a continual study and evaluation of our program—herein or at sometime in the immediate future.

Attendees at the meeting agreed that these purposes could be best accomplished through formulating three committees. All attendees were invited to work on either the committee concerned with graduates and dropouts, the committee concerned with the present school population, or the committee concerned with the adult population. Teachers served as chairpersons of each group. Each committee was charged with developing a "plan of attack" related to its own topic. Byas served as the coordinator of all the committees.[40]

Beginning in October and continuing throughout the year, the school and the community devoted substantial nonpaid time to committee work. For example, the teachers on the committee on dropouts and graduates decided to meet every school day, except Friday, at 3:00 P.M. and work for a minimum of forty minutes; on Fridays, they had an abbreviated schedule, working for only thirty minutes after school, and on Tuesday nights, they convened with the community members who were also part of the committee. In a similar pattern of time investment, the committee on the present school population met on Tuesday, Wednesday, and Thursday afternoons of each week, with Wednesday night being the "most suitable night for the meeting of the entire group." Their thirty-five committee meetings included two extra months of activity, presumably beyond initial projections, to tabulate the results of standardized tests. The final group met twice weekly after school for two to five hours for six months. At its end, they had devoted more than twenty-two hours to compiling and analyzing community surveys.[41]

All three of the teacher work groups shared similar characteristics, as the activities of each group adhered to common standards of evaluative research. Each generated school concerns, converted concerns to survey questions, and distributed surveys to members of the school community. Group 2's report on standardized testing provides an example of the activities that characterized all groups. The report details activities such as ordering and reviewing standardized tests that could possibly be used as instruments of data collection, soliciting and making group decisions about appropriate questions to use on the group's own two planned questionnaires, crafting a plan to distribute questionnaires to students and parents, planning a process for tabulating results, piloting sample tests, and generating a plan for an appropriate sample. A similar orchestration of people and materials is evident in group 1's attention to school dropouts. Committee members collected data on dropouts from permanent record files, collaboratively developed and revised separate questionnaires for dropouts and graduates, and agreed to interview as many dropouts as possible rather than merely sending questionnaires.[42]

Because much of the committee work involved the need to contact community members beyond those already working with teacher groups, Byas used Fair Street's school newspaper, the *Clarion*, to invite community ownership of, and commitment to, the completion of the survey. In the December issue, as the curriculum survey was taking shape, Byas used the paper to describe to parents the events that had transpired thus far, emphasizing his own commitment to seeing that the "educational needs of [their] children will be met. For unless this is done, there is no justification for the existence of a Fair Street or any other school." The article then appealed directly to the community for help: "We think you can help us to determine the experience areas to be provided (or as many of you have said, 'the courses to be offered'). Knowing that it will take too much of your time to meet with us, we thought it wise to ask a committee (composed of your faculty, interested adults and students) to come to you. We would like to know what you think about Fair Street Junior and Senior High School; its strong and weak points. We hope to use your suggestions as a guide in changing our experience areas courses." He then explained the division of the project into three subcommittees and recounted the purpose of each committee. He noted that by this time members of the school community had "no doubt" seen the questionnaires, and he expressed his hope that they have returned them to the committee. He also emphasized the importance of their response by noting that their answers would be "tabulated, and the committee will use your answers as a basis for determining the educational needs of the youth served by this school." The article ended by explaining to this black community, which had never been involved in any similar project, that these activities were called a "Curriculum Survey" and that they were providing their "best thinking" to help their children "for tomorrow."[43]

The process of completing the curriculum survey did require the full school year. At its end, the professor requested money from the superintendent to publish the results. Since no money had been expended that year for a truancy officer, the request seemed a reasonable one. However, the superintendent reported to the professor that he did not have the money to support the publication of results. Presumably, the superintendent had given little attention to the process and was unaware of the magnitude of the effort or the extent of school and community collaboration. Visibly unperturbed by the superintendent's recalcitrance, Byas requested funds from the Parent Teacher Association (PTA) at Fair Street. With its financial backing, he had professionally printed three hundred copies of the curriculum survey at the cost of twenty-five cents a book. The document was thirty-two pages long, with a table of contents, acknowledgments, introduction, report and recommendations of each of the committees, and recommendations to superintendent and board of education. It also included copies of surveys and tables documenting results. Byas then delivered a copy of the document to the unsuspecting superintendent.

At his office, the superintendent slowly reviewed the document. As the black community had indicated at the outset, dropouts were indeed a problem in the school. According to the report of the committee on dropouts and graduates, the dropouts were seldom from the top quarter of the class, and fewer than 50 percent had repeated a subject. Importantly for parents seeking a truancy officer, 78 percent of dropouts reported that they received parental support to stay in school, a finding confirmed by results that showed that 85 percent of parents insisted on seeing students' report cards. However, parental support was mediated by economic concerns. Seventy-eight percent of the dropouts had held jobs while in school, and 40 percent believed that they did not have adequate spending money. Additionally the dropouts were students who were deemed by the committee "to have [had] too little participation . . . in extra-curricular activities."

The report of the students who dropped out could be contrasted with the report of graduates. Thirty-five percent had had one to four years of college, but 43 percent reported that they were financially unable to attend college. A full 50 percent of students believed that they had not had adequate courses in high school, and 55 percent believed that they needed courses that they were unable to take in high school. To address the concerns raised, the group cited the need for expanded curriculum in home economics; typing; science, particularly physics and chemistry; and physical education, the last being required by state law rather than being highly ranked on the student list. They also point to the "dire need for a visiting teacher" as a way of addressing the problem with keeping students in school.

The results from the committee on the present school population echoed the desire of black students for an adequate high school education. The committee reported that 77 percent of students wanted to finish high school and 68 percent wished to go to college. From the parental survey, the committee also determined that parents had similar aspirations for their children, with 77 percent noting that they planned for their children to attend college. This aspiration for their children occurred despite the fact that only 12 percent of the reporting parents had been to college and as many as 50 percent had not finished high school themselves. Similar congruity between students and parents was also revealed in areas of curriculum, with 40 percent of students identifying typing as a central curricular need, followed by driver's education and foreign language. Likewise, 76 percent of their parents identified the need for commercial courses in the school, and 24 percent noted the need for driver's education.[44]

The professor waited patiently while the superintendent read the survey results. Byas reports that when this leader of schools in Gainesville got to the section on the results of the standardized tests, he was particularly perturbed. Of the thirty students then enrolled in grade twelve, not one student was on grade level in achievement tests in reading, mathematics, and language. Twenty-nine were more than one grade below, twenty-eight more than two, and at the end of the spectrum, ten students were more than five grades below level. Similar distributions in reading, mathematics, and language occurred in grades seven through eleven. Standardized tests in social and related science were no more encouraging. After presenting a tabulation of scores in the areas of U.S. history and government, physical science, and biological science, the committee concluded that most of the students "fell in the first percentile, which is very low." The Mental Maturity Test showed students typically scoring in the high average to low average, with most of the distribution toward average or below. As with the standardized achievement tests, the committee reported high student scores in nonlanguage than in language, which they concluded to indicate "a deficiency in reading, spelling, and vocabulary usage."[45]

The superintendent's shock and dismay soon became a verbal reprimand to the new professor. As Byas remembers the interaction: "He said to me, 'This is bad here. Look at these test scores. This is a reflection of you and your predecessor.'" Rather than acknowledging the problem in the black school as originating in the less than adequate resources, the superintendent preferred to shift the blame for the educational incompetence to the new black professor and, by extension, his staff. Byas was unrattled. As he recalls his response, "Mr. [superintendent], in all due respect, you and your predecessor have been in charge of the school. And, uh, you all have to take some of the blame if blame is to be given out." Byas patiently explained, "I have been here one year, and I take one year of responsibility. [But] somebody else has been in charge of these schools the other time."

The superintendent now had a massive problem much more complicated than the singular request with which he had initially been confronted. With the completion of its curriculum survey, the black community now had a documented list of needs. Indeed, far from the paltry sum of two hundred dollars he might have expended on an uncertified truancy officer had he heeded the parents' initial requests, the superintendent was now faced with requests in writing that would require major financial expenditures. Rather than a truancy officer, the members of the school community now requested a visiting teacher *and* a guidance counselor so that the students' potentials could be developed "to the fullest extent." They wanted an expanded curriculum that included commercial education, chemistry, physics, advanced biology, foreign languages, and physical education. They also wanted materials and equipment for new courses, new teacher support as needed to implement the courses, and money for teacher workshops. Lest their requests be unclear, the curriculum survey ended with a series of overall recommendations to the superintendent. They emphasized that these recommendations resulted from a joint meeting of all groups, where the recommendations of each group were discussed "point by point" and where each group was required to present a factual finding to support a recommendation.

So much for "holding them back." The list in the superintendent's hands was extensive, well documented for its overlap in committee recommendations, and straightforward. The result of his self-interested, hastily approved plan to allow the new professor to engage the school in a curriculum survey had allowed ample time for the professor to lead an effort that crystallized a vision across varied constituents of the black school community and that provided a formal venue through which the school community could present well-formulated and adequately substantiated requests. Far from "holding them back," as the superintendent initially envisioned that he would, the professor had masterfully generated a more costly and complete list of needs for the black school and squarely placed before the superintendent and school board the onus of responsibility for fulfilling those needs: "the following are areas in which we are making to you, the Superintendent of Schools and Board of Education of the City of Gainesville, Georgia, for your consideration."[46]

Confronted with a damaging portrait of his black high school, the superintendent worried about the possible implications of insubstantial support of a black program if the survey results were made public, and thus his immediate response was to repress the information. "I hope no one has seen this" is Byas's memory of the superintendent's effort to conclude the matter and control its repercussions. The superintendent's concern that the results not be publicly disseminated likely reflected two concerns, one personal and the other professional. On a personal level, he is critiqued by professor Byas as someone who had not embraced the changing climate of race relations that characterized some of the other white citizens of Gainesville and even some members of the school board. Byas reports that this superintendent was one who still refused to use the titles "Mr." or "Mrs." when interacting with his black teachers. Coupled with his refusal to grant the community's request for a truancy officer, the superintendent's obstinacy to support improved educational efforts for the black high school may reveal either his personal beliefs or his perception that he represented a constituency that expected him to affirm the status quo as a measure of his job performance. Professionally, the concern may have been linked to legal implications. Like the problem in Hutchenson the previous year, in a post-*Brown* era, public visibility of the plight of the black school could generate the grounds for litigation, a response neither he nor the school board would welcome. As at Hutchenson, this climate worked to advance the cause of the black community when properly exploited.

In responding to the superintendent's query about the publicity the results had received, Byas blithely lied, although he adds that he thought it was a good lie. Appearing to be sympathetic to the dilemma posed by public knowledge of the document, Byas answered the superintendent as though he were confessing: "I just dropped off a couple of copies to the local press." According to Byas, the superintendent was "*sho* sorry he had done that." Meanwhile, Byas left the superintendent's office and set out to convert the lie to truth immediately. Heading directly for the local Gainesville newspaper, the *Daily Times*, he entered the office and dropped off a copy of the curriculum survey. Although he had no prior relationship with the editor, the results—as he had hoped—became the major school news in Gainesville for several weeks, thus creating a public record of the black school's needs.[47]

"It was the most comprehensive survey to ever be conducted in the Gainesville schools," the *Daily Times* led in its series of front-page articles, all of which focused on bringing wide visibility to the needs at the black high school. One headline article, published May 2, 1958, was titled "Fair Street Curriculum Study: Students Rate Poorly in Biological, Physical Sciences." Its lead began by noting that this is "another in a series of a reports" on the Fair Street Curriculum Study. The article then provided detail on the numbers of surveys utilized and return rates, as well as the time members of the committee had invested to achieve a completed report. Most important, the paper also included the recommendations of the committee, including adding driver's education, engaging yearly testing of students, and adequately funding the school library. Thanks to the newspaper editor, who would later describe Byas as an "innovative genuine community leader," the plight of the school became public conversation during an era when whites needed to demonstrate the equality of black schools if integration was to be avoided. Moreover, the data substantiated the black community's needs as far exceeding a truancy officer.[48]

The school community had reason to be proud of its efforts. Publicly pressed, the school board acted, beginning with typewriters and business education. The chairman of the board approached the professor explaining a cost estimate of $5,500 to outfit a typing class. Although reportedly more open to funding the black schools than the superintendent was, the chairman was looking for confirmation that the students were not going to "tear up the stuff" or destroy the equipment. In response, Byas brought the board member to talk with a local black businessman, who slowly and dryly, but with sharp mental acumen, refused to give the chairman any assurance of the children's behavior but affirmed that he wanted the board to supply for the black children the same equipment it supplied for white children. It was the kind of statement an independent business owner could make, and although Byas does not make a direct connection, he surely knew it when he steered the chairman in the direction of this particular community member. The board member must also have recognized the statement as an implied expectation for equality in the distribution of funds between the white and black schools, an expectation that could not be unilaterally dismissed.

Byas reports that by the beginning of the next school year, the school board had spent $6,500 for typewriters and had added to the budget adding machines, calculators, and an extra line for the hiring of a typing teacher. Pitts quotes the total cost of the new initiative at $6,800 to the school board, including desks and equipment, and adds that by the fall of that same year, 124 Fair Street students were enrolled in their first typing class.[49] According to Byas, this was his whole eighth-grade class. Within two years, all of the requests in the curriculum survey would be met. More than the reprimand of a truancy officer, black students soon had a curricular incentive to stay in school.

The strategy utilized by a professor in his first year in the community was successful. Although he appeared to be accommodating, Byas coupled his understanding of community norms with his educational expertise to find a way to propel a resistant superintendent into making needed changes within the school. Moreover, he had harnessed the momentum of the community to create a single vision of the school's needs. Byas reports that the staff and community members who worked on the curriculum survey believed that they had worked harder on this than on anything in their lives but that they had learned something and enjoyed it. In particular, after the newspaper ran its series of front-page editorials, people really "stuck out their chest." The Curriculum Study was a document "everybody could take pride and ownership of."

Viewed through one lens, the entire episode is an exemplar of school and community collaboration. Though the professor and the community were initially in disagreement about the expected ends, the project generated mutual ownership and a collaborative vision for school needs. As will be discussed in the latter chapters of the book, the professor intentionally approached the school and community in a manner that was professionally and culturally appropriate. In response, the community coalesced in support of his plan, despite the fact that no evidence exists that they understood the ways the outcome would be used to serve directly the needs of the school. Interpreted through this rubric, the episode provides a model of the triangulation of leadership, school participants, and community members converging around a single vision: namely, to engage in activities that would produce the best education for black children.

Viewed through another lens, the curriculum survey was also the result of a deliberate leadership style whereby the professor resisted inequality by collecting data and using the results to leverage financial investments in the school. Examining the activity through this lens demonstrates the ways in which Byas presented a demeanor of acquiescence to the superintendent while using the survey to cultivate a plan of resistance. As Byas recalls: "He [the superintendent] is the one who has to evaluate me at the end of the year. He has got to believe I'm doing that little nothing he wants me to do."[50] The strategy was not unlike the Brer Rabbit saga repeatedly embraced in African American literature. Brer Rabbit, without the physical strength to defend himself, uses his tenacity and mental acumen to outsmart his would-be captors. Such was the game played by black professors, although they called it Dr. Jekyll and Mr. Hyde. The academic descriptor defining such behavior has been captured by scholars such as Darlene Clark Hines and Kevin Gaines. Quoting and extending Hines, Gaines explains the culture of dissemblance, in which educated blacks might create the appearance of disclosure "while actually remaining an enigma to whites." In Gaines's explanation of this tactic, dissemblance is "more than a guarded demeanor." Rather, it is a "weapon . . . a source of strength" for African American men and women that was central for their survival "in a racialized world not of their own making."[51] The description aptly depicts the behavior of the black professor in the era of de jure segregated schools in the South.

The pervasiveness of the game is captured in a 1967 article in the *Herald*. Although the writer, W. F. Crawl, a professor at Walker Elementary School in Athens, notes that the changing climate of the late 1960s made the game no longer necessary, his commentary also effectively establishes the credibility of the report of black professors on the use of the game. He writes, "Yesteryear, perhaps our images were a little tarnished because of the environment in which we HAD to operate. Perhaps we HAD to be Dr. Jekyll and Mr. Hyde in some instances."[52] He notes that financial needs forced the professor to joust with superintendents and school boards instead of speaking forthrightly about the needs they confronted. They were after all, Negro men first, and principals second. Engaging even the most undereducated superintendent required that prevailing norms of race relations in the South be fulfilled. In this context, there could be no conversation among educational peers, at least not when the Negro professor was overtly raising questions about the highly valued southern system of school segregation and inequality of the races.

Yet, the plan of the black professor to undermine his captors was not a mere expression of fear for job security. In the highest intellectual circles was also a recognition that the difficult problems faced by blacks in the struggle for equality required myriad tactics to obtain solutions. In the *New South* in February 1964, the address of Roy Wilkins, executive secretary of the NAACP, to the Southern Regional Council on November 29th provides "advice to civil rights fighters" at a meeting in Atlanta. After challenging craven tactics and uni-racial assaults, he queries:

> Is it too old-fashioned to suggest that we may need more flexibility in our campaign? Where our opponents have been most inflexible, they have been most vulnerable and we have won undisputed psychological victories, even though practical advances may have been delayed. When the Trojans found a frontal assault ineffective, they used a wooden horse. Hannibal surprised the Romans by bringing elephants the back way across the Alps . . . A bulldozer can excavate for a foundation, but a block and tackle is required to get a piano into the ninth floor.

Wilkins concludes this particular argument by observing that "the plain lesson is that we must use every method, every technique, every tool available."[53] Although his argument is aimed at the tactics of a larger movement and purists would cringe at a comparison of the two disparate leaders, it also reflects the psychological repertoire Malcolm X would advise during the same period: by any means necessary. For the black professor, in the days before a frontal attack on inequality at the local level could be mounted, Dr. Jekyll and Mr. Hyde worked rather well.

Of course, establishing the presence of the Dr. Jekyll and Mr. Hyde game does little to explain how the black professor understood how to play the game. Its unwritten rules required a combination of deceit, communicative skills, and educational expertise in the interaction with the superintendent that were not directly taught in administrative coursework. Thus, to understand the professor's capacity to play the game requires an unraveling of the personal and professional worlds of the black professor. Themselves products of the segregated schools they led and often victims of the same poverty their students confronted, the professor was an exemplar of the black student who could advance beyond the limited circumstances of childhood and through variegated, even co-incidental opportunities, become participants in an expansive educational world that focused its energies solely on helping black professors learn how to save black students like themselves.

For Byas, this personal and professional world reveals three interlocking influences. One influence is his personal background, which includes his familial circumstances, educational experiences from grade school to graduate school and his early teaching practices. The other two are explained by amplifying the activity of his national and state professional networks, most visibly the Association of Schools and Colleges and the Georgia Teachers and Education Association. As explained in the three chapters that follow, each of these worlds help explain the making of a professor.

From High School Dropout to Classroom Teacher

Ever since I have known myself, if I had a problem, I looked first inside myself to find the solution.
— *Ulysses Byas*

The autobiography of another Georgia principal, John R. Harris, who titles his story *Defying the Odds: The Inspirational Story of a Poor Farm Boy Who Overcame Incredible Odds to Become a Successful Educator*, is a memoir of the nuances of family, community, and culture that birthed educational accomplishment in his life during the years preceding desegregation.[1] Like Harris, Byas experienced poverty and poor schooling as a child and adolescent. As both stories demonstrate, a saga that ends in the accomplishment of becoming a professor does not begin that way.

To deconstruct the behaviors of Byas during his Dr. Jekyll and Mr. Hyde episodes requires first, as Harris provides in his work, a recounting of the familial and educational influences of Byas's life prior to his becoming a professor. In his segregated childhood world, where limited financial reward constrained interest in high school diplomas, future professors could be created or could become school dropouts. Fraught with false starts, Byas's career is deeply influenced by his past life of creative solutions to poverty as a child and young adult and by the multiple educational opportunities that shaped his vision of practice. Unearthing the details of these influences, however, requires dissecting his childhood and schooling experiences in Macon; exploring the significance of two higher-education institutions he attended, Fort Valley, a historically black college, and the elite white graduate school at Columbia, and examining his early experiences as a teacher/professor-in-training. The compilation of these life events explains, in part, how Byas was able to become a professor with the commitment and savvy to refuse to be confined by the limitations of a segregated world.

Growing Up in Macon: A Story of Harnessed Ingenuity

Professor Byas was a creative and ingenious child born of poverty and seg-regation but encouraged by motherly values and a school curriculum suf-ficiently expansive to include industrial education for students unlikely to attend college. Born in 1924, he grew up during the Great Depression, and his childhood and adolescence reflect that era. Half or more of black workers in Georgia were unemployed, and the policies of the New Deal, which brought economic relief for many citizens in Georgia, were none-theless inequitably distributed for black workers, a situation that caused some blacks to refer to the policies as NRA, or Negroes Robbed Again.[2] For Byas, the woeful economic realities of the era were compounded by the particulars of his family circumstance. He was the second child of eight, coming of age in the textile town of Macon with a single mother who struggled to pay rent and to provide for the material needs of the family. Byas recalls never being certain where home would be, as they lived in more than ten rental properties during his years growing up. He and his siblings shared beds and clothes, and all family members neces-sarily worked together during this period when amenities such as plumb-ing and electricity were still aspirations.

The realities of the financial needs in the home instilled in this second son an overwhelming and driving need to "help mother" as she struggled to provide for the growing family. Despite child labor laws in Georgia since 1914, Byas was employed by the time he was six, including selling the evening newspaper on a street corner downtown and picking up scrap iron, rags, and bottles to sell to the "scrap man." Laws against child labor were unevenly enforced generally in Georgia, and in 1920 the state had led the nation in the employment of children under fifteen. Indeed, Horace Mann Bond reports that as many as 80 percent of rural black children were employed. Though fewer urban black children were employed, Byas maintained steady employment throughout his young life in the city of Macon, including such menial tasks as sweeping the floor at a candy store downtown.[3] His employment record vividly demonstrates how depress-ingly difficult maintaining economic stability could be, especially when one was growing up fatherless and black in Georgia in the 1930s.

Byas should have been a statistic. His was, as he would later learn in graduate school, a prototypical "broken" family. However, as Byas would argue about the depiction of himself and his family many years later at Teachers College, Columbia, he never perceived his family or his childhood as broken. To the contrary, he contended that he and his siblings were "lacking in material things" but that they were surrounded by loving and caring and sharing in the home environment. For him, the poverty of material circumstances could be distinguished from a poverty of personality, with one failing to constrain the possibilities inherent in the other. Poverty produced resilience, or as Byas would term his values, an ongoing belief that if he looked within himself, he could always "find a way" to address any needs he might confront.

A counterexamination of the circumstances of his childhood helps substantiate the validity of his claim that he could always "find a way" to solve problems he faced. Even at the age of six, on one occasion when he was selling newspapers on the street corner, the young Byas discovered that he could use his wits to generate income that would exceed that of the neighboring boy with whom he had to compete to sell the papers. Asked by a white businessman how each boy would use the money received from selling papers, Byas's competitor described the ways the money would fulfill a personal need. Byas countered with a more empathy-generating response. He piped up that he intended to use the money to help his mother pay the rent. The rent was typically from fifty cents to one dollar a week, but even that amount was difficult for a single mother to pay. It was a coincidence perhaps, hardly possible that a six-year-old could have intentionally exploited the sympathy of the buyer. More likely, Byas's response simply reflected the truth. He did intend to use the money to help pay the rent that would be due at the end of the week. But the agency developed as a result of having the buyer purchase a paper from him instead of his companion perhaps also generated the seedling idea that responses, rightly presented, could influence the outcome of behaviors.

An episode sweeping the floor at a candy shop provides further evidence that some capacity of creative problem solving germinates from his early experiences. The period was one when Georgians warmly embraced the election of Governor Eugene Talmadge, who openly and unashamedly baited racial animosity. Many whites accepted, and benefited from, the mores that defined race relations even as they assuaged their consciences by "helping" those blacks in their employment. Byas's employers' form of "help" was to give to their little floor sweeper the leftover candy in the afternoon, an action they surely assumed would satisfy the sweet tooth of a child and perhaps generate loyalty. Byas, however, quickly learned that the gift of candy could be converted into profitable revenue. Taking the coveted gift home, he used a cardboard box to create a makeshift candy store front. He placed the "candy shop" on the side of his house and sold the individual pieces of candy to the neighborhood children. As candy sold, his meager salary from the job was supplemented by the money he made as a miniature business proprietor.

Part of Byas's ability to find ways to help his mother was generated by the daily press of economic need; however, his childhood solutions also reflect a creative spirit that refused to be squelched by the numerous dictates of segregation. When he and his friends were denied the opportunity to have a swimming pool during the lazy, hot days of a Georgia summer, Byas dammed the small branch of water running through the back of his yard and created a cool place they could all splash and play. Until his sister reported his mischief to their mother, whereupon he was "given a beating" and ordered to dismantle his "pool," the makeshift water park provided enjoyable recreation to black children denied public facilities.

Building his own radio is another indicator of Byas's childhood creative spirit. Although he does not describe the motivation for his desire for a radio, his was the era when Joe Louis and Jessie Owens were champions among blacks for their ongoing capacity to defeat whites, thus demonstrating to the world that blacks could excel in integrated sports arenas. Marian Anderson was likewise a widely admired singer. However, participating vicariously in the exploits and talents of faraway heroes required a radio, which neither Byas's family nor many families on his street were able to afford. In Georgia in 1940 only 51.7 percent of all families had radios, with the percentage of black families presumably falling far below this figure.[4] Byas's solution was to buy a comic book that provided information on creating a crystal set radio, spend a dime for an aerial wire and the other few materials needed, and assemble his own "radio." His feat was so surprising that neighbors gathering around to listen pronounced with pride and amazement, "Byas done built a radio." Over the years, he fashioned bicycles from old used parts, installed two poles between his house and that of a neighbor so he could learn to pole vault, and demonstrated other early forms of resistance to his constrained circumstances. He is at a loss to explain his ingenuity. In the absence of the theoretical framework of "resilience," which educators would later use in reference to children like himself, he employs the explanation that most closely matches his cultural and religious values. "I fault God for it" is one of the few explanations he offers to explain his childhood creativity.[5]

By the time he was a teenager, Byas's experiences crafting solutions to segregated life and economic constraints could in fact have begun to generate the simple, but profound, belief that he could find solutions to anything if he merely looked inside himself. But the single-minded focus he maintained on creatively helping his mother, and himself, in their economically limited world did not come without expense as a school student. His school record from the Bibb County Public Schools provides an erratic portrait of scholarship, whose only trend from his entrance into first grade during the 1930–31 school year seems to be a downward turn as he progressed through the years. Some few grades of excellence are recorded; however, these are accompanied by the opposite extreme, including an F+. His teachers' comments are instructive. They range from "smart" and "brilliant" in the early years, to "good," "tries hard," and "apt" during the middle school years, to "fair," "mischievous," and "playful" during his high school years, by which time he had settled himself into a good average C performance.[6] As far as Byas was concerned, school was a waste of time. He frequently misbehaved, and he developed into an art form the timing of his disruptions so that he could miss as much school as possible. For example, if he challenged the teacher during a particularly disdainful subject, he would be sent home to get his mother, a walk that would have to be multiplied by two to account for the journey home and back. By the time he and his mother returned to the school, as he gleefully explains, he would have missed all of that subject, which he says was his plan from the beginning. No wonder some teachers saw him as "mischievous." In high school, he was irreverent about the utility of Latin verbs, failing to see their relevance for his life. Though he had been deemed "good in studies" in earlier years, his eighth-grade teacher assessed his academic performance as only "fair." For different reasons, twice he was a school dropout, and for the same reason twice he repeated a grade.

Despite the efforts of black educators to salvage children such as him, Byas primarily credits his educational salvation to his mother. Though she had only the seventh-grade education available to blacks in Macon at the time she was a child, she was determined that all her children would receive high school diplomas. The desire was a gallant one but fraught with difficulty. Compulsory attendance laws, in existence in the state since 1916, were unevenly enforced by local authorities, a disparity that helped contribute to the fact that black children were among the majority of those children not in attendance in Georgia. Moreover, with only 46 percent of black children enrolled in schools in 1941–42 and 30 percent of black children enrolled in first grade, she was pushing against the odds with her dream of seeing all of her children graduate. These impediments notwithstanding, Byas's mother, like many blacks during the era, subscribed to the belief that education was the key to her children's and the race's future. In so doing, she unwittingly mirrored later academic arguments about the centrality of family in nurturing strategies that would help black children resist the devaluing effects of race.[7] Although his mother did not require him to make As on his report card, she seeded in her creative and mischievous little boy the idea that he was smart in "book learning," and she held high expectations that he would learn. Indeed, she was so adamant that he actually be educated, and not merely promoted, that when the school passed him in second grade after he had missed much of the spring quarter, his mother insisted that he be held back, or flunked. She had kept her child home for these spring months as a form of silent protest after discovering welts on his body, the result of an overly harsh spanking by a teacher. However, she was emphatic that he be taught the material he had missed, despite the fact that he was given a C for the year and promoted. "He's missed too much," she maintained, and she remained outside the principal's office until the staff relented and he was detained. The report card confirms that Byas repeated second grade, despite showing a passing grade the first time.

In later years, disillusioned with the need for education, Byas pressed his mother to be allowed to dispense with school altogether. Finally obtaining reluctant approval, he formally dropped out of school on April 29, 1939, just before the completion of his eighth-grade year. Elmer Dean writes that black youths were often induced to drop out of school because of the easy availability of jobs as porters, elevator operators, hotel workers, waiters, stockroom clerks, and so forth. However, Dean also notes that the jobs were plentiful precisely because of the "sectional wage differential which places wage rates for Negroes at the bottom of the wage scale."[8] Byas learned this differential firsthand. He worked hard for very little money, and his mother insisted that half the money be used to supply household needs. The combination of hard work, low pay, and little personal enjoyment of his wages created a dropout career that lasted a mere four months. With the financial contributions to the household weighty and his entrée into full-time work demanding, he was glad to return to school the following year. Back at Hudson Industrial School to reenroll her son, his mother echoed her script from his second-grade year. Accompanying him to the high school, she insisted that he repeat a year to make up the work missed, thus creating the record of two eighth-grade years also on his transcript. His mother's influence in his public school years was so significant that he freely admits that his high school diploma, received June 6, 1943, was for her. His mother had indeed beat the odds in producing a high school graduate. As late as 1950, the median number of years of school for Georgia blacks over twenty-five was reported in the census as 4.9.[9] Yet Byas and all his siblings completed high school.

Despite Byas's attribution of influence foremost to his mother in explaining his graduation from high school, to dismiss the influence of the Hudson Industrial School as a silent collaborator in contributing to his diploma is to ignore the contribution of industrial education to his development. Like many black high schools that never participated in the ongoing intellectual debate on the merits of industrial education versus classical education, Hudson offered its students a comprehensive curriculum, believing that all students should be exposed to a variety of ways to earn an income. This idea was consistent with much of the literature on segregated schools, which shows that schools unashamedly embraced both classical and industrial education. For Byas, Latin verbs held no interest, but the trade shops at school did attract his attention. In the expectations and activities of the trade shop, Byas saw a direct relationship between schoolwork and income potential. For a child who had a family member and a few neighbors who had high school diplomas but were still employed as domestics, seeing this relationship between school and increased job opportunities was important to create aspiration. Such was a conclusion black teachers during the era hoped students otherwise uninterested in school might reach.

Byas took the introductory course in industrial education during his first year in high school and was exposed to a variety of skilled areas. He eventually settled on carpentry and building construction as an area of expertise. Consistent with school policy, he took courses in this area the remainder of his years in high school, becoming sufficiently skilled to be among the top three or four students who were offered employment by the professor to help build houses on the weekends. The pay was minimal, fifteen cents an hour, but a school activity was now helping to fulfill his need to make money and to help his mother. He was even allowed to peddle bookshelves and other items constructed in class, sometimes receiving five dollars for an item that cost him two dollars to make. To Byas's

teenage mind, this type of schooling was logical. Although the significance he attributed to it was not as great as the credit he gave his mother,
these activities also explain the steady C student he became in his later
years of high school. Moreover, although Byas was an eager learner in
industrial education who wished to dispense with the preliminaries and
"take wood and start building," the industrial teacher required a variety of
project proposals that incorporated mathematical and literacy skills before students were allowed to build extra projects. Without Byas realizing
it, the teacher's requirement was also increasing his scholastic competence.[10]

The influences of his mother and of the industrial education curriculum loom larger as explanatory factors than the influence of individual
teachers. He recounts his admiration for a particular elementary school
teacher, Eva Phillips Lee, who taught him for two years and instilled in
him a desire to learn. In later years this teacher would attribute the success of her former student to his "fine home training" and his willingness
to ask questions "about anything and everything of which he wasn't absolutely sure." The teacher believed the student made her a better teacher;
Byas in turn is convinced the teacher made him a better student because
she made him want to know. Unfortunately, however, this one teacher's
influence was not sufficient to deter him from dropping out, suggesting
strongly that the capacity of individual teachers to care for individual students could be undermined by larger economic factors that could prohibit student interest despite anything a single teacher might attempt.

Importantly, neither his mother nor the school is alone sufficient to
explain Byas's attainment of a high school diploma. Without the influence of his mother, Byas would have become a permanent dropout in the
eighth grade, before he could have been sufficiently lured by the school
to learn a skill. However, without the industrial curriculum offered by
the school, the ability of a classical curriculum to compel him to remain
a student through high school would be questionable, especially when
he was so motivated to help meet familial needs. Although the account
of his childhood depicts tensions between his mother and the school in
ways uncaptured in the fond memories of many students of segregated
schools, such as conflicts over discipline and criteria for promotion, it
does depict a familiar scenario in segregated schools, where the school
enables the parent to accomplish a vision that the parent would not be
able to accomplish independently.[11] Working cooperatively, if not inter-

dependently, mother and school harnessed ingenuity and provided Byas sufficient opportunities to begin a new stage of life.

The Young Man of Promise, Unfulfilled

Byas's childhood establishes his resilience when confronted with difficult circumstances and, potentially, his future concern for student dropouts at Hutchenson and Fair Street, but in many ways it seems a mismatch with his later life. How does a creative youngster, but unwilling academic, transform into a college graduate and achieve the master's degree? Without the transformation, his natural creativity might have generated the mother wit to want to outsmart the superintendent, but he would have been handicapped by his lack of knowledge. Alternatively, without the education, he would never have been in a position to be employed as a professor, thus making the need to outwit a superintendent a moot point. For Byas, the transformation was initially spurred by the opportunities that were generated by World War II. A chronology of his life during this period powerfully depicts the salience of the opening opportunities for blacks in the post–World War II era and the vexing dilemma of whether to participate in a world that continued to constrain opportunities for blacks or to resort to old antics that had helped buffer him against the harshness of life as a child in Macon. Though the opportunities to develop leadership skills at a historically black institution would later propel him to graduate school, the years between high school and college helped invent the new person he would become.

During the years of World War II, America was internationally embarrassed by the continued disparity between its rhetoric as defenders of democracy and its inequitable treatment of its own citizens at home. This contradiction generated baby steps toward equality that opened a new world of opportunity for black individuals, particularly men. The steps were indeed small, and contradictory. On the one hand, historians indicate that the U.S. Navy began allowing black men to serve in general service and even reluctantly started to train its first black naval officers in the years after the United States officially declared war in December 1941. On the other hand, for most members of the navy, the segregated practices continued, including the irony of being a part of the U.S. Navy but never being taught how to abandon ship because the segregated pools where black soldiers could have been taught to swim were missing.

Byas entered this contradictory world shortly after high school. When he finished eleventh grade, which was the last year of high school during this era, he worked as a carpenter, first being hired as a carpenter's helper and then being quickly promoted to carpenter as the foreman recognized the extent of the training he had received in high school. Given the dearth of skilled labor in Georgia during the period, the rapid promotion is unsurprising.[12] He likely would have spent his whole life as a carpenter had national politics not intervened. However, within three months of full-time employment, Byas was drafted and began service in the U.S. Navy.

Since he was black and from Georgia, and since perceptions about race affected how people in the armed services thought and acted, no one expected much of Byas's performance on the required tests. However, Byas surprised the administrators, his peers, and himself when he was among the highest scorers on the achievement tests. He remembers studying "a little funny book" for about three months, taking the test, and scoring "something like a 3.65 on a 4 point scale." His white colleagues were surprised. In military mental tests, 80 percent of all enlisted blacks, as compared with 30–40 percent of enlisted whites, tested in the lowest two categories.[13] Byas's success primed a young mind. Perhaps his mother had been right, and he was smart in book learning after all. Of course, it is equally possible that the mathematical calculations required by his industrial education teacher were paying off. Either way, the idea that he might be smart was a new one to him. Byas relished the fact that his score countered the negative images his fellow sailors had of blacks and Georgians, and for the first time he singularly focused his energies on a responsibility other than helping his mother financially.

Assuming a public stance birthed by a new vision of himself, Byas was elected to a leadership position within three months. In rapid order, he made third-class cook, then second-class cook, then first-class cook, and finally chief cook. Eventually, he was elected chief of the watch, with all the cooks of various classes reporting to him, and with the responsibility of overseeing 8,000–10,000 men per meal. His responsibilities also included serving as an officer's cook through his years in the navy. Although being designated an officer's cook and leader honored one's leadership and culinary capacities, the post was still a reflection of the segregated practices of the era. For example, like many other smart black men in the navy who were relegated to jobs as cooks, he was denied combat experiences. Indeed, each time Byas was to be transferred to active duty, the captain declared him as essential to the operation of the base and sent someone else in his place. However, the result of the discriminatory World War II practices was the development of an accomplished cook and an acknowledged leader who could coordinate the behind-the-scenes functions of food production and distribution.

When Byas was honorably discharged, he joined numerous other black veterans for whom World War II had reinforced the belief that they should be treated as citizens. Unfortunately, however, he and they immediately confronted the second-class status assigned to them as part of their American heritage. Byas exhibits two responses to this reality, the first demonstrating his desire to become a participant in the democracy in which he was born and the second reflecting his disillusionment with its entrenched racial divide. Byas's first response was to engage the new world of opportunity he perceived to be unfolding around him. Perhaps still inspired by the new belief that he was smart, he had exited the navy with a desire to use the GI Bill to further his education and had been accepted at the Philadelphia College of Pharmacy and Science for the fall. During the interim, he began working in Manhattan in a skilled occupation that drew upon his high school training, woodworking. However, he soon discovered that while the expectations and risk on the job were those of a skilled journeyman who should be making three to four dollars an hour, the pay he received was minimum wage. He was also disgruntled to discover that the arrival of the shop steward meant that his employer handed him a broom and told him to sweep, unwilling to let it be known to the union representative that his skill was being utilized in other, more dangerous ways. Unimpressed with the combination of risk and pay and spurred on by the loss of his wallet—which meant he had no money to enter school—Byas gave up on New York and his belief in the opening world of opportunities.

Back in Macon, Byas resorted to a second response to the contradictory practices regarding race in the post–World War II South. Now overtly disdainful of a system that devalued his skill because of race, Byas was not inspired to pursue more gainful employment in Macon or even to seek schooling opportunities when he returned to the South. Since his unemployment benefits provided him pay comparable to that he would receive if he accepted one of the jobs relegated to black men in the South, Byas invented a way to avoid the demeaning practices that challenged the recently elevated beliefs about his ability. With the benefits, he could receive twenty dollars a week without working at all. For a calculating mind, living in Macon and paying his mother rent netted more financial reward than receiving the minimum wage from dangerous employment in New York, where rent was a whooping eight dollars a week.

Byas turned unemployment into a game. With the shrewd calculation that allowed him to miss as many days of school as possible as a youth, he now became skilled at maintaining the requirements for eligibility for his unemployment check, without having to accept a job. The government required that his papers be signed by potential employers, a documentation that demonstrated he was seeking employment as a criterion of continued weekly benefits. The loophole Byas exploited, however, was the caveat that benefits would not be stopped if he was not hired. Thus, Byas made it his new business not to be hired. Instead of donning attire appropriate for the job he was seeking, he consistently arrived for blue-collar interviews in a suit, tie, and Sunday shoes. While he explained to potential white employers he had been sent by the employment agency and answered their questions about his work history and experience, he simultaneously carefully brushed lint off himself and examined other aspects of his dress. Byas was intentionally sending a subtle, disdainful, and deceitful message that he was uncomfortable in the surroundings in which he found himself. Although such a message contradicted the reality of his prior work experiences and employers surely knew this history, they consistently responded with a "Boy, you not gonna do no work."

Predictably, the external persona Byas presented clashed with southern white potential employers, who were likely already suspicious of this former navy man and the new breed of black men he represented—one unwelcome in the South. Despite his prior experience as a carpenter and cook, these aspects of his work history could be dismissed if the man himself did not fit their concept of an appropriate employee. The white employers refused to hire him. The response is consistent with historian Leon Litwack's interpretation of white employers during the era. They believed that employing black servicemen would not be a benefit, ostensibly either for themselves or for a southern economy unwilling to participate in America's slowly changing stance on race relations. Undeterred and respectful, utilizing the "time-tested strategies of . . . subtle resistance," Byas acknowledged that he understood and asked whether the rejecting employer would sign his card to prove that he had sought work.[14] Unsuspecting, different potential employers repeatedly signed the card, and Byas departed having successfully met his goal of remaining unemployed. His performance successfully concluded, Byas was free for two more weeks to enjoy life without the constraints of employment.

And a good life it was. Byas had become adept at playing pool while in the navy and now spent many a leisurely afternoon in the local pool hall earning extra income from opponents unaware of his expertise with the game. Apparently with no long-term goal, this saga continued until his benefits were almost completely exhausted. Having drawn forty-eight of the fifty-two weeks of possible unemployment benefits, he was finally forced by the looming loss of income flow to become proactive, and he decided to enroll in nearby Fort Valley State College, the newest of the historically black colleges and universities (HBCUs) in Georgia. He would be one of the 142,133 veterans who would enroll in institutions of higher learning by 1954.[15] For Byas, however, becoming a student implied no special interest in education. It was simply another way to keep the money coming. If he enrolled in school, he could get seventy-five dollars a month, and that salary seemed to him a whole lot better than working.

Byas is emphatic that he had no particular life plans at this stage of his development. However, the combination of his actions portray a strong sense of a perceptive young man unwilling to be exploited by a systemic structure that refused to validate his potential. In his first experiences with full-time work, when he dropped out of school in eighth grade, the combination of hard work, low pay, and little personal enjoyment had eventually compelled him back to school. A similar pattern replayed at this stage of his life. Ironically, despite his latent academic ability, the navy experiences and work challenges in the post–World War II climate continued to communicate the same message that he had received as a youngster—that blacks should work hard, receive low pay, and have little personal enjoyment. As he had been adamant about not going to school when he could not see the financial reward, so he had become adamant in the post–World War II years about not participating in an economic structure that yielded him few rewards. One could argue that the same ingenuity generated by a childhood of economic need provided the impetus that allowed him to craft his new, also creative, form of resistance to a democracy that devalued his potential as a worker. Byas contends that Fort Valley ignited his untapped potential. In the challenging but supportive climate of an HBCU, he came to view education as a tool through which he could exercise his potential, even in a segregated society. The experiences at Fort Valley turned the creative young man into an educator with conviction.

Byas Outwitted; or, The Salience of the Fort Valley Experience

Slightly south of Macon, the campus of Fort Valley boasted buildings named after icons in the struggle for black equality in Georgia during an earlier era. Among them was H. A. Hunt Hall, a monument to honor the black president who had publicly pretended to honor the wishes of white philanthropists in order to channel money into the school but who several years later was the impetus for a renewal of agency and advocacy for black education through the auspices of a renewed black teachers' association. Eventually, a building would also be named for Horace Mann Bond, the black scholar well known for his publication of *The Education of the Negro in the American Social Order* who was also the president of the institution in the years before Byas's arrival. One day there would also be a memorial to the current president, well-known educator in the state C. V. Troup, who was a leader among the black teachers' group both at the time Byas was a student and during later years when Byas was a professor.

None of these names meant very much to Byas in the beginning. He arrived on campus in March 1947 with no particular vision, unpacked his clothes, settled into a dorm, and reviewed courses to determine how these years might be used. He was older than the approximately seven hundred other students on campus because of his career in the navy, a fact that would later contribute to the campus leadership he would exercise. As had always been the case in his life, he also needed ways to supplement his income. With a plethora of experiences and now the determination to actually secure a job, he was soon engaged in employment as a cook on the weekends in a small restaurant close to campus and as a stage carpenter for the Players' Guild during the semester. Aside from the continuation of these skills brought from his earlier life, almost all the other opportunities for education and leadership were new.

Byas identifies four critical incidents in his life at Fort Valley that compelled the creation of a new man. None relate specifically to the school curriculum or to his declared education major per se. In fact, on paper, the influence the school had on his transformation would not be evident. According to an unpublished dissertation of the period, the courses Byas would take for the general college requirements would not have been substantially different from those of HBCUs in other parts of the state, Albany State and Savannah State. Comparing the course requirements across the schools reveals that Byas would have been required to take additional courses in rural sociology and minority problems at Fort Valley as part of the forty-two hours of coursework and student teaching required for social studies. However, Byas makes no reference to their import in his world, with the exception of acknowledging the significance of practical experiences student teaching provided.[16] Overall, the strength of Fort Valley that, according to Byas, would "change his whole perspective" emanates more from a combination of professorial direction and selected experiences. At Fort Valley, Byas was inspired to want to become educated, given opportunities to exercise leadership, introduced to teaching, and encouraged to believe that success on its premises could generate success any place he went.[17]

Byas's evolution began shortly after his arrival on campus. The academic scene was new for a young man unfamiliar with college norms, so Byas was surprised when they were calling him "smart" within a few weeks. By the end of the first quarter, he was likewise amazed to discover that he had been the only student to make an A in elementary statistics. Success bred desire, and the former dropout began to pursue studies with the same zest with which he had previously avoided them. This pursuit, fueled by the influence of several individual teachers, undergirds his first explanation for the role Fort Valley played in his development: that it generated a desire to become educated and to do quality work.

One of his most admired teachers was William Boyd, a scholar who taught history and political science and who held a Ph.D. from the University of Michigan. Coincidentally, Boyd was also president of the state National Association for the Advancement of Colored People (NAACP), an activity that likely infused race into lectures in his history and political science classes. Boyd was dismissive of Byas's calculating regurgitation of facts and challenged him to learn to think. When Byas entered his office to complain that other students had copied from his paper and received a better grade, Boyd was unrepentant. "Byas," he reportedly explained, "you have all the facts, but you have them all jumbled up. If you can't say what you know, you don't know it." The instructor explained to his petulant student how to list the facts in the margins of the paper, organize them, and create a cogent argument. The concept was a new one to Byas but a profound one, he thought, as he mulled it over in his room. Over the course of the semester, the teacher continued to drill organization and presentation, and Byas eventually learned how to present his thoughts in an organized way in writing.

Another instructor stressed attention to detail in submitted work. Although having points deducted for an uncrossed *t* or an undotted *i* seemed nonsensical to Byas at the time, its overall effect was to make him aware of the importance of perfection in his work and the need to pay attention to details if perfection was to be achieved. Years later, he would continue to quote the mantra he learned in her class from the Handy Craftsman's Creed: "I am only a piece of work. After I leave your hand, you may never see me again. Put into me your best. . . . Say to them through me, 'I know what is good.'" The learning of the poem and the perfection required in written submissions were minuscule demands in a craft class, but their collective message challenged Byas's work ethic. "If you making something," he explains, "if it's good, folk will see that."[18]

The sense of high standards imposed on him by his teachers eventually morphed into high standards for himself as a student. For example, although French is not reported as a required course in the 1951–52 Fort Valley bulletin, Byas enrolled as a senior because by this stage of his career, he believed he should know a language if he was going to be well educated. Despite making a D the first quarter, one of only two during his Fort Valley stay, he reenrolled in the class the next quarter against the advice of the teacher, just to prove to himself that he, like his peers, could learn the language. Despite the warning of the instructor, or perhaps because of it, Byas struggled through and managed a C in the second course, eliciting the teacher to proclaim, "Mr. Byas, you made a good strong C. I guess you'll be back." In response, the forthright Byas intoned, "No, I'm not willing to work that damn hard. I proved whatever kind of point I was trying to prove. I'm not coming back in here." As in the case with Dr. Boyd, the student Byas could be forthright and sometimes abrasive. However, the episode demonstrates his evolving commitment to becoming well educated rather than merely attaining a grade. During his discussion with the previous teacher, his concern was that he was not being given the grade he believed he deserved; by the time of this episode the grade mattered less to him than that he actually knew the material.

In addition to teachers inspiring learning and a desire to be well educated—he was on the honor roll most quarters—Fort Valley also reportedly built upon the leadership skills he first practiced as an officer's cook in the navy. Some forms of leadership at Fort Valley brought with them day-to-day responsibilities, such as being selected by the cafeteria manager, Mrs. Fambro, to be the head of the table for the family style of serving meals in the cafeteria or being elected president of his senior class by his peers. Others taught more direct lessons about standing by convictions, and the costs associated with such a stance, especially if he spoke his opinions in the forthright manner that was becoming his trademark but failed to temper the telling with an awareness of power differentials.

One critical incident illuminates the lesson he learned about the cost of speaking forthrightly and adhering to his convictions. Byas was elected by his peers to become one of two student members of the Disciplinary Committee during his junior year. The Disciplinary Committee was charged with responding to students who had violated campus rules. He functioned successfully as a student representative for this committee of faculty, in the process surely learning the language, behaviors, and values that characterized faculty administrative talk and decision making. However, when two senior females decided to violate college rules by going across the street from campus to get food at an eatery, the College End, on a Sunday night the tension erupted.

The dean of women reportedly watched the students leave campus, spend ten minutes getting sandwiches, and return with the food. Since gender differences made leaving campus without permission a particularly heinous crime for women, the dean referred the case to the Disciplinary Committee. Byas was the student representative when the case was discussed, but he voiced his concerns directly. "I asked the dean, I said, 'Didn't you see them headed toward that way? Why didn't you stop them?' You set up there and you watched them and you watched them come back. You're not accusing them of doing anything illegal or anything. They just walked across there and got something to eat.'" As a student, Byas sympathized with the girls, especially since he had his own opinions about the quality of the Sunday evening meal in the cafeteria—a sandwich and a piece of fruit—and his opinions were none too positive. However, he also believed strongly that the women were being treated in a way that was unjust, despite the violation of the rules. As far as he was concerned, the dean of women should have reprimanded the students on the spot rather than waiting to refer them to the Disciplinary Committee.

The faculty members on the committee did not concur with his observations. They suspended the woman from college, thereby creating a massive campus uproar and demonstrations. Alerted that the student body was requesting that its student representative speak at a protest meeting, the academic dean reminded Byas about the confidentiality of the proceedings of the Disciplinary Committee. Byas was the only student member of the committee, as the second student member of the committee was a senior who completed his requirements the quarter before and no replacement had been elected. Responding to the dean's veiled threat, Byas retorted: "Those [students] are my constituents; they elected me," he explained, the knowledge from his political science major in evidence. "If they ask for a report, I shall report." And report Byas did. By the time President C. V. Troup returned to the campus, the students had initiated a strike and sixty to seventy students had been brought to the Disciplinary Committee with charges of rebelling.

Byas was not invited to be present during the meeting when the students were being suspended. When he was finally solicited, he entered the room to discover that other committee members were already seated around the conference table. Never at a loss for words, he blatantly addressed the group: "You all are forgetting one thing," he began, no evidence of repentance in his voice. "I am supposed to be a member of this committee." The comment resonated with the confidence acquired by his broad experiences in the navy, his success as a student, and, possibly, his failure to be intimidated by those seated, having himself participated in deliberations with them at earlier meetings. It is also consistent with his other forthright dealings with professors in which he seldom yielded to their authority but was unremitting in making his own points. The chair, however, was not amused. "Mr. Byas," he reportedly admonished, "this is of a serious nature, and we wish you would govern yourself accordingly." Byas responded with the expected apology for his opening remark but was nonetheless suspended indefinitely and asked to leave the campus immediately.[19]

The bull-headedness, as Byas calls his behavior, that was carefully concealed during Dr. Jekyll and Mr. Hyde games is captured in his response to the dismissal. Back in his room, Byas reviewed the official telegram notifying him that he was indefinitely suspended because of his actions, and he then composed a letter requesting immediate reinstatement, noting that the telegram he had been sent did not specify the time requirement intended by the word "indefinite." He then carried the letter to the dean. Apparently unclear about how to respond to the request, the dean conferred with other administrative officials and eventually referred the matter to the college president, who had been away during the events. As the conversations went back and forth between college officials as to who should take the letter and when, Byas settled himself into the office: "I am going to stay here until you all decide," he announced. His letter and self-imposed "sit-in" were perceptive in pressing the loopholes in the correspondence and suggest that he was beginning to learn the power of the written word to redress issues. However, his calculated strategy of defiance failed to account for the power differential between himself and members of the Disciplinary Committee. Moreover, he failed to appreciate the extent to which members of the administration might have intentionally used the incident to teach their bright student a lesson about authority. Before the end of the day, Byas was dismissed. In fact, he was not even given the mandatory bus fare for the trip home, an oversight that may have been an administrative error or that may confirm the extent to which the administration was determined to curb his behavior.

The time Byas spent home did not teach him the skills to use different methods to achieve his ends. Nonetheless, he did learn he could suffer a personal penalty for failing to consider power differentials in instances of injustice, or he could decide that a higher end might require that he conceal some of his disdain and pretend to accommodate. Initially, the dismissal merely fueled anger. He spent one quarter at home because he was suspended, then stayed at home another quarter because he was "mad." He considered completing his degree at Wayne State University, even going so far as to visit the campus; however, by this time in his college studies, he was on a fast track to graduate from Fort Valley and had his eye on using his money remaining from the GI Bill to support graduate school at Columbia. After he learned that he would lose a substantial amount of course credit by transferring, his desire for the degree trumped defiance, and he returned to Fort Valley.

These episodes with faculty members who inspired high standards for knowledge and administrators imposing constraints on brash leadership surely provided a foundation for Byas's later grappling with ways to win when issues of power prohibited the collaboration and disagreement of equals. However, at this stage of his development, a speedy verbal response to perceived injustice was still ingrained in his character. As he reminisces, he explains that the forthright response he utilized as a student may not have helped his situations but they sure did him "a whole lot of good." Eventually, the forthright character would be sufficiently harnessed to provide a calculated response that would best serve the situations of injustice he would confront. However, this skill would be developed over time when issues larger than himself would be at stake.

The challenge to become an independent learner and the opportunities to lead were also complemented at Fort Valley by an introduction to the world of teaching. Despite not having entered Fort Valley with a desire to teach, Byas was invited by a business professor to assist with an in-service class for black teachers on Saturdays at the pay rate of thirty-four dollars a month.[20] Byas accepted and began for the first time to plan classes. Although he was not the instructor of record, his full-time teaching in the class mirrored the report of in-service classes of the period in which the student assistant assumed major instructional responsibility.

When teachers in nearby Macon learned that their own product, Ulysses Byas, was teaching one of the Saturday classes at Fort Valley that would meet new state requirements, they reportedly flocked to his class, ballooning the numbers in the first few sessions from thirty to seventy-five. The Macon teachers' assumption presumably was that familiarity with the teacher, one who was a product of their own system, would breed more lax standards. Their suppositions were premature. Students, many older than himself, soon discovered he was "hard" when they performed poorly on two or three unannounced tests. A complaint was filed with his mother: they just didn't know "what had happened to Ulysses down there." He was summoned home by his mother to discuss his performance as a teacher, but Byas was undeterred. He adamantly told his mother that "those folks don't want to study" and had taken his class only to make an easy grade, an ironic comment given his less than stellar interest in schooling while a student in Macon. However, time had passed since they knew him, and the new Byas was determined that they imbibe the same spirit that had compelled him to want to become well educated. He was determined the teachers, instead of merely place holding, would actually learn something in his class, and his mother relented. The episode contributed to Byas's belief in the importance of strong teaching and his conviction that "if you are going to spend your time on something, you should have some residual when the time passed." In other words, the effect of good teaching was that students should actually learn something. This burgeoning idea, fermenting during this early teaching setting, would reach maturity during his years as a teacher and later, as a professor.

The shift to education as a profession also occurred during a teaching opportunity given to him by another professor. In addition to his work as an in-service teacher in the business department, six hours on his transcript reflect his teaching in the adult education program during his junior and senior years. As a sophomore, he had taken a three-hour course in adult education, performing so well that the professor solicited him the following quarter to work as a volunteer in the school-sponsored adult education program. This experience fueled in Byas a passion for the personal rewards of teaching and the need for meaningful adult education. Byas recounts with particular pride his success in teaching a man, a Mr. Kersley, who was illiterate at the beginning of the program but attended faithfully through storms or sunshine and eventually, successfully, "writ all over the back of that check" after being asked to make his X mark at the bank. Inspired by his student's success, Byas knew "from then on" that he was "going to be a teacher and do something about adults and education." Although teaching certainly represented one of the few professional outlets for educated blacks during the period and was a logical choice for a major, Byas attributes his interest in the field of education to these experiences at Fort Valley that instilled in him an understanding of the gratification a teacher feels in successfully transforming the lives of others.

The closing act at Fort Valley that completed Byas's transformation was his adoption of the unwritten campus mantra: that he could be a master at anything to which he set his mind and that a degree at Fort Valley could send him anywhere he decided to go. Since he was a first-generation college graduate, a logical choice at the end of his academic career would have been to accept the offer he was given to become a professor directly out of school. This opportunity had germinated from an unlikely source: Mrs. Fambro, the supervisor of the school cafeteria who had selected him to serve as a table leader throughout his undergraduate tenure. In the norms that characterized black school environments, Mrs. Fambro apparently closely observed her students to determine those she deemed to be particularly capable of a successful career, and her recommendation carried greater weight than Byas realized when he first began to work with her. When he became a senior, Mrs. Fambro recommended him to an area white superintendent to fill a job as professor, or "fessor" as the community called them, of an elementary school. Byas was surprised but went for an interview with the superintendent, performing so well that he left with a tentative job offer. The job expectations set forth by the superintendent were minimal. Betraying his lack of interest in black children actually being educated, and thereby unwittingly reducing the receptivity of Byas to his offer, he conveyed his expectation that if Byas went to the school and made sure the students stayed quiet, he would be doing a good job.

Had the offer come at an earlier stage in his development, perhaps he would have taken the job. But the superintendent now confronted a calculating almost-graduate who believed in the power of education for himself and for others. He was amazed that he could be solicited as an administrator with so little experience, and he was disdainful that the expectations of the job and its pay could be so minimal. He was being offered $170 a month to work with seven to eight teachers and four hundred students. As he counted his own income as a student, he included the $15 a month from the Players' Guild, the $10 a month for assisting a teacher in the business department, the cooking on the weekends that netted $35, plus his income from the GI bill to conclude that the job was not financially feasible. Indeed, the offer was a new iteration of an old scenario, and the combination of hard work and low pay were insufficient incentive for a student now emboldened to believe his success at Fort Valley could make him successful anywhere. Although he told the superintendent he would come the following Tuesday, he did not keep that appointment. He waited instead for his offer of admission from Teachers College, Columbia. If somebody thought he could be a professor when still a college senior, he began to believe he could be a real professor. He would not be the kind who would simply keep the superintendent happy and school-sit the children. Rather, he would become a stellar professor, with all the appropriate academic credentials. This drive to attain more education to do an even better job was a far cry from the man who had come to Fort Valley so that he would not have to be employed.[21]

Finding a Voice in Education without Segregation: Teachers College, Columbia

Byas's mother was no longer the catalyst in his desire to continue his education. "I had a hard time trying to make you go to school. Looks like I'm going to have to get the police to stop you from going to school," she reportedly lamented as her son explained he was going to graduate school. She was surprised that he was turning down full-time employment, commenting that he had been the "least likely one [of all his siblings] to go on to college" and implying that he should be grateful to have a degree. The idea of graduate school was beyond her comprehension. The roles now reversed, Byas patiently explained to her the concept of a master's degree.

Byas's decision to enroll at Columbia surprised even his college professors, as he was setting a course different from that of most black educators at the time. In 1949–50, 871 black teachers had used scholarship aid provided by the state of Georgia to pursue graduate work outside the state; although the program they desired to complete was offered to whites at a Georgia state-approved institution, comparable opportunities were not available to blacks. This financial assistance was provided by southern states to adhere to segregation mandates that prohibited black teachers from being admitted to southern white graduate schools. According to new research by Donna Jordan-Taylor, the program was devised by southern and border states as early as the 1920s as a way to equalize educational offerings between blacks and whites. By 1955, the number of black teachers using the scholarship program would have so substantially increased that the cost of the program in Georgia ballooned from $1,044 in 1944 to $208,217.90 and the number of recipients increased from 5 to 1,790.[22] Thus, Byas's choice to attend a northern graduate school was consistent with the pattern of other black educators in the state. However, one aspect of Byas's matriculation at Columbia diverged from the expected pattern of black teacher enrollment. Typically, black teachers with graduate student stipends studied in the summer, usually attending classes for four summers to obtain a master's degree. With GI money still left, Byas elected not to pursue the option for state aid and summer study and instead enrolled in Columbia as a full-time student. He reportedly was one of only two blacks who were full-time students that year, the other being George Richardson of Oklahoma City.

Some teachers at Fort Valley had discouraged him from going immediately to Columbia after graduation, saying that he should get some experience before enrolling. Byas finished college one month and began graduate school the next. In those days to go to graduate school "fresh out of college" was something "nobody did." However, one professor encouraged him to continue immediately to graduate school, and the encouragement of the one exceeded the naysayer voices of the many. Byas reports he was only one of two entering students who lacked teaching experience in the administrative degree program. He recalls that the average number of years of teaching experience in the group was twelve, and the average number of years of administrative experience was six. Despite his status as a neophyte compared with his classmates, he dismisses the advice about getting experience by noting that his experiences wouldn't have meant much anyway, as he was soon taught at Columbia that "the average practice in the BEST schools in the country was fifty years behind the theory in the field." Byas decided that if that lag was the case throughout the country, then Butts County, Georgia, where he had been invited to come be a professor, was probably two hundred years behind, and so the experience there "wouldn't have done [him] a bit of good."

Although he had been admitted with deficiencies, Byas performed well at Columbia. To be admitted with deficiencies at Columbia meant that he would need additional coursework to compensate for his perceived poor training. Because Fort Valley was only ten years old in 1950, the year of Byas's matriculation at Columbia, and because it was an HBCU in the South, Byas was told he would have eight to sixteen points in deficiencies, with the exact number to be determined after his first semester of matriculation. Being assigned deficiencies motivated Byas. He "decided to study hard and get good grades," and at the end of the first semester, he was given the minimum number of deficiencies and told that he could take the additional coursework at any institution he chose, including Fort Valley.

An analysis of his reported and documented behaviors as a graduate student reveals the increasing confidence of a black student applying his intellect for the first time in an integrated class setting and learning to reconcile norms for graduate school content with his experiential knowledge of black communities. The growth in this development is best documented in his educational foundations class with the well-known and controversial scholar Harold Rugg. Rugg's course covered a variety of topics, including American education, economy, and politics in the postwar world; sources of social and racial conflict in America; democracy and the battle for an informed public opinion; the nature of culture and the problem of social change; social frontiers; new horizons in science, technology, religion, and ethics; frontiers of art and expression; the idea of a democratic society; and a new design for American education in a new world. The class provided a basic reading list and utilized lectures and small groups to "reinterpret and amplify the introductory topic statements, in the light of current developments." Its thirty-nine-page bound syllabus, with the myriad required books, was a new form of teaching and learning, especially for a student coming from an HBCU where the curriculum and teaching delivery were constrained by limited resources.[23]

The required written responses to the course demonstrate his expanding capacity to state his conclusions straightforwardly, without muddling those ideas in educational jargon. For example, his earliest journal responses provided one to two sentences of critique of the class or readings, and these statements are steeped in educational verbiage, almost as though the young graduate student had not yet discovered his voice. Shortly thereafter, in response to a lecture on social and racial problems in America, he extended the length of his response to a paragraph, apparently focusing more on summarizing the discussion of the group rather than on providing his own individual analysis. However, as the class continued, his statements on democracy and the battle for an informed public opinion became more forthright. "Teachers," he argued, "must take the leadership in the battle for public understanding and counteracting propaganda." The teachers' groups and the curriculum of the school "must infuse the people with understanding," he continued, "which is paramount in a democratic society."

Although he may have begun the class with a belief that his responses should summarize the perspectives of others and mask his own opinions, his statement on teachers and their role in democracy production is demonstrative of increasing confidence in his analytical voice. By the time the class discussed "social frontiers," Byas unabashedly engaged the class and professor with the type of critique assumed to be the basis of superior graduate education. Apparently somewhat miffed, he wrote: "I feel that much more could have been accomplished if each group had been given a specific frontier to investigate so that all aspects and problems connected with this frontier could have ascertained some solution of said problem. From the analysis of social frontiers, Mr. Rugg should have evolved questions of classification and procedure, however, such was not the case resulting in a drifting mass of teachers without any guide as to the surveying and crossing of social frontiers." His tone implied an irritation with a lost possibility. A later critique of student conversation is also evident: "I received the impression, both in the smaller and larger groups that the students were groping for a concrete approach to the problem of using science to better the lives of all people but were unable to find a starting point." The sigh almost evident in the text, he tempered his criticism of his white colleagues' limited address of the problems of social justice by noting that "the awareness of the problem is in itself a step in the right direction."[24]

Coupled with his description of himself as having become an avid reader during this year, the evolution of his voice reveals the way Byas continued his desire to learn at Fort Valley by buttressing it with newly developed ideas about appropriate ways graduate students entered the discourse on social and educational problems. Though he must surely have engaged similar topics in his political science major at Fort Valley, the setting of the conversation at an HBCU would have involved professors and peers who shared culture and oppression and perhaps presumably shared similarities in vision about the nature of the problem. At Columbia, Byas had to develop and articulate a solo response. He took Rugg's course in 1950–51, during his first semester as a graduate student. He was reportedly the only black student in the class.

The course content at Columbia also challenged Byas to reconcile his lived experiences with the academic descriptions of black life. His reported public disagreements with professors on the "broken home" provide an example of the ways the world of academe and black segregation mated in his evolving response to educational issues. He reports that he liked the conversations on families and extended families but strongly critiqued the characterization of some families as "broken." Describing the sharing of clothes among children, he emphasized in his all-white class that his one-parent family was the only family he knew and that it was not broken. He reported this family instead to be one full of caring and sharing and love, even though it was poor in material things. Moreover, he argued, in direct contrast to the pressing beliefs of the day that lessened the possibilities of black children because of their familial circumstances, that "material things are not inhibitors unless you let them be." Although his rebuttal foreshadows that of other black students in the 1970s who would complain of having to represent the black point of view in an integrated class, Byas's willingness to speak forthrightly is representative of an intellectual wrestling with poorly conceived educational ideas and a willingness to counter those ideas in public settings. He was developing a capacity to allow his experiential cultural norm to inform his educational professional norm.

Some of his newfound comfort in this intellectual world, as well as his critique of it in light of his own experiences, is evident in his final evaluation of Rugg's class. He described American society as "characterized by racial prejudices, private enterprise . . . people living in poverty when the system can give plenty." The ideas are resoundingly similar to the circumstances he experienced as a boy seeking to help his mother pay rent and living in a world that restricted his opportunities because of race. However, he also emphasized that people formulating questions about these difficulties should "understand [a] situation before a plan of action is approved." This idea would form the basis of his own effort to manipulate a recalcitrant superintendent and gain funding to help students victimized by racial prejudices and private enterprise, both of which excluded their full economic participation. He continued by arguing that this strategy is especially important when people are operating in a democracy. As required, Byas ended his paper by offering critique of small-group discussions and noting changes in curriculum he would make in any school if he were given the opportunity to do so. Suggestions included his desire to prepare students to become citizens of the world, to introduce orientation courses for teachers and parents to discuss their common problems, to encourage better student-faculty relations, to give student counsel groups freedom from the heavy restrictions of advisers, and to introduce courses in music and arts for student appreciation of the "finer things in life."[25] Each of these ideas reappears, in some hybrid form, in subsequent years of his professional life.

While documents from Rugg's class demonstrate the development of the graduate student in his capacity to engage educational ideas about race, another professor provided a second central ingredient that would inform his life as a professor: that of learning to ground theoretical ideas with the reality of environmental constraints. For this lesson, he credits Ruth Strang. Byas reports that Strang, a professor who had authored "thirty or more books," was one of two authorities in the country on counseling during the era, the other being Carl Rogers of the University of Chicago. He expresses distaste for her appearance—in fact, thought she dressed like a "maid" because of the "green two-piece suit and white stockings" that were her staple outfit. The intensity of his criticism is likely informed by the norms of black teacher dress during the era, when clothing was a visible way black teachers conveyed professionalism. Strang's appearance would have been inconsistent with that of the black teachers with whom Byas would have been most familiar and would explain his surprise when first confronted with a teacher who didn't attend to the details of professional dress. However, despite his initial amazement at her appearance, her lesson about applying knowledge in ways consistent with the dictates of local circumstances resonated.

Strang had given students the entire semester to write a guidance program for a high school, and Byas was convinced he had developed "an airtight program." He was surprised and disturbed to be asked to report to her office and to be told that his paper was a good theoretical paper, such as one might expect of an undergraduate, but that it lacked an application of the testing techniques to a particular school setting. "You told me how familiar you were with all the various techniques and the latest in the field," Strang reportedly explained. But after querying whether he intended to go back to Georgia to work and receiving an affirmative response, she continued, "Well, I doubt whether there is anybody in the whole state of Georgia who can administer the Rasch, much more interpret it." She emphasized that Georgia was one of the poorest states in the Union and that neither the expertise nor the resources would be available to execute his plans.

In asking him to rewrite the paper, Strang explained her desire to have him select a geographic location, a school within that location, problems within the school, and specific ways he could solve the problems, including inhibitors and ways he might circumvent them. The reassignment was revelatory for Byas. Although he made an A in the class, as he reports having also made in other classes, his embracing of the ideas in the class assignment far exceeded the professor's attribution of his learning as evidenced by a grade. "And from then on, my whole philosophy of that thing changed," he remembers. "There is going to be some good stuff you know to do, but because of circumstances [those ideas can not be implemented]." He points out that "our job is to identify inhibitors in the learning environment and then to propose solutions within our resource availability to solve them." The idea, he explains, is one that was prompted by Ruth Strang.[26]

At this stage of his education Byas had in his arsenal an understanding of the language of democracy and the ways he might engage that conversation, a capacity to blend community knowledge and educational knowledge and use one to critique the other, and an understanding of how educational ideas could be constrained by local circumstances. Although he does not note other specific instructors, Byas also benefited from other professors and graduates at Columbia who produced a substantial body of scholarship on democracy, civic education, and race. Like others before and after him, Byas embraced these concepts and extended them to include himself and black children in the South. Since he never allowed Columbia to strip him of the cultural heritage that defined his life as a child, he was able to blend these cutting-edge educational ideas with the needs of the black community that produced him and to use the ideas to advance an agenda beyond the imagination of the faculty that taught him.

However, the new lessons did not erase two continuing aspects of his personality. Both his creativity and resourcefulness when facing monetary challenges and his confrontational manner in response to perceived injustices were still intact at Columbia. Byas's creativity is exemplified in his choice of a job during his year as a student. Upon arrival, he sought and received a job in the school cafeteria, where his employers quickly learned of his culinary skills and promoted him to cook. The job choice worked perfectly to supplement his meager income. On any day he was cooking, Byas was assured of a meal. However, on days when he was not working, he would visit the cafeteria, speaking to co-workers along the line and accepting the samples of food they offered along the way. "By the time I left," he recalls, "I'd had a meal." Though not as evidenced at Fort Valley, the episode at Columbia demonstrates that the creative problem-solving capacity of Byas in times of need was still intact.

The confrontational spirit, evident in many of his encounters at Fort Valley, also still lingered at Columbia, demonstrating aptly that direct confrontation was still his solution to perceived injustices, whether he was battling white or black administrators. For example, Byas describes being "mad as hell" in his verbal altercation with the registrar who challenged whether he had sufficient hours to graduate, showing again his willingness to go home rather than staying another semester to take classes he was being told were required. "I told them I already had [a] job offer . . . and I didn't need the master's degree anyway." Although the episode ended with the registrar explaining that the credits could be fulfilled even if he was not in residence, Byas's vehement response suggests a belief that a black man could express himself as an equal and that he was willing to pay the price if he could not. Later, Strang's counsel about adapting plans to fit the realities of a situation would become part of his repertoire of educational tools, and he would develop new ways to harness his temper while continuing the spirit of the fight. But the idea of a different response to injustice was not a lesson Columbia could teach. For that model, he would need to be taught by the black professors in the South who had mastered it well.

Coming Full Circle: The Trickster Back as a Teacher and Professor-in-Training

Byas left Columbia after eleven months, completing his final requirements from the small town of Elberton in northeast Georgia, where he had accepted a position with James Hawes at the unheard-of teaching salary of five thousand dollars. For the first time in his life, Byas experienced a direct relationship between educational attainment and income potential. The principal who hired him was known for recruiting the best black teachers he could find for the Blackwell Memorial School in Elberton, Georgia. Himself a native of Macon and a graduate of Fort Valley, Hawes was familiar with Byas's expertise as a carpenter and knew he was completing a master's degree at Columbia. The combination of industrial skill and educational expertise exactly fit Hawes's needs for a self-contained seventh-grade teacher who could also teach an evening class for veterans in industrial education and residential building construction. Hawes contacted Byas's mother to obtain an address, telegrammed a request, and, without difficulty, lured Byas to accept a job offer. Byas is adamant that he did not even know where Elberton, Georgia, was located but that the salary was sufficient to compel him to find the small town northeast of Atlanta, near the South Carolina border. And find it he did.

The former school dropout was now responsible for the education of children much like himself. His only remaining requirement at Columbia was to submit a third point paper, a requirement he could easily complete from afar. Byas thus settled into full-time teaching. Echoing the practices of his graduate coursework, he devoted considerable energy to lesson planning and evaluation and to introducing ideas about democracy. Perhaps because of Byas's belief in the potential of groups and the disdain he had developed at Columbia for ineffective groups, or, more likely, because he understood that self-regulating groups were a precursor to democratic participation and he wanted his students to imagine themselves as part of a larger world, he devoted considerable time to outlining and evaluating the behaviors of individual students in small-group settings. His lesson plans reveal the ways he allowed students opportunities to work in groups, including assigning chairpersons for each group; outlining the sequence of drills for a day, such as the relationship of the activity to the previous day's assignment; and prompting questions for discussion. In one set of lesson plans, he concludes by noting his own objectives: "This lesson or general study is to give the children some experiences (as all are) on working together in a group. It is hoped that an understanding of the germ is obtained as well as some ways whereby the spread thereof can be reduced." Although the planning detail of other groups varies, the format is consistent. Echoing his own assignment in Rugg's class, he also included the requirement that each group was responsible for keeping a cumulative record of all work and maintaining a scrapbook.

Much as he critiqued the functioning of student groups at Columbia, Byas also enthusiastically captured the behavior of his student groups as he worked. Beginning with October 8 and continuing through November 8, there are fourteen handwritten pages of notes on individual and group behavior, many intriguingly aligned with the field note dictates of an anthropologist. For example, on October 8 Byas writes that students are "pointing in the books. I believe they are studying. Occasionally one or the other will ask a question." Like a good ethnographic researcher, he carefully distinguishes between behaviors he sees and his responses to those behaviors. He writes that he had explained to the group chair how to "guide the lesson" and that the student is "extremely good" despite the fact that he has "been having trouble trying to get him to pay attention."[27]

Overall, the notes describe students sitting, standing, holding string in their hands, having books open, having backs to the teacher, walking and speaking with other students, rearranging papers, and engaging in other distracting behaviors. They depict instances of engagement with him as well as his intrusion as a teacher into individual and group conversations. Most notes are extraordinarily detailed, some even including a parenthetical note: "I think he is conscious of the writing that I am doing. I'll stop for now." Together, the notes provide a window into the engagement of students during his group work and illustrate his interest in conducting fieldwork in school settings. The teaching materials also reflect what will become an ongoing professional interest in civics education. The introductory notes for one unspecified lesson begin with the question: "What is it that makes 'us' so different?" The outline continues with descriptors of materials related to Georgia, the United States, the United Nations, and various countries, specifically Iraq, Iran, and Egypt. He also includes a "World News of the Week" map and then devotes the rest of the space to writing the word "Democracy."[28]

Supplementing his daily instruction, and perhaps remembering the importance of his own mother's role in his attainment of a high school diploma, Byas also establishes himself as a classroom teacher who communicated directly with parents. While a professional norm existed among black teachers and professors that encouraged home visits, Byas's records provide the first examples of written communication with parents. Carefully written, recopied, and hand-delivered, his formal communication conveyed to parents his belief in the partnership that should exist between the school and home, his praise for acceptable aspects of student performance, and his suggestions about ways parents might facilitate future student development. Of one student, he writes that she is "among the best in the class." Nevertheless, he reminds the mother that the student needs some social development. "She is getting of the age now where some time should be given her to attend some of the social activities given by the school—even if it means bring her yourself—some parents do. . . .

On this point I would like to talk with you." In contrast, another student is commended for her social development: "She is a very good mixer," he writes. However, he expresses concern that she be given guidance about "some places in the community that she should not go—you know where these are—for I believe they are not the sort of things to make for the kind of girl we hope she will be." He encourages the mother to teach her about growing up: "You as her mother should tell her about her body—give her a complete understanding of everything that 'you' know. For I really do believe that this sort of thing will aid her in staying in school."[29]

Overall, his letters demonstrate pride in academic performance and concerns about poor academic performance, sometimes comparing the academic average of a student (in precise numbers) with that of his or her peers. Not surprisingly, given his own history, he raises concerns about attendance, suggesting to one parent whose child had missed forty days of school that the child's withdrawn manner and compromised school performance might improve "if you could help her to cut her absentee rate at least one half." He also appears to be astute in observing economic need, telling one parent that he had concluded from his conversation with the child—one who appeared "shaky and tight"—that the child needed free lunch at school. Several of the letters indicate that the written comments follow previous conversations with the parents at various times during the school year. Given his directness in addressing student needs, the letters suggest they are written versions of an ongoing conversation. Intriguingly, but without explanation, where letters concern the behavior of male students in the class, he directs his communications to the male parent.

The extensiveness of Byas's efforts to work with students and their parents to ensure success in school and to demonstrate to students their place in a world structure suggests a strong teaching commitment to helping black students become participants in a world less restricted than the segregated one the teacher and parents knew. While World War II had taught him that blacks were not yet welcome as equals in that world, Columbia had shown him they could participate and succeed in an integrated setting. Moreover, Fort Valley had given him the confidence to believe he could participate in any world, segregated or desegregated. Many of these ideas are embedded in his teaching, both in his pedagogical strategies—such as groups with designated leaders and freedom to perform tasks—and in his overt curricular emphasis. While no complete record remains of all the activities throughout the two years he taught or the array of parental communications, the available materials confirm his belief that "black children had been educationally cheated" and that he always wanted students to understand that they had been robbed so that they might have some indignation about having that which was taken returned to them.

Blackwell Memorial School in Elberton, however, was far more than a teaching laboratory for Byas. Although he expanded his daily teaching by teaching carpentry skills to adult veterans at night, including leading them in building and rebuilding houses on the school's campus, Byas was learning a good deal more at Blackwell than how to teach. While a teacher in this setting, he also began to practice his eventual role as a professor. Before the first year was over, Byas had become Hawes' protégé. As the young teacher demonstrated his capacity, Hawes allowed him to become his confidant, freely discussing with him the mechanics of school administration, delegating routine administrative tasks to him, and often taking him to meetings of principals across the state and introducing him as his "young whipper snapper." The fact that both were from Macon and both were veterans, Hawes having served as a World War II veteran, 1st Lieutenant, United States Army and Byas in the United States Navy as an officer's cook, may simply have enhanced the communicative styles, cultural norms, worldview, and professional beliefs that made the mentorship a very good match.[30]

Although Byas is less descriptive of the nuances of the professorship he observed in Hawes during these up-close encounters, Hawes's mentorship appears a critical incident in his transformation. As the two worked closely together, Byas would have observed the manner in which black professors implemented professional ideas in local settings, especially as he began his own participation in the network of professional black teachers and observed Hawes interacting therein. In a very real way, Byas surely observed the differences in the professional facade black professors deliberately assumed, dependent upon whether they were addressing black or white audiences.

At the time, however, other teachers were unaware of the extent of his learning in the informal apprenticeship. His fellow teachers at the school were sometimes critical of the senior professor's methods. "Byas," they reportedly said, "[has] gone up to Columbia and got this master's degree and he's sitting up there doing all this work for Mr. Hawes for nothing." Byas's perspective, however, diverged. He considered himself "fortunate to be with a man who, even though I had to put in hours and it came off my tail" was doing him a favor. "I was learning something about how a school operated. I had only studied it," he recalls. Unspoken is another likely conclusion: In addition to learning the mechanics of general school administrative tasks, Byas was particularly learning the nuances that accompanied the administrative responsibilities of running a successful black school.

Byas's return to educational life in Georgia as a teacher and professor-in-training brought him full circle. His journey reveals the unlikely transformation of a crafty child into a committed educator. It also demonstrates the convergence of national events and governmental funding that pivoted him to an HBCU, where he in turn learned that a world of scholarship awaited him and where he was encouraged to believe he could participate in that world. Coupled with new understandings about democratic participation, a different person returned to Georgia in 1951 than the one born there twenty-seven years before.

To seek to understand his actions as professor apart from the embedded cultural and educational context that shaped his demeanor makes it impossible to understand the zeal for excellence in black education and the capacity to undermine constraints that limited excellence that characterized his career. Both the Dr. Jekyll and Mr. Hyde personas were possible because of the educational expertise and the commitment to community and black schools that evolved from his lived personal and academic experiences. The examples of creativity ingenuity, masking with the superintendent, group organization, data collection skills, and communicative capacity with parents that provide the foundation for the successful implementation of the Curriculum Survey are all skills that can be ascertained in his experiential and educational world. And yet, the foundation that explains his activities does not end here. The skillful teacher and professor-in-training was also welcomed into a professional network of black educators that reinforced and extended the understandings he already had. This complex and interconnected professional world is equally central to unveiling the making of a professor.

In Spite of
This Old Devil
Segregation

*From the moment I decided
to be a principal, I decided I
would be knowledgeable about
what was going on in high
schools throughout the country.*
—*Ulysses Byas*

Two interrelated forms of professional development help explain Byas's vision as a professor. These professional development opportunities placed him in a network where his educational expertise could be extended beyond his collegiate and graduate training and where the ideas could be imported into forms that would be useful in his segregated school setting. As significant as were his personal and cultural experiences in shaping his character, so were these two forms of professional development in shaping his vision for leadership. On the national level, the most significant of these opportunities was related to the processes of school accreditation.

Byas's first introduction to this national network of professional development came in 1951–53 while he was still a teacher and professor-in-training at Blackwell Memorial School in Elberton, Georgia. Under Professor James Hawes, Byas was introduced to the rigid standards for black schools seeking an "approved" rating from the Southern Association of Colleges and Schools (Southern Association). The Southern Association was the accrediting agency that established standards for white schools and colleges throughout the South. Although this group accredited white schools that participated in the self-study process and passed the standards of its Evaluative Criteria, black schools using the same standards could not be considered "accredited" by the Southern Association. Instead, the Southern Association listed black schools who met the criteria as "approved."

The Southern Association also did not invite leaders of black schools to become part of its membership or attend its meetings. Rather than joining the Southern Association, black schools sought their approval rating from the Southern Association under the auspices of a separate body, the Association of Colleges and Schools. The "Association" as it was affectionately called by its members, was the black counterpart of the Southern Association. Most black educators knew the Association existed, though few likely understood its intellectual web or its history. They did know, however, that participating in its process of self-evaluation and receiving an "approved" rating gave a black school a distinguished and coveted status. Fewer than 17.5 percent of black Georgia high schools had undergone this process and been approved at that time; even four years later, 82 percent of the black Georgia schools would not have sought approval.[1]

As Professor James Hawes's administrative assistant, Byas learned through immersion the process of seeking and renewing the approval rating for a black school. During the year he arrived as a teacher, the school was involved in the self-study that was part of its preparation for an impending visit from an outside team of evaluators. The self-study required an intensive self-examination of the school population and community, basic data on pupils, enrollment, withdrawals, educational intentions, test results, occupational status of adults; the agencies influencing education in the community; the faculty philosophy, objectives, and programs of study; and myriad details on library, school plant, and staff and administration.[2] In assisting Hawes, Byas brought his Columbia credentials, which would be a merit in the faculty descriptions of the school and which may also explain why Hawes was so anxious to recruit him. However, he also brought the sweat labor of someone who wanted to learn how to run a school. He "stayed up late at night and didn't get paid" as he helped prepare reports and construct tables that would meet the stringent expectations of the Southern Association's Evaluative Criteria of 1950.[3]

In the process, Byas became so comfortable with the criteria for evaluation that when he left Elberton in 1953 to assume his first professorship at Hutchenson, he immediately initiated the process of self-study with his own faculty as preparation to apply for an approved rating. Byas did not remain long enough to see the school actually approved. However, shortly after he left Hutchenson for the more prominent and lucrative position at Fair Street in 1957, Hutchenson would be approved under the name of its new facility, the Robert L. Cousins High School. For this feat, Byas deserves partial credit.

Importantly, when Byas assumed the leadership of Fair Street, he accepted the helm of a school already on the Southern Association's list of "approved" schools. Fair Street was one of the thirty-seven Georgia schools on the list and had been since 1946. Although his intimate knowledge of the process of approval likely created some of the dismay he felt about the constrained curricular offerings when he arrived, the 24 teachers and 595 pupils at Fair Street could nonetheless boast that their school was among the earliest black high schools in Georgia to become approved by the Southern Association, with only nine schools having been approved prior to 1946 and five schools joining it during the year it was approved. Three hundred and eight black schools were approved across the southern states, and Georgia ranked fourth among southern states with the most approved schools.[4] While this number of black schools was far below the 234 white schools in Georgia accredited by the Southern Association, the black schools in Georgia were behind only Florida in the total number of approved black schools.[5] As the new professor of a school already approved, Byas became part of a group to which many other professors hoped to belong: professors of approved black schools. With his admission also automatically came certain membership and voting privileges.

The first privilege of membership was evidenced in the fall of 1957, at the same time the Fair Street School and community were deeply involved in completing the curriculum survey. During this period, the professor received his first invitation to an Association meeting. The meeting was convening that year in December in Richmond for its twenty-fourth annual convention and would boast 232 delegates and visitors in attendance. Attendees represented a membership that included 13 states, inclusive of the District of Columbia; 60 four-year colleges; 4 two-year colleges; and 308 high schools.[6] They were all leaders in schools that appeared on the list of black schools "approved" by the Southern Association. With an invitation to join this group, since only professors who led approved schools were invited, Byas was entering into the membership of an ongoing consortium of well-educated black principals, college presidents, and selected college faculty members. The result was a rather elite national club and one that would substantially influence the professional ideas Byas would later implement in his school.

More than any other national body, the Association provides a window through which to glimpse the educational stimulus provided for Byas and other black professors through its annual meetings, professional activities, opportunities for leadership, and printed materials. Indeed, this group provides the primary form of professional development on the national level that crafted a vision for Byas on effective ways to educate black children. Byas's affinity for its contribution to his development is unique; indeed, he distinctly contrasts the vision and activities of this black professional network with those of its white counterparts, the Southern Association of Colleges and Schools, the National Association of Secondary School Principals, and the National Educational Association (NEA). During meetings of these other associations, he perceived little attention being devoted to issues concerning black children, and he came to believe he was an unwelcome guest at their meetings. At the former, he was in his intellectual home.

We Hold These Truths: The Political and Educational Agenda in the History of the Association

Although Byas was new to the group in 1957, the work of the Association greatly preceded his entrée. Four years after he was born, the Association had begun its work of improving educational opportunities for black children and spurring quality educational experiences. The Association traced its origin to 1928. Prompted by dismal results of a "Survey of Negro Colleges and Universities," released earlier that year by Arthur J. Klein of the U.S. Office of Education, a group of black leaders approached the white Southern Association of Colleges and Secondary Schools for help in elevating black schools. Deeply moved by the report's recommendations to improve programs at the black colleges and schools, the black leaders sought to become part of the Southern Association's machinery in the South, a machinery that had functioned since 1895 to set school standards by providing institutional accreditation for schools that completed the self-study and passed the review of the visiting team. The goal of the 1928 meeting was to determine the willingness of the white organization to lend its support in helping to improve black colleges and schools. The black leaders understood that the process of meeting criteria the Southern Association set for accreditation was a means to foster excellence in all schools, and they believed the "vigorous steps" they were taking toward meeting the measures of the white agency was "one means of accelerating a program for self improvement" in black schools.[7] Though unrecorded in their materials, the strategy of the black educators is consistent with the strategies of the Dr. Jekyll and Mr. Hyde in that behind its benign request was an intent to force the Southern Association to assume some responsibility for elevating black education.

The response of the Southern Association to the request of these black educators was positive, even if constrained by an acceptance of the parameters dictated by the segregated practices of the era. As its minutes record, the Southern Association was assured by Thomas E. Jones, president of Fisk University, that the black group did not desire a "joint meeting" between the blacks and whites but only "experience and leadership . . . in formulating and putting into effects standards for Negro schools." Convinced that the request was not a means of challenging racial separation, the Executive Committee of the Southern Association at its annual meeting in December 1928 in Fort Worth, Texas, set in motion a form of interaction with the black group that lent the Southern Association's structural support to the process of evaluating black schools, but the committee delicately avoided an integrated gathering. Utilizing the services of an approval committee and later an ongoing Liaison Committee, black schools would be evaluated through their own autonomous organization, first called the Southern Association of Negro Colleges and Secondary Schools, using the Southern Association's standard Evaluative Criteria.[8] Schools that successfully completed a self-study and external team visit would be placed on an "approved" list of black schools. Such were the dictates of racial norms during the era.

In fact, race is the defining variable that best explains the psychological diversion of educational agendas between the two groups over the years. For the Southern Association members, some ongoing relationships with their black colleagues were necessary because of their commitment to perform a professional service to black schools by allowing them to be evaluated using the Southern Association's Evaluative Criteria and placing them on a list of "approved" black schools. This commitment had not come without debate and shifts in attitude among the members of the Southern Association. For example, Theodore H. Jack, dean of Emory University, initially believed the Southern Association "had no responsibility in the matter of examining and accrediting Negro schools." Later, he shifted this stance to agree that the Southern Association did have a professional responsibility in the matter, and he even became part of the first committee of appointees to function as a liaison with the black group.[9] However, despite the Southern Association's individual and group concession to professional responsibilities, its records do not provide evidence of a desire to disrupt the status quo of race relations and schooling.

In contrast to the white Southern Association, members of the black Association, from its outset, identified its "main purpose [as] professional growth, with the ultimate aim of gaining membership in the Southern

Association."[10] Having the Southern Association's assistance in requiring similar educational standards *and* gaining full membership in that association were clearly articulated agendas among the black educators involved in the group, though both goals were mediated by time. In the short term, black educators were critically concerned about addressing the needs of education for black students in an exemplary and sustained manner. They believed this goal could best be accomplished through applying the standards of the Southern Association to its own schools. From the time when the first black colleges were first placed on an approved list in 1930, Association members insisted that their schools be measured using the same criteria that were used for white schools. Black leaders believed strongly that the same evaluation standard was necessary, as J. T. Cater, dean of Talladega College, argued in 1935, to serve as "a yardstick . . . for improving the work of the school." In 1940, the black sentiment on this issue was captured in one of the Association resolutions at the annual meeting in Atlanta:

> The Commission on Secondary Schools commends the manner in which the committee on Approval of Negro schools has conducted the accreditment of Negro secondary schools in the Southern states. The commission, however, desires to stress the vital importance of careful and frequent inspection and reinspection of our secondary schools; first, in order to guard against the lowering, for Negro schools, of standards with reference to any of the criteria of accreditation; and second, in order to stimulate the continued growth of schools already approved.

Some members were adamant that they did not want a paternalistic modification of standards that would allow "Negro institutions [to] pretend to be what they are not."[11]

However, the insistence on the same evaluation standards was also a sublime act of resistance. Practically, and in the short term, employing the same standards for black schools that were used for white schools had the effect of leveraging additional funds from reluctant white school boards and superintendents. The Southern Association's Evaluative Criteria assessed library materials, pupil-teacher ratio, teaching load, school term, science equipment, school plant, and training of faculty. Because black educators were aware that black schools during this era fell "far short of meeting some of the more important standards," their insistence on evaluation by the same measure was a calculated means to stimulate white superintendents to provide the necessary materials that would enable their schools to qualify for approval.[12] Though carefully veiled behind educational rhetoric, the thrust to assure measurement by a comparable standard was a covert mechanism to advocate for equality of resources.

In another short-term goal, black educators saw black institution building and professional development as central in efforts to elevate the black race through education. From its inception, black educators viewed the Association as "an autonomous organization which could more effectively deal with their own peculiar problems," a view that recognizes the need for an organized body to focus specifically upon the problems that challenged the black community. They were explicit in their recognition that they were engaged in a "struggle" for greater educational opportunity for a huge number of blacks. They spoke openly of their desire to improve "the quality of . . . service to education, especially for Negro youth." For example, early reports in 1935 note that the Association's purpose was to "make studies and investi[gate] problems affecting the higher education of Negroes." This process involved a six-month task of outlining problems and seeking solutions for those problems. More than merely making the material relevant for the black social and political needs, the black leaders specifically equate their activity with lifting a race, a process they believed would lift America. Quoting a 1965 Teachers College report on Negro colleges and universities written by Earl J. McGrath, the Association's institutional history emphasizes the "unconquered and unconquerable faith in education for all the people to lift the level of a group and make America stronger and better." According to Leland Cozart, who was secretary-treasurer throughout the life of the Association and the writer of its official institutional history, in this New Deal era "education for Negroes was so related to the direction and velocity of change that it was futile for a body of educators to attempt to find solutions in a purely theoretical vacuum." Like black educators before them, members of the Association believed their activities would generate support "in the interest of the Negro and the nation as a whole."[13]

However, to view the short-term goal of building strong black institutions with adequate resources, people, and professional development as the ultimate goal of the group is to misunderstand the significance of its self-identified long-term goal. From its earliest meetings, the Association resisted its segregated organizational status. Its members discussed at length whether they should become a branch of the Southern Association or their own autonomous group, debating skittishly at times the advantages and disadvantages of each approach. The historian of the black Association describes its rebirth in December 1934 at an Atlanta meeting where participants chose to evolve the earlier body, the Association of Colleges for Negro Youth, into a more expanded mission that would include high schools as well as colleges. He provides detail on the salient organizational and practical issues that confronted the "educational pioneers" who headed the earliest organizations and notes that as early as this meeting, the organization was "charged with the zeal for ultimate membership in the Southern Association."[14] This long-term goal would seem in contradiction to the conciliatory tone of the president of Fisk in 1928, who insisted to the Southern Association that the group of black leaders did not want integrated meetings. However, since the report of the black president's statement is among the minutes of the white Southern Association but not among the black Association minutes, proceedings, or institutional history, the stance may be an example of Cozart's description of black leaders during the era as having to "come to grips" with the alternatives available to them. Sometimes these alternatives required "the pragmatic approach, sometimes a prophetic role, often a compromise," he writes. However, they were "never yielding to the complacency of becoming embalmed in a segregated situation cursed with the implication of inferiority."[15] This agenda substantially distinguished this group from the rhetoric and goals of its white counterpart.

At the Richmond meeting to which Byas was invited, the short-term goals of the black Association were being fulfilled. The same evaluation criteria were uniformly applied to black as well as white schools, and their application had helped provide many black schools with needed equipment and staff and would continue to do so over the next decade. Moreover, the black institutions had developed their own capacity for schooling directly linked to their segregated circumstances. As Horace Mann Bond described the black schools during a meeting of the Association in 1954: "Inured to hardship the will to survive had to come from within," he emphasized, applauding the "veiled quality of these institutions to inspire hope and aspiration in Negro children in spite of 'this old devil segregation.'"[16] On the measures of institution building and professional development, the Association was enjoying some short-term success. However, the long-term goal of integration with the parent body was not fully accomplished.

The Centrality of Segregation in Professional Settings

The Southern Association and the Association were still meeting separately in 1957, despite the fact that they were meeting in the same city. The Association gathering included an impressive array of well-educated black professors who spoke with expansive vocabularies and were meticulously dressed. Members of the intellectual elite were also among the attendees as guest speakers and, sometimes, as members of the Association. The term "intellectual elite" refers to black college presidents, deans, and teachers who held advanced degrees, most often from white institutions. These attendees populated the leadership of black colleges and, very often, were in the forefront of research efforts and organizational efforts to provided equality of opportunity for black children. In the absence of a professional conference for black researchers during this period, the Association provided an important space for intellectual exchange.[17]

Despite their elite status, the black attendees at the Association meeting were still constrained by segregation and deemed insufficient to become full members of the Southern Association. They were instead invited to hold their meetings concurrently with the white group. That is, the two groups met in separate locations but in the same city at the same time. This segregated arrangement dated from 1950, at a previous Richmond meeting, when the Executive Committee of the Southern Association recommended that the Association be invited to hold its annual meeting "in the same city and at the same time as the meeting of the Southern Association of Colleges and Secondary Schools." The black meeting usually began one day after the white meeting, an arrangement that allowed the Association to engage some of the key speakers of the Southern Association for presentation at the black meeting.[18]

Both groups were gathered in Richmond the first week of December 1957, although the policies of segregation dictated that the two thousand delegates to the white Southern Association could convene in the comfortable quarters of the John Marshall Hotel in the downtown business district. Most sessions of the white gathering were in the meeting rooms of the hotel, with the exception of the general session and discussion groups, which were held at the white and segregated John Marshall High School. The program of the Southern Association attendees invited them to avail themselves of the city's major attraction. On the front cover was a "cordial" invitation from the Liggett and Myers Tobacco Company to have delegates visit the City's "greatest industry in actual operation," with hosts who would "escort visitors through the plant and . . . explain how cigarettes are made."[19] In contrast, the black registered attendees of the Association met west of the central city, approximately fifteen minutes away, at Virginia Union University. In 1957, Virginia Union was still part of a thriving black community. It had been founded as a Christian institution in 1896 to provide "moral and intellectual uplift [for] Afro-American youth," and it was nestled amid black middle-class homes where attendees at the conference could be boarded by willing community members. This arrangement sometimes required sharing a bed with another professional colleague.[20] The black delegates received no publicized invitations to visit the tobacco company.

The segregation of the annual meetings of the white and black groups was customary, having been violated on only one traceable occasion. Two years after the 1950 recommendation to hold meetings during the same time period, the two organizations orchestrated a joint gathering on Tuesday, December 2, at 3:00 at the white Metropolitan Baptist Church in Memphis. For both groups, this joint event was one of many sessions in their otherwise segregated meetings. Addressing his biracial audience, platform guest William H. Kilpatrick, professor emeritus of education at Teachers College, a Georgia native, and a familiar figure among black teachers, noted that "this joint meeting of the two Associations is a milestone and indicates that we have come a long way educationally." He believed the gathering was "a monument to the progress" the two organizations were making. The young John Hope Franklin, already an emerging scholar in African American history, was a keynote speaker for the afternoon. Preliminary assessments on the value of the integrated gathering provided by members of the Liaison Committee for each group were positive. Discussing the feedback at an Association meeting in Atlanta in April 1953, the report of the Liaison Committee indicated that "the first joint effort was successful both as to professional growth and the revelation that such a thing can be done without apparent difficulty."[21]

However, hopes for more integrated gatherings were premature. Although the black and white representatives of the Liaison Committees had reached a point in their discussions where they suggested "making all sessions of the two associations joint meetings," the proposal was stymied when members recognized that they were scheduled to return to the segregated city of Memphis, where a simultaneous gathering of blacks and whites in the same venue would be problematic. Although members of the Liaison Committee "thought [that] it might [be] possible to arrange for some joint committee meetings during the Memphis sessions," the black Association was incredulous when it received a note the following September from the executive secretary of the Southern Association saying that facilities in Memphis made a joint session impossible. The white executive secretary's letter concluded with the following paragraph:

In conclusion, let me say that the Executive Committee of the Southern Association in session July 9–11, 1953 considered this whole problem of the two associations, the relationships between them and the nature of the program for our next meeting. They are all sympathetic from a professional standpoint to the values which might be achieved through joint professional meetings. At the same time, they have to face practical situations of the facilities available to us this year. Maybe in some future year, and in some other place, we can do some of these things.

In other words, the white Southern Association was capitulating to the racial norms, with the noncommittal last sentence a hint that some of the pressure to conform may likely also have emanated from within its membership. The pressure to which the document alludes was real. As Byas notes, the Southern Association received its money through the annual dues paid by southern school districts. This dependency eradicated any direct voice it might have assumed and, instead, created a symbiotic relationship between the Southern Association and its constituents. To violate the mandated segregation laws in southern states would directly inhibit the flow of money that kept the group in existence. Violation of those laws was not an option for the white association at that time in the proposed city. Thus, the executive director concluded by suggesting that some of the members of the Association might wish to "avail themselves of the privilege of hearing some of our outstanding speakers" by "cutting" some of the sessions at their own meeting.

In curt reply, the black Association sent to the Southern Association six copies of its own planned program, noting that it would "happily welcome the presence of any of [the Southern Association] delegates" at its own meeting. To further illustrate their disdain for the dismantling of plans for integrated gatherings, in discussions among themselves, the members of the Executive Committee affirmed that the Liaison Committee would continue to serve as "our medium of communication . . . [on] problems of mutual concern" but that the black Association's own "time and place committee [would] decide upon the time and place for [the] 21st annual meeting without reference necessarily to the place and time of the meeting of the Southern Association of Colleges and Secondary Schools."[22] By the 1957 meeting, concessions had been sufficient to allow both groups to convene in Richmond at the same time and with some shared speakers. Of course, the black meeting would still begin one day later than the white meeting—an arrangement that continued to allow the segregated process of sharing some speakers who discussed issues considered to be germane to members of both the black and white groups. The ideologically overlapping but physically separate setting was disdainful but, as Byas recounts, was "a practical solution to a complicated problem." In this convoluted context, the point remained that interracial gatherings would not be permitted.

The Agenda of the Black Association Meeting

The agenda of the Richmond meeting of the Association to which Byas was invited was typical of the activities, people, and talk that had dominated its meetings for the previous twenty-three years. Each year the leaders carefully crafted a theme they believed would address the needs of black children. For the members, the theme was no flowery statement of ideology. Rather, for attendees, the conference theme was always considered to be "a trumpet call to action." The theme this year was improving the quality of education for black youth.[23] As Byas would soon discover about the themes, attendees embraced the conversation with vigor.

On Monday evening, the program began with an opening session that included an address by Dr. Buell Gordon Gallagher, president of the City College, New York City. Gallagher waxed eloquently on his "intellectual contempt and pity" for the "mental myopia" that allowed one citizen to reject "his neighbor because he doesn't like the neighbor's skin color." He acknowledged that "these remarks may be offensive to some ears," since "the voice of conscience . . . is seldom welcome." But he acknowledged that he was "not profoundly disturbed by those who [would] not listen neither to reason nor to persuasion." While they were "being dragged kicking and screaming, into the twentieth century . . . life will flow around them and pass them by," he emphasized. "To cling to the values of the Middle Ages in a day of democracy is to threaten our entire culture with the disruptive forces of strife, dissension, violence, anarchy." Sharing the program with him that evening was the chorus from neighboring black Armstrong High School, a fitting accompaniment to a speech that repeatedly highlighted the "contradiction between faith and practice which any form of racial segregation presented."[24]

Tuesday morning was devoted to commission meetings, both of the High School Commission and the College Commission, with each discussing the ways in which the theme of quality education was operationalized at their institutional level. Tuesday afternoon and Wednesday afternoon included two other major lectures, both also aimed at improving quality education. On Wednesday morning, the opening session began with a panel discussion led by Alonzo G. Moron, president of Hampton Institute. He was joined by William Brown, the director of educational research at the North Carolina College at Durham, later to become Central University; Norman Burns, a professor at the University of Chicago; and Sadie Yancey, the dean of women at Howard University. Together, the panel considered a number of concrete ideas deemed to be important to spur the retention of black students in college. Among these were attention to counseling, study skills, orientation to college, job information and placement, quality faculty, and student personnel.

In the panel on standardized testing that convened earlier in the day on Thursday morning, the ideas of quality education focused more directly on secondary education and generated sustained audience interaction. Charles H. Thompson, dean of the graduate school at Howard and longtime Association speaker and participant, was the moderator of the panel. Thompson was the editor of the *Journal of Negro Education* and had received his doctorate from the University of Chicago in 1925. As important, he had figured prominently in the debunking of questions of black inferiority as a result of standardized testing that had permeated the black scholarly community since the publication of Carl C. Brigham's study of intelligence in 1923, a study that unequivocally concluded that the difference in black and white army test scores was genetic. In previous work, Thompson published a survey that documented the rejection rate of white registrants for the army in South Carolina and concluded that this rate was four times as high as the rejection rates of blacks in Illinois. He had used these and other data to argue that the impact of environment on differences in educational opportunities implicitly negated Brigham's conclusions.[25] Joining him were other panelists. One, Dr. Warren G. Findley, a regional advisor for the Educational Testing Service, provided meticulous detail on the nature of the achievement gap between black and white students. The other, Dr. Martin Jenkins, president of Morgan

State College, focused specifically upon the factors he believed motivated student achievement at Morgan State.

Findley led the conversation. He outlined the results of the tests of twenty-five thousand white and black children using the Stanford Achievement Test (grades four and six), the Iowa Every-Pupil Tests (grade eight), and the Essential High School Content (grade twelve). His detailed conclusions showed that, despite some overlap with white student scores, only 2–10 percent of black pupils were meeting the standard on the various tests, that the scores of the black children were falling progressively further behind as they advanced through school, and that white teachers were also showing better performance on all the tests than black teachers. Findley concluded that cultural background, inadequate facilities, poor teaching, and low individual competence explained the poor achievement. Rather than blaming the students and the schools for the inadequacy of student performance, the president of Morgan State College, following Findley's presentation, provided practical ways his college addressed the entering students at his school who typically scored in the seventh percentile, including discussions of such measures as freshman orientation programs, freshman English programs, reading clinics, test seminars, and so forth.

At the conclusion of the panel, the conversation was piercing. The question "How do we account for the superior achievement in college of the students of low socio-economic status?" was immediately posed to Findley. After a brief answer, the next question was presented: "Dr. Findley, would we get a more accurate picture of the intellectual powers of these children in a raw socio-economic status by varying the instruments of testing?" When the question was perceived to have not been answered by the guest speaker, the delegate rephrased the query: "Dr. Findley, I did not make myself clear, I am sure. I was not referring to achievement tests. I was referring to the tests of the intellectual ability on which we base our diagnosis of children's readiness to learn. Would you comment on that?" As the minutes ticked away, the questions continued: "How can you overcome the problem of bringing the low performing group up to acceptable standards with the same number of teachers? Wouldn't one have to have more teachers working with these groups? Has a study been done on pupil-teacher ratio in this connection?" The report of the meeting is not sufficiently expansive to determine how many of these questions were raised by professors in the audience, although the practical challenges embedded suggest that at least some may have come from professors. On some questions, notably those of some college presidents, the secretary-treasurer of the Association recorded names associated with particular queries. For example, the president of Benedict College in South Carolina, J. A. Bacoats, asked: "Were there any Negroes represented in the administration and evaluation of the Atlanta tests?" From Nelson Harris, president of Shaw University in North Carolina: "Do you feel that the low scores made by the Negro pupils at the various grade levels were affected by the less favorable opportunities to learn in the school themselves as represented by double sessions and lack of facilities?" As the session wore on, the presenter of the findings, Findley, responded to the last recorded question on promotional policies, "I may have to shout for help . . . before I finish this one." It may have been a genuine request for assistance or the unintentional truthful unveiling of the exhaustion the Educational Testing Service representative felt after an intensely engaging interaction.[26] Throughout their days, as these descriptions and others indicate, the presidents, professors, and those in between intensely engaged their theme: improving quality education for black children.

The session ended on Thursday evening with the closing banquet. The president of Howard University, Mordecai Johnson, was the keynote speaker. As Johnson rose to dominate the podium, his speech was expected to issue the final challenge before all attendees would return to their respective states, schools, and immediate problems. At the head table with him was Virginia Union's president, the well-known Samuel D. Proctor, who would later become president of North Carolina A&T in Greensboro. Present also were Benjamin E. Mays, president of Johnson's undergraduate alma mater, Morehouse College in Atlanta, and John E. Codwell, a former student from Howard who was now principal of Phillis Wheatley High School in Texas and had been recently elected to the presidency of the Association.[27] Although the men made certain Johnson received an appropriate introduction, one was hardly needed. Johnson was the first black president of the first black school where black students could receive graduate training, and he was well known to the black and white intellectual and political world of this era. His savvy congressional negotiations would net Howard $7 million when he retired three short years hence, up from the $35,000 the school received prior to his arrival. He was known for his willingness to agitate in the college domain to improve academic excellence, including bringing to the institution brilliant black scholars, raising faculty salaries, and strengthening admission standards. One of his hires had been Charles H. Thompson, the Association member who had moderated the panel on standardized test scores earlier that day.

Surely not lost on some attendees—especially S. M. Nabrit, president of Texas Southern University and brother of James Nabrit, a Howard-trained lawyer for the National Association for the Advancement of Colored People (NAACP)—was the fact that Johnson was also intimately connected to the Association's gaining its long-term goal of inclusion in the Southern Association.[28] Across town, the Southern Association was voting at its annual meeting on admitting selected black schools to accredited status in the organization. Just the previous year, the Southern Association had established a Joint Sub-Committee on Colleges for Negro Youth to begin the process of screening applicants for full admission into the Southern Association. The goal of the committee was to complete its work of transferring black institutions from approved status to accredited status within a five-year period. At their meeting this year, the Southern Association would decide to admit fifteen black colleges to full membership in the Southern Association. Of course, inclusion did not yet encompass the other black colleges or the black secondary schools. However, the expectation was that all other "approved" schools would be added at the end of the five-year period, in 1961.[29]

That the white Southern Association was even contemplating this decision was directly linked to the climate ushered in by the *Brown* case, which was inextricably linked to the evening's speaker. Johnson was the gutsy Howard president who, only two years after his own appointment, had spurred the creation of a first-class law school by hiring Harvard-trained lawyer Charles Hamilton Houston and giving him the latitude to reinvent the law school, despite objections from some older graduates. From that new law school, a cadre of lawyers had been trained who had been responsible for the defeat of the school segregation laws in the historic *Brown v. Board of Education* case. Indeed, NAACP attorney Oliver Hill, also a resident of Richmond, reports that he chose to matriculate at Howard Law School precisely because he wanted to be part of the mechanism that would defeat legal inequality.[30]

Thus, the Southern Association's capitulation to the black Association in agreeing to admit black members was likely less the result of twenty years of interactions with the Association, despite the advocacy of the black members of the Liaison Committee, and more likely indicative of the climate of impending racial integration following *Brown*.[31] Johnson was clearly aware that his foresight helped make the anticipated accredited status possible. During a speech before this same group four years earlier, the December before the 1954 *Brown v. Board* decision, Johnson had paid effusive tribute to the "Negro lawyers and the gains they have made," noting that South Carolina had been required to hire a former presidential candidate in the person of John W. Davis because "he [was] the only man [they] could find able to stand against Thurgood Marshall." His comments had generated rousing applause from the audience, and his speech had continued with his admonition that they must all use every avenue available to eliminate segregation in the South. "Without relenting and without animosity, we must sweetly sue them, sweetly vote against them, argue against them." Johnson believed firmly that the forthcoming *Brown* decision would be a "wise one because the Supreme Court realizes that segregation is inconsistent with the laws and well-being of the nation."[32]

The Southern Association may have been less convinced than Johnson that its plans for inclusion were constitutionally justified, but it prepared to heed the ruling of the high court immediately after the May 1954 ruling.[33] However, owing to the tempered *Brown II* ruling in 1955 and the rise of southern resistance to any efforts to integrate southern schools, meeting the 1960 merger deadline the Southern Association first envisioned no longer seemed crucial. With the new climate, the Southern Association reverted to its default position of segregation, and the actual merger of the two associations would not be fully accomplished until 1964.

The night of Johnson's speech, mindful that the Southern Association had debated the status of black schools across town at its meeting, this icon in the struggle for equality for blacks prepared to address his audience. Johnson was among friends and colleagues in the banquet room at Virginia Union. The Howard president was a member of this group; Howard had received its "approval" rating in 1934, with only three other black colleges having been approved before it. He had been speaking before the group since 1937, when he critiqued the educational system as a "warped instrument" that was "stumbling along in relative blindness waiting for a revision which it knows it must have but which it is not quite certain how it would lay hold upon it." Though Johnson did not have as intimate an involvement with the Association as some of the other eighteen college presidents who sat in the room, apparently delegating more active committee work to his dean, O. W. Holmes, he was clearly no stranger among the group either. In the banquet room that night at Virginia Union University, he was not merely a member of the intellectual elite; he was among colleagues.[34]

Perhaps because they knew him, the members of the audience could appreciate Johnson's opening joke. Before becoming a college president, Johnson had served in West Virginia as a Baptist minister. In his opening remarks, he drew upon that training and imagined himself turned away from the "beautiful kingdom" and sent back to earth—to Mississippi—to spend another lifetime learning to make twenty-minute speeches. Apparently, everybody who knew Johnson was aware of the fact that he had the reputation as someone who, as Byas describes it, "could talk all night." Johnson's opening remarks suggested that he might have the same reputation in the heavenly place. But, despite the opening jest, Johnson's speech was no joke.

Captivatingly and eloquently delivered, Johnson allowed his audience, including N. L. Dillard of Caswell County High School in North Carolina, to eavesdrop on his conversations with British ambassadors and engage his response to great books from professors at Columbia College. He shared ideas that had "come to [him] one day while . . . standing on a shore of the Mediterranean Sea looking across to North Africa." He guided his listeners through a history of the Middle Ages and the Protestant Reformation, talking of Jesus and Thomas Jefferson and arguing that they both converged in the belief that all people were worthy of respect and teaching. "God helping me," he resounded, "I'll never do anything to thwart, to check, to humiliate, or deal contemptuously with [this] precious life. However I may touch you, I am going to salute you, serve you, lift you up and do everything I can to establish on this earth in a world wide way . . . that great society which I know to be possible because of the possibilities that are in people like you and you and you."[35]

As he developed his argument—the speech was indeed lengthy—Johnson addressed the theme of the convention, quality education, directly. He argued the need to restore the "inherent dignity and high possibilities for every human individual." Perhaps inspired by the integrated world he and his colleagues imagined would soon be upon them because of the judicial victories, Johnson argued that the black leaders in the room needed to help not merely their friends, and not just blacks. Rather, he challenged them to commit to teaching any student coming to their institutions. This sentiment echoed a prominent belief in the organization that a truly democratic schooling would necessarily be an integrated one.

Moving, finally, toward a conclusion, Johnson appealed to the importance of audience members identifying themselves with the children they sought to help. His points suggested resoundingly that the attendees had risen above constrained educational circumstances and that they had in their knowledge base the tools needed to help others succeed in ways they had. Thus, the goal of these leaders must be to imagine the possibilities in the children and help them likewise succeed.

> What is the meaning of the Negro sitting in this room? We have come from the humblest segment of the human race. Men have measured our heels and said what was in our brains because our heels were long. Men have measured the thickness of our lips and limited our minds because our lips were thicker than theirs. Men have measured our heads and because some of them shoot up this way and some of them go up that way, and told their children what are the limits of the possibilities of those brains. But we have seen a Negro with a head that shoots up like a "squozed" watermelon go to Harvard University and come out with a M.D. and Doctor of Philosophy degree. . . . Our existence here tells not only what is possible for us but it tells about the nature of human nature because we have come from the bottom of humanity and we have climbed every stairway that it is capable for human foot to tread. We have touched every shore where human intelligence and the human heart and the trained aesthetic power can touch. We know, don't we? We must be the agents of what we know.

As Johnson sat down, he did so to the applause of a speech that compelled respect for the value of every individual person and celebrated the possibilities of an integrated world while simultaneously challenging his colleagues to identify with, and connect themselves to, the uplift of people who had the same potential that they had. Johnson believed that what was more important than decisions about curriculum was that his listeners could be the primary agent to help the masses who had not yet become successful. In minutes of the proceedings, the Johnson lecture would be deemed "one of the high moments of the conference."[36]

The World of Black Professional Development

The 1957 Association meeting opened for Byas a new world and beckoned him to become a participant in an ongoing conversation about educating black children. The topic of black students and testing that provided much of the conversation of this meeting provides one example of an issue that was part of an ongoing debate in the black professional community. Among the many black scholars who conducted research and published articles debunking black inferiority was Horace Mann Bond, former president of Fort Valley, who had appeared on a panel at the Association meeting of 1954 with J. M. Nabrit, who was then the secretary of Howard University. Bond emphasized the characteristics of black institutions, noting their capacity to "inspire hope in spite of the threat of despair." To ignore this climate in the face of interpreting testing data was to ignore his theory of multiple causation in explaining the test scores of black children. In part, Bond's analysis of a *New York Times* report noted:

> This study seems to me to be an example of single causation which is bad science. It said that they had tested a certain number of Negro high school children in the South and found that only 2 per cent of them were qualified to compete with white students of Northern colleges; and this was due to the fact that these were segregated high schools. It seems bad science . . . to take one part of the complex in which all of us are involved and say this is it. And, it also seems deadly to the hope and aspirations of Negro children for some time to come.
>
> I believe, if we made a study of these children in terms of their limited culture items, (Allison Davis of University of Chicago has done a great deal about it) we would discover that some of us have known for thirty years that these tests are not tests of native intelligence, but of the environment and the culture. And instead of arraying the probability scores of these children in terms of what Northern white high schools or Northern Negro high school children might be expected to achieve and then array them in a probability curve against graduates of more fortunate high schools. As a matter of fact, a lot of us whose parents were illiterate have made it. When the chips were down and desire motivated, we found we could do it. The findings of the simple causation principle falsely imply inferiority and rule out the salient quality of inspiration, which those who have muddled through had the power to give.[37]

His conclusions reflect his assertions in the Clark Foreman study conducted in 1932, in which his findings also indicated strongly that the improvement of the environment for black children markedly improved their test results.[38]

The way this topic was part of an ongoing conversation is also exemplified by the repetition of testing as a central facet of the meeting the year after the Richmond gathering. One year later, when the Association would meet at Central High School in Louisville, Kentucky, noted scholar and authority on testing Allison Davis would challenge listeners to move beyond mere testing and to consider other variables that would facilitate success for black children: "We are not going to learn apparently very quickly that intelligence tests will not predict what children will do in college or high school or elementary school; and secondly, that they are culturally loaded. They don't measure intelligence in any direct or simple way because of the cultural bias." Rather than focusing on the poor results, Davis would provide avenues that would facilitate student success. Among these were references to the importance of students being able to identify with the teacher, to teachers locating materials that would be related to the lives of the children they taught, and to school educators accepting children as they came to school.[39]

A second topic reflected in the ongoing dialogue Byas joined was related to democracy and citizenship. This was an area of concern already reflected in Byas's graduate training and teaching. In her dissertation, Patrice Preston-Grimes raised the excellent question of how black teachers taught citizenship in black schools during this era. Her results indicate that black teachers were very aware of the trends of social studies educators and sought to utilize these ideas in their classrooms.[40] However, the classroom behaviors she uncovered find their intellectual home in the Association conversations. For example, lectures at the 1935 meeting directly raised questions about the relationship between curriculum, citizenship, and black needs. Without damning U.S. policy or romanticizing the activity in their schools, speakers focused on defining citizenship and functional citizenship, noting the role of courses in preparing black citizens, critiquing the general apathy of Americans and blacks on citizenship issues, and touting methods being used in some schools to create blacks cognizant of their roles as citizens. Among these methods were offering classes in citizenship, requiring black students to help in political campaigns, and inviting city officials to lecture on various urban and rural problems. The speakers at the meeting describe utilizing community institutions and assisting students in making local records of black communities' living conditions and incomes. Cooperative activities such as these were to be mechanisms through which black college students would "know what citizens should do and . . . learn how to do it." One speaker also forcefully noted the limitations of society: "Even in those places where [the Negro] is allowed to vote, [he] is seldom as interested as the white people since they seldom expect to get anything out of it. In these sections where they are disfranchised, citizenry is a mockery."[41]

The theme of blacks and citizenship was more directly addressed at this meeting in a subsequent panel, held later in the day, where participants included Horace Mann Bond; John W. Davis, president of West Virginia State College; Rufus E. Clement, then president of Louisville Municipal College; and Charlotte Hawkins Brown, principal of Palmer Institute in North Carolina. The discussion directly addressed the question of "the responsibility of the schools for citizenship status of the Negro in America." Answers to the question embraced curricular initiatives but made clear the difficulties for blacks attempting to participate fully in the responsibilities of American citizenship. One participant, W. T. Gibbs of North Carolina A&T in Greensboro, noted that "citizens have the right to hold office which Negroes do not." Citizens, likewise, were allowed to enjoy the liberties, duties, and privileges of ordinary Americans. Contrariwise, he noted that "the Negro's position is unsatisfactory from both of these points of view." He argued that black colleges must not develop black students for citizenship through a single course but that all courses should "operate in [the] direction" of citizenship preparation so that students would know "duties and rights and opportunities and privileges and responsibilities at every turn of the game." In settings where the next generation of professors were then being prepared, he encouraged blacks to move beyond loyalty to the government, such as fighting honorably in World War I, as a measure of citizenship. His sentiment was echoed by others such as A. L. Kidd of Florida A&M, who spoke directly of the propaganda that was used to "discredit Negroes as citizens" and argued that the college must develop the kind of leadership that could "look at trends and movements and attempt to point the way in which we should go."[42]

Closely related to conversations about citizenship in Association meetings were sessions centered on the meaning of democracy. In particular, in 1940, immediately prior to America's entrance into World War II, the question of the role blacks should assume during the world conflict consumed the conference agenda. Ralph J. Bunche, professor of political science at Howard University, led the discussion with his talk "The Negro's Stake in the World Crisis." Bunche emphasized that the conflict had immediate significance for black citizens, as he believed a world revolution was in progress, and that the "Negro loses if Hitler wins." He was echoed in a discussion of "Not Made to Die," a talk presented by John Temple Graves, editor of the *Birmingham News*. Seeding the ideology that would prevail among black newspapers during the period of the conflict, discussants argued that America would "not have a complete democracy until it has set its house in order." Moreover, he argued, "this [was] not a time to overlook differences, but to correct them so that we can have a democracy that we cannot lose by default."[43]

Discussed repeatedly over the years, these conference themes directly address the intent of the Association to provide professional development sufficient that professors of approved schools throughout the South would be able to prepare black students to become full participants in the nation. In part, the Association addressed these needs by frankly examining the present state of black youth and critiquing American values that maintained limits on the students' potential. However, equally important as a realistic assessment of the confining southern context was the need to raise the educational level of parents and teachers by being certain attendees were abreast of current educational trends. In addition to topics infused with the needs of black youth, many sessions covered traditional curricular topics such as guidance, vocational education, scholarship, and athletic subsidies. Even these conversations, however, were contextually and culturally interpreted. Thus, a discussion of vocational opportunities tabulated offerings in colleges and secondary schools and compared them with occupational opportunities for blacks.[44] Throughout the years, the conversations centered on the needs of black children and ways to ensure their success.

In part, the capacity of the annual meetings to link cutting-edge theoretical ideas in education with black needs was elevated because of the presence of the intellectual elite among the attendees and speakers. In 1935, for example, scholars such as Ira De A. Reid, Abram Harris, and Charles S. Johnson joined twenty-four other attendees to study the problems of higher education for blacks and to prepare a report for the next meeting. At the same meeting two appointed committees were chaired by Charles H. Wesley and W. E. B. DuBois. Over the years, speakers and participants at the meetings included Mary M. Bethune (1936), Ralph Bunche (1940), Ambrose Caliver (1944, 1956), Rufus Clement, and Benjamin Mays (1942).[45] Indeed, the presence of well-known blacks such as these and others at annual meetings was an attribute that characterized all of the thirty-one annual meetings held during the life of the Association.

Importantly, the Association was not the only national agency that expended its efforts directly on black children. The American Teachers Association (ATA) also represented a convergence of people and ideas that helped to solidify an agenda for black education. Older than the Association, the ATA was founded in 1903 and served as the black national counterpart to the National Education Association (NEA). The NEA was founded in 1857 and served as a "platform for the explication of ideas and ideals by the nation's leading educators."[46] Mirroring the activities of the NEA, professional development also served as a primary focus of the ATA. For example, a Georgia delegate to the ATA meeting in 1962 would report to colleagues who did not attend: "We enjoyed vibrant sessions and group meetings in which we shared problems, exchanged ideas, and related methods and techniques of teaching."[47] The delegate's summation echoes the ATA's goal, according to the ATA history, of allowing the information at the meeting to serve "as points of departure and suggestive guidelines for the initiation or the development of school and community programs."[48]

The Association and the ATA also overlapped in other ways. Generally, the ATA and the Association agreed on the educational agenda for black youth, that being the desire to elevate professional knowledge and to apply these broad educational ideas to the needs of black children. The ATA's professional magazine, the *Bulletin*, provides an example of the issues addressed in 1954. In this edition, articles focused on the progress of the education of blacks between 1870 and 1950 and devoted substantial time to understanding the legal status of segregated schools. At meetings in other years, topics included studies on testing and grading, programmed learning, language labs, curricular improvement, and other topics that reflected the educational trends of the era and the needs peculiar to educating black children.

In addition to topics, attendees of the ATA and the Association meetings overlapped. Some of these included the professors who attended both meetings. However, the intellectual elite were also among the participants of both groups. For example, Charles Johnson of Fisk, who was a presence at the Association meetings, was a presenter at the ATA's twentieth annual meeting in December 1953, giving a talk entitled "Next Steps in Education in the South."[49] The fifty-ninth annual convention in Miami,

Florida, in 1962 captures the intent of these meetings. Among the eminent scholars present were Kenneth Clark, Allison Davis, and Whitney Young. Consistent with the conversation at Association meetings on testing and the difference a school or teacher (or both) could make when high expectations were held, Clark directly addressed the concerns of black educators. Adhering to the importance of high standards and encouraging black educators to meet the challenge, he argued that the black teacher "must work twice as hard to compensate for past educational deficits and injustice." "Negro teachers and Negro students," he maintained, "can not be excused for shoddy performance because they are a Negro." Allison Davis echoed the challenge by pointing out that "the school is one of the most powerful factors in changing their culture and their way of life." He posited that children who were, in the terminology of the period, considered to be "culturally disadvantaged" needed "most of all teachers who [would] encourage them to try, to hope, to believe."[50]

Finally, records indicate that the same people were often leaders of both groups. This overlap created a consistency of vision for the ideas the black educational community should be embracing. Mordecai Johnson, for example, was president of the ATA in 1929. H. C. Trenholm, president of the Alabama State Normal School at the time and an attendee at the Association meetings, was elected president in 1929. Rufus E. Clement, then president of Atlanta University, was also president in 1936 and an active member of the Association. Other individuals serving as leaders of both groups were Mary M. Bethune, Horace Mann Bond, Charles H Thompson, and L. S. Cozart.[51] The overlap in leadership makes the similarity in ideas discussed unsurprising. It suggests that the binding agent, though operationalized under different institutional names, was the intent to utilize organizational structures to address egregious problems facing black schools.

Given the similarity in focus, one might imagine that both the Association and the ATA would figure prominently in Byas's national network of influence. However, the ATA figures less prominently in Byas's network as a form of professional development. Byas explains that the ATA charged only $1 for individual dues in contrast to the Association, for which school boards were sometimes paying in excess of $200 a year for membership for their black schools. The small fee paid the salary of an executive secretary but in Byas's opinion limited programming. Moreover, while school boards were willing to approve school dismissal and travel for professors to attend Association meetings, similar approvals were not automatic for the ATA. Most significant in comparing Byas's perspective on these two groups, his emergence as a well-respected professor in the state after his employment at Gainesville also coincided with the demise of the ATA. Officially considered to have "merged" with the NEA in 1962, the ATA sacrificed its independent programming and its commitment to a black educational agenda and became part of the larger white educational group. For all these reasons, the Association emerges as the most significant form of professional development for Byas on the national level.

However, the contrast in the ATA's agenda and that of the NEA would be important foreshadowing for Byas's later perspective on the NEA. Despite the structural similarity, the ATA and NEA operated with differing fundamental missions that echo the dissimilarities between the Association and the Southern Association. Much as the Association existed in relationship to the Southern Association but had its own agenda specific to the education of black children, so the ATA existed in relationship with the NEA but with its own separate educational agenda for black children. Specifically, as Wayne Urban notes, the NEA historically focused on educational issues. Where inequities were considered as important agenda items, these inequities were related to gender. Even when data on racial disparities were part of its database, the NEA was silent. Neither the ATA nor the Association would have been silent.[52]

The Ways the Association Served the Professor

Several particular characteristics of the meetings of black educators endear this professional development setting of the Association to a professor like Byas. In their most basic purpose, Byas believed the professional meetings planned by blacks with the needs of black children dominating the agenda provided a structural forum through which local professors could become linked to the national ideology about racial uplift and the national educational ideas that could spur new educational possibilities in their schools. The meeting structure, in imitation of that of the Southern Association, included two separate commissions—one on colleges and one on high schools—that allowed attendees to interact with their peers across secondary schools and colleges. Through this arrangement, college teachers served on the High School Commission and high school principals also served on the College Commission, a format that encouraged joint discussion of mutual problems. Moreover, both high school professors and college presidents and some faculty were participants in the array of small and large group gatherings that defined the meeting, although proceedings reveal that college professors and administrators held more visible roles than high school principals.

As a professor new to the Association in 1957, Byas saw this differentiation as well. He remembers that principals generally "looked up to the colleges as leaders." Byas also reports that the college presidents sometimes had "heads like horses," imagining that they "they knew it all." His comments suggest some of the nuances of the interpersonal interplay that surely characterized the meetings. Nonetheless, the gatherings must also be recognized for the ways in which they provided intellectual spaces of mutual engagement around ideas affecting them all. The fact that high school professors, as well as college presidents, could serve as leaders in the organizations, and records indicate that they did, also helped to stimulate cross-institutional interaction. Moreover, the limited educational opportunities for blacks meant that many of the attendees were graduates from the institutions or had previous relationships with the college presidents represented. This history assisted in creating an environment in which many attendees had other relational experiences and potentially diminished some of the distance between presidents and professors. In speeches, these interpersonal and institutional relationships are sometimes publicly acknowledged.

The significance of the collegial exchange at these meetings for a younger professor such as Byas cannot be overlooked. In addition to expanding his knowledge base about educational issues by listening to the voice of various educational experts, he also had the opportunity to expand his professional repertoire of strategies that could be used in his own settings as he became increasingly familiar with strategies working in other geographic regions. A perusal of attendee lists provides some illustration of the extent to which participants were able to engage in conversations with other professionals across a wide geographic region. The attendee list of the 1959 Association meeting is illustrative of the norm. Despite a lack of gender diversification, the group was geographically well represented, with representatives from each of the southern states, although North Carolina, Virginia, Florida, and Georgia were frequently among the states with the most representation. The meetings also were rather evenly represented across colleges and high schools. The result was that the Association meeting brought together stakeholders across the educational spectrum to tackle issues germane to black education. For example, in 1957, 6 high school professors and 14 college presidents from

Georgia are listed in attendance in Richmond. However, Byas also had access to the other 212 attendees who were not from Georgia. Purposely, the structure of the meetings invited mutual accountability between the black intellectual elite, who represented the best scholarly thinking of the era, and the local professor. While no data reveal the extent to which the intellectual elite reshaped their research based on these interactions, the ongoing relationship between professor and college leader necessarily required the elite to remain informed by the practical realities of black schools. Through these structures, scholars and school principals did not live on the periphery of one another's world; instead, they lived overlapping lives in this segregated context where the good achieved would serve to raise the status of both them and the communities they served.

Another characteristic also marks the importance of these national and regional gatherings in the life of the professor. In addition to the structured interaction delving into topics confronting black schools and school children, Byas reports that he valued these Association meetings for the more personal opportunities for collegial support and individual professional growth. By this, he means that the setting provided a space for professors of the best black schools across the South to learn administrative strategies from one another. On the importance of their collegial interchange, Byas explains: "I got a chance to meet at least once a year for three days with the top leaders among blacks in elementary, secondary, and higher education in seminars and in groups to discuss problems plaguing us as a unit of the association. . . . And I got a chance to try out [my school ideas] on what I thought was top educators when I'd go to the meetings." Byas notes that in this setting, people in the "best of secondary schools in other states that were segregated shared solutions that they had worked out—that they thought were working and shared some of their action research." Byas too, as he became acclimated to this group, began to share his ideas for school development:

> I came up with an idea once that I could improve student achievement by coming up with a schedule that decreased the number of daily preparations, academic preparations. . . . Then I tried that out on some of my colleagues at some of these meetings. If I was impressed with a certain principal from North Carolina, from Tennessee—say C. C. Barnes who ran a good school in my opinion, I'd say "C. C., got a few minutes. I want to try something out on you." See I am a young duck [and I wanted their advice on ideas].[53]

**ASSOCIATION OF COLLEGES AND SCHOOLS
ANNUAL MEETING ATTENDANCE, BY STATE/DISTRICT,
1957**

State/District	College	High School	Unknown	Other	Total
Alabama	6	1	1	1	9
District of Columbia	3	0	0	1	4
Florida	5	21	3	3	32
Georgia	14	6	3	3	26
Illinois	2	0	0	0	2
Kentucky	1	2	0	0	3
Louisiana	5	5	0	0	10
Maryland	1	0	0	0	1
Mississippi	13	2	0	0	15
New York	1	0	0	1	2
North Carolina	20	23	0	1	44
Ohio	1	0	0	0	1
South Carolina	10	7	2	0	10
Tennessee	10	2	0	0	12
Texas	6	5	0	0	11
Virginia	19	22	1	1	43
Unidentified	—	—	2	—	2
Total	117	96	12	11	236

Source: Proceedings of the Association of Colleges and Schools, 1957.
Note: Universities, junior colleges, and institutes are listed as "Colleges."
"High schools" include lab schools, prep schools, and academies.
"Unknown" refers to attendees who are named but who are without
an institutional affiliation. "Other" includes agencies or state groups
affiliated with a particular school.

Byas's summation is affirmed by Cozart, the author of the official history of the Association. He writes that the "exchange of points of view as to what constitutes good educational practice and swapping information as to what was going on in the several institutions, no doubt, provided stimulation to do better the desirable things they may have been doing already and to introduce better ways of serving the Negro youth of their generation."[54]

The meeting accommodations for black academics and professors, necessitated by segregation, also had the unintended consequence of ensuring that some of the leaders of the race had opportunity to "practice what they preached" about the importance of maintaining connections with students and the community. In particular, the theme of staying connected to the community undergirds their gatherings. Rather than viewing their status as college or community leaders as an accomplishment to be personally lauded, speakers continually reinforced the shared problems the black race confronted and the need for attendees to remain connected to the community in an effort to solve the problems. Mordecai Johnson's speech in 1957 captured this theme when he challenged listeners to remember from what they had transcended to become the "agents of what [they] knew." Yet his words and actions were reinforced by others. Two years later, in his keynote address, Horace Mann Bond also linked himself with the needs of the community. "Our lives are devoted to the improvement of the educational performance of children like me; like you; who were first schooled in the School of Families and Communities of the Underprivileged, the Sub-Standard." He closed by urging attendees to "make our educational institutions the instrument for improving the educational performance of under-privileged youngsters to an almost infinite degree above present expectation."[55]

In the opportunities for collegial exchange these meetings sponsored, the admired traits of the "educated" black leader were clear. He or she was to be capable of negotiating expansive language and familiar with the classical and historical references and to have cutting-edge knowledge about educational ideas. Yet the leader was to function within this wide intellectual vision while simultaneously remaining an interconnected part of the black community. Even more, the leader was to become the champion for community, proving a visual example of the capacity of blacks to achieve and utilizing moral persuasion to encourage others to do likewise. These ideas are embedded in the attendees' descriptions of leadership.

Segregation thus imposed the compounding of rhetoric and reality in ways that may have exceeded the practices of the attendees' white counterparts. Black professionals were typically forced to convene at black colleges or in high schools in black communities, and student groups routinely provided entertainment. Sometimes, the student body of the visited school was invited to listen to a selected speaker during the meeting. In this world confined by the limitations of segregation, the students and institutions they led were never physically far from the conversations academics held about them at their professional forums.

The outside black community also influenced the education professionals who gathered at the meetings. Whereas white educators returned to individual hotel rooms, some black educators—dependent upon the city in which they were meeting and whether black hotel accommodations were available—would need to return to the homes of black community members who had opened their homes to the educators who could not be accommodated otherwise. Byas reports that in some cities, such as Louisville, hotel accommodations were available. In most cities, however, young black attendees had to obtain from older colleagues who had been in attendance in previous years the names of people who had extra rooms in their homes and who would allow them to board.[56] This environment created a duality of intimacy. It allowed the professionals to continue their conversation together in the confines of sharing a bedroom and, as Byas reports, most often a bed. However, their presence in the home of local black community members also mandated continued interaction with the people whose children they were to serve. In the intimacy of a home, they were forced to maintain an awareness of appropriate cultural norms in conversation and behavior. Moreover, they could observe the interactions of professors senior to them in their exchange with community members, in effect, seeing an exemplar of the ideas about community connectedness that were affirmed at the meeting and having the opportunity to model the behavior. The physical limitations imposed by segregation thus manufactured the unanticipated outcome of continued connection to the community rather than distance from the black community. This connection was maintained despite the differences in educational level that could have stifled communication had the better educated been unwilling to assume the norms of the community.

In Byas's professional development network, the Association is the group that assumes dominance on the national level. The Association regularly placed leading local professors on the crest of the tide of the ideas for uplift espoused by the intellectual elite. Well-known intellectual leaders of the race were not disconnected from the professors who shaped the struggle in local states and communities. Rather, the black professors of segregated schools in the South existed in close philosophical proximity to the race's intellectual leaders. The meetings created a cross-disciplinary, institutional access to people and ideas centered on educating black children. In this shared space, educational ideas were both disseminated to and shaped by the black professor. By working in relationship to one another, members of higher education and professors in public and private segregated schools remained mutually accountable as they collectively, though in different spheres, sought to advance the cause of the black race.[57]

Over the years, Byas became intricately involved in the activities of the Association, participating in small-group sessions and sharing with his colleagues across the states ideas that were working in his own school. Indeed, just before the Association voted itself out of existence in 1964 in anticipation of pending integration with the Southern Association, Byas had become so visible in its network of activity and sufficiently known by its members across the southern states that he would be elected one of fourteen Association members who sat on the Commission on Secondary Schools.[58] This election meant that Byas would be the leading representative of professors from the state of Georgia. For Byas, the world of the Association became his professional world also.

Professional Meetings with Whites

The significance of the national black professional world can be better understood in the context of contrasting Association activity with the professional meetings of whites. Byas's response to these integrated professional meetings with whites provides a sharply contrasting view to his perception of the values gained in the black meetings. Like his colleagues, Byas believed in attending white meetings as these meetings became increasingly available to him in a desegregating world. He believed that if he was going to be a good high school principal, he should know what top high school principals across the country were doing. As he repeatedly emphasizes, knowing what was happening in education was an important agenda item and one that black educators did not take lightly. In fact, he reports attending these meetings because of the desire he and others had to "stay abreast of what was happening in the field of education." He argues that attendance at the white meetings was crucial because he understood that when his children would graduate from high school, they would go "everywhere," and principals and teachers needed to "be aware of what was going on" in other places so that they could prepare the students for these environments."[59] Black professors reportedly saw themselves as being "duty bound to know what was happening in secondary education throughout the country and that [they] were duty bound to know something about what happened at the college because [they] were feeding people into the colleges." Moreover, because it was deemed a "big responsibility" that many people "did not take lightly," attendance at white educational gatherings was an important avenue for professional growth.[60]

Unfortunately, however, Byas's response to the influence of the integrated setting on his professional development strikes a dissonant note. The professional meetings to which he refers are the national meetings of the NEA and the National Association for Secondary School Principals (NASSP). Although the NEA would continue to maintain segregation in its organizational affiliations at the state level during most of the period Byas was a principal, the national meeting was open to black attendees. The NASSP, which focused specifically on providing pertinent information that would improve the secondary school, also allowed black participation, and Byas had been a member of this group since he first began working as a seventh-grade teacher for Hawes in 1951.[61] Both of these settings were ones that presented professional ideas and the potential for collegial interaction and exchange of ideas across race.

Although journals indicate a level of professional talk and the inclusion of black educational leaders in the professional meetings of whites, these desegregated professional settings did not allow the opportunities for advancing collegial support, crafting definitions of leadership in a segregated world, or staying connected to the black community that were familiar staples in the black meetings. For Byas, attendance at the white meetings provided exposure to educational ideas, but these meetings were without the educational climate in which he was accustomed to operating. For example, Byas attended NASSP meetings expecting full participation and communication across a wide variety of people. Yet upon arrival and attending his first general session, he was immediately concerned: "When I went the first year, I expected to see all the black brothers from the East and North and South and West, but to my surprise, there were practically none who were high school principals. All the high school principals were from the segregated states . . . the only people who looked like me that were present were from the southern states." In his words, the "democratized states, where we [other black principals] thought they were the models, had no one who looked like me. And that was a negative impression on me. I thought we'd have blacks all over the place."[62] After his first meeting of the NASSP in Philadelphia, he continued to pay his dues but never went to another meeting. He claims that the conversation assumed monetary resources not available in black schools and generally ignored attention to the practical issues he needed to confront in the segregated South. Without colleagues there who would extend his professional network beyond the one currently available, Byas was without incentive to continue attending. He emphasizes that he "wanted to go to meetings where, from a practical point of view, [he] could learn something and be realistic about it."

Byas's summation of the NEA is little better. Although he was an active participant in one NEA conference, maneuvering skillfully with other southern black school leaders at national meetings to insert "free legal counsel" into an NEA amendment, his visceral and intellectual response to the lack of black leaders present was much the same as with the NASSP. Commenting on the five thousand or more delegates present sitting under banners from states across the country, he lamented: "Nobody looked like me who sat under those banners." As with the NASSP, Byas was concerned about the lack of black participants from northern states and concluded that "there must be something wrong with folk up there."

The sense of exclusion Byas reports should not be attributed to lack of comfort in integrated settings, as evidenced by his life as a graduate student at Columbia. Rather, the collegial interaction he expected was handicapped by a stark impression that integration in this national meeting was an integration of invitation but not an integration of participation. He was surprised and disturbed that the so-called integrated states did not have representatives in leadership positions who were black in the ways he was accustomed to defining leadership in his southern black segregated world. In the integrated setting, he saw little opportunity for a cross-fertilization of ideas in ways that were not already available among his black colleagues in the South.

In additional to his concern about the lack of professional colleagues with whom he could exchange ideas in these settings, he was equally concerned that the talk did not reflect an educational agenda that included equality and fairness in a democracy, at least not as those conversations influenced black education. He believed the meetings' participants had a general commitment to the education of students, and this commitment is reflected in an accounting of the topics in the program, but he did not view the topics discussed as focusing on the needs of black children. Byas could not see that problems he confronted in Georgia were part of the conversation, leading him to conclude that he "didn't need to come up here." He explains that as a member of a black professional group, he already knew what black schools were doing, and he had no need to expend his limited travel funds "to hear people discuss problems not [applicable] to me."

Byas believed certain structural barriers handicapped the white actors and limited their capacity to discuss issues of importance to black children and administrators. He posits that the meetings were attended by white southerners who would have refused to participate if the organization advanced any stance for equity. "You had a lot of southerners in high positions," he reports. "And they were not going to do anything to infuriate the folk back at home and the politicians so they just left that thing alone."[63]

Historian Wayne Urban's characterization of the NEA during this period confirms Byas's perceptions. Urban argues that the NEA did not act to support or encourage professional relationships between white and black members, that it opposed politicians who were noted for their efforts to assist oppressed groups, and that it lacked a commitment to assisting efforts to achieve equity for black schools and teachers. He notes further that the executive secretary of the NEA, William Carr, was "quite sympathetic to the views of the white southerners." He was unwilling to "offend state education officials from the South and members of the white southern affiliates." Although the ATA history reveals a more conciliatory approach, its descriptions of agency on the part of the NEA relate primarily to the joint committee the ATA had with the NEA and to the actions of that committee. Furthermore, the ATA written history was sponsored by the NEA, potentially an inhibiting factor in the author rendering a portrait of the NEA that was less than supportive.[64] The unfortunate result of the failure to address educational and equity issues for black children because of the mores of southern educators was a setting in which differing professional ideologies limited the commitment of Byas as a black educator. The opportunities for collegial exchange were diminished, and examples and discussions of the importance of connections with the black community were omitted.

Byas's appointment to a standing committee in the NASSP, which should have secured an insider status and enhanced the exchange of ideas, merely solidified his distaste for the agenda of these meetings. As documented in the NASSP journal, Byas was appointed to serve on, of all topics, the curriculum committee. However, despite the fact that he reports maintaining contact with the leaders after the meeting by sending them materials related to curricular developments in his own setting, he says he was never called to a meeting of this committee. He reports that the committee did nothing and concluded from his experience that the problem was one of "massive tokenism." His presence was tolerated but not his ideas. Byas was unconvinced that his colleagues were interested in fairness and equality in exchanges between black professionals and whites. This concern likewise lessened his intellectual engagement.

Byas did find that, unlike the meetings, the professional publications of white organizations and institutions were useful, as they provided interesting curricular ideas. He posits that he "valued the literature" because it offered him the insight he desired into practices across the country. Throughout his years as a professor and into retirement, he subscribed to the NASSP journal. Among others, he also subscribed to *Teachers' College Record*, *Harvard Educational Review*, and the *Journal of Creative Behavior*. The last of these was short lived, but he repeatedly notes that it was an excellent journal. Byas is emphatic that these journals provided professional development for him and not mere office decoration. "You TAKE the time to read," he posits, recoiling at the suggestion that the journals would be received but their contents ignored. "I always believed that if you are working in an area, you ought to try to keep up with the literature and what is being done both locally, statewide, and nationally."[65] Reading, therefore, unlike the conversation at the meetings, proved a useful means through which he could derive information from a broader range of professional sources that would inform his school setting.

But, of the meetings themselves, Byas concludes that he was "shocked" by how they were operated and that he "didn't gain as much." He emphasizes that black folk could come to the meetings but they were expected to sit and listen, whereas he was accustomed to being a "full participant" in the black meetings: "I was on committees and I led discussions and I listened to folk and they listened to me." The difference between the groups was not in how panels, seminars, and speakers were organized but in the invitation to ownership and participation. In the white group, there was no "personal interplay" with colleagues who might share their ideas. Instead, it appeared to Byas he was merely decoration. He explains, "These people thought that Ulysses Byas as a professional ought to be pleased when somebody asked him to sit up on a subcommittee. In [the black Association] there were no such limitations. . . . So I wasn't worried about going back to that. And I said, well I can do my own thing by going to my own organizations that are controlled by blacks."[66]

This black professional development setting on a national level is an intricate part of Byas's educational world. The professor did not operate in a solo capacity as some communities imply. Rather, the actual professional world he inhabited was expansive and interconnected, and its vision for black education was resoundingly shared. Although the black professional world's structures paralleled those of white educational world, its focus did not. For black educators, examining the particular needs of black students as victims of segregation and finding ways to deliver a quality educational product served as the unifying vision for their professional activity. The task was one they embraced with commitment and vigor.

Understanding the actions, beliefs, and ambience of this world is important because they constitute one of the several factors influencing Byas's behaviors as a professor. Nested in this cocoon of ideology about black education, he received continued validation of his cultural and professional beliefs and reinforcement of the ideals that should dominate black leadership in local settings. For example, reinforced here were ideas about staying connected to the community and using cutting-edge knowledge to inform student development. Both of these extended his beliefs as a member of the black community and as a professor well trained in educational jargon. Had the Association been his only world, he would have imbibed educational ideas useful in his school setting. However, the Association and other national meetings were just one part of the layering of influences that defined his professional world. Another professional circle, equally as intricate and as central to his development, also awaited his return to Georgia.

The new principal in Douglasville. Byas's first position as a professor was in Douglasville, Georgia, at Hutchenson Elementary and High School. Shown here in a principal's office reportedly so small he could "see all the way outside" when he opened the door, Byas used these cramped quarters to craft his first version of the Dr. Jekyll and Mr. Hyde game. (Photo courtesy of Ulysses Byas)

Ulysses Byas's mother, Marie Smith Byas Sharpe. Byas attributes his return to high school to his mother. Since no high school was available for blacks in Bibb County when she finished elementary school, she was emphatic that all of her children would have a high school diploma. During Byas's brief time as a high school dropout, she reportedly made his contribution to the household so great that he was happy to return to school the following year. (Photo courtesy of Ulysses Byas)

Ulysses Byas high school graduation photograph. A former high school dropout, Byas graduated from Hudson High School in Macon, Georgia, in 1943. (Photo courtesy of Ulysses Byas)

President of Fort Valley State College, C. V. Troup, speaking to the GTEA delegation. Troup, who had approved Byas's dismissal from Fort Valley as a reprimand for Byas's failure to maintain confidentiality regarding the proceedings of the Student Disciplinary Committee, was a major speaker when he and Byas met as colleagues at the GTEA convention in Macon in 1957. (Photo courtesy of the Horace Edward Tate GTEA collection)

Byas in World War II. Byas (center) credits his high test scores and successful leadership in the U.S. Navy with beginning to shape his belief that he could be smart. (Photo courtesy of Ulysses Byas)

School Masters Club, Georgia. The ideology of the Association was transmitted to some local settings through the auspices of the School Masters Club. An elite group that Byas joined in 1957, these professors all led schools approved by the Southern Association. Byas, a "youngster" among the group, is in the middle row, the third person from the right, seated behind the table with pencil in hand. (Photo courtesy of Ulysses Byas)

Audience at the Georgia Teachers and Education Association convention, Macon, 1957. The year Byas assumed the principalship at Fair Street School in Gainesville, the GTEA convention was held at the Ballard-Hudson High School in Macon. The former Hudson High School, from which Byas had graduated, was one of the two schools that had merged to form the new high school. Shown here is a portion of the audience at the Friday morning session. (Photo courtesy of the Horace Edward Tate GTEA collection)

Roma Gans delivering the keynote address at the GTEA convention. Gans was a professor of education at Columbia, the school from which Byas received his masters' degree. Educators from outside Georgia who spoke at the GTEA meetings were a part of Byas's intellectual world. (Photo courtesy of the Horace Edward Tate GTEA collection)

E. E. Butler High School in assembly. The students at Butler were very proud of their new school. (Photo courtesy of Ulysses Byas)

E. E. BUTLER HIGH SCHOOL
Gainesville, Georgia
IDENTIFICATION CARD
SCHOOL YEAR 1963-64

SIGNATURE

ADDRESS AND PHONE
ULYSSES BYAS
PRINCIPAL

SEX   HEIGHT   DATE OF BIRTH

WEIGHT   EYES   HAIR   RACE

Photo by
HEWETT STUDIOS, INC.

Byas's identification card. After the Fair Street facility became too cramped to hold the expanding student body, Gainesville erected a new structure named after a prominent physician and black school board member, E. E. Butler. All students and faculty were required to carry an identification card. (Photo by Hewett Studios, Inc. Card supplied through courtesy of Ulysses Byas collection)

Athletic Association in Gainesville. Engaging parents to support activities in the school was a critical aspect of the job of the professor. The Athletic Association is one example of the ways Byas organized parents and community members to support the school program. (Photo courtesy of Ulysses Byas)

Ulysses Byas Elementary School, New York. When Byas abruptly resigned from the principalship in response to the politics of school desegregation, his departure opened the door to two superintendent positions. Shortly after he left Gainesville, he became the first black superintendent in any of the southern states. He retired as superintendent from Roosevelt Union Free School District in New York. Shown here is the school named in his honor upon retirement. Newly reconstructed in 2008, the school continues to operate. (Photo courtesy of Ulysses Byas)

Byas with his family, 1966. By the time Byas was a professor in Gainesville, he was married and the father of four. Shown here at their home (from left to right) are Byas; his wife, Annamozel; Alisia (baby in arms); Melanie, Eric, and Laverne. Byas credits his wife with providing the family support that allowed him the time to function successfully as a professor. (Photo courtesy of Ulysses Byas)

Byas with his siblings. Although professors at Columbia labeled Byas the product of a dysfunctional home, he and all of his siblings completed high school and retired from successful careers. Shown in this photo (left to right) are Robert (contractor who assisted Byas with the subdivision in Gainesville), Ulysses, Sarah Louise (caterer), Richard (automotive administrator), Carl (executive chef), Dr. William (professor and minister), Albert (physical education teacher and coach), and Emily (caterer). (Photo courtesy of Ulysses Byas)

In Georgia, Where I Am Free to Express Myself

You thought of teaching as a profession. [Attending meetings] was just the thing to do.

—*Ulysses Byas*

For the professional educators leaving national black meetings and returning to the segregated schools throughout the South, the task they confronted and embraced was one of connecting the national ideology to the needs in their own state. While historian Kevin Gaines, in his significant portrayal of black leadership in *Uplifting the Race*, accurately describes some of the disconnection between the black intellectual leaders of the period and local communities, his assessment fails to explore the role of the organizational structures within states and the black professor as the person who allowed intellectual leaders of the race to be physically and ideologically present in local settings.[1] Byas explains the relationship, as the educators perceived it, between the black intellectual leaders and themselves: "The icons [national black leaders] tried to prick the conscience of society. They set the problem in philosophical terms. But the grassroots leaders [professors] were there with the problem. Their goal was to try to pick up the least of these, those on the floor. At the floor level you ask, 'What are the problems facing this individual?'"[2] The relationship was one of mutual responsibility but also a division of activity. In this cooperative enterprise, the black intellectual elite directly influenced the black community and shaped its development, but their influence was mediated through the leadership of professors who recrafted and shaped educational missions to fit the needs in their own settings.

In Georgia, the professional development activity most central to echoing the ideology of the Association conversation and helping Byas frame practices in his school existed through the School Masters Club. In the School Masters Club, Byas had the opportunity to discuss and implement ideas seeded at the Association meetings through a structural mechanism that united all the professors of black approved schools in Georgia. The Georgia Teachers and Education Association (GTEA) delivered the other more comprehensive form of professional development. Together, the two assured that national beliefs about educating black children remained within local reach.

The Association Reinvented in Georgia:
The School Masters Club

The School Masters Club was the formalized way black professors of approved schools in Georgia could extend the conversation of the Association meetings into their state setting and mesh the ideas discussed at those meetings with the needs they understood to be salient in Georgia. Like its parent organization, the School Masters Club was the most exclusive black professional group in the state, since membership was limited to professors of approved schools. In effect, the School Masters Club was the mechanism through which these professors directly brought the Association home.

Some people inferred that the members of the club were somewhat snobbish. Perhaps they were, as the professors, initially all men, constituted an elite group who held a certain status in the community as a result of the "approved" schools they led. Only later would one female, Dr. Bettye Smith-Calhoun, join the group. Like Byas, some of the professors had master's degrees, and all held high standards for their schools. But they were not the only ones who thought highly of membership in the School Masters Club. Principal J. L. Powell of East Depot High School in LaGrange, Georgia, provides an example of the value membership held with black educators across the state. In the 1956 report of the LaGrange Teachers Association in the GTEA journal, the *Herald*, the writer notes that East Depot High School was one of two high schools approved by the Southern Association that year. The writer also notes that "membership in the Southern Association of Accredited High Schools is the highest honor that can come to a high school." Like many community members during the era, the writer did not have a clear understanding of the distinction between the two associations — specifically, the fact that although the Southern Association was the organization that granted the "approved" status, its black counterpart, the Association, was the organization to which black professors belonged and whose meetings they attended. However, the process of approval by the Southern Association is accurately articulated: "[Approval] is determined by the school plant and equipment, the course of study, the faculty, the records of the school's graduates in college, and efficient administrative and supervision of the school." Moreover, the writer demonstrates an understanding of the relationship between approval and the School Masters Club. "Mr. J. L. Powell is principal of East Depot High School," the writer notes, "and automatically becomes a member of the School Masters Club." Attaining membership in the club was a goal to which many professors aspired.

The article also provides some description of the purpose of the School Masters Club. The writer explains that at its meetings principals could hold clinics to prepare themselves for reevaluation.[3] In part, the author is correct. However, the School Masters Club went beyond mere preparation for reevaluation. In this setting, professors were committed to working together to address the problems discussed at the Association meetings, and thus they talked about general issues in education, requirements for integration, and other topics of interest for those principals interested in achieving good schools for black children. In its by-laws, Section II, the club records as its purpose to provide "professional, cultural, and social enrichment experiences for its member institutions." Club dues were expected by October 15 of each year; officers were elected for two years; three meetings were held a year, once during the last week of January, April, and September.[4] Association reports show fifty-two schools in Georgia on the approved status list; a photo of the 1960 gathering of the School Masters Club shows twenty-seven principals in attendance. Meetings were usually held in Atlanta two to three times a year because "everybody wanted to come to Atlanta." Of course, Atlanta also had a large number of approved schools, and Atlanta was a setting where accommodations were available.

Byas provides three explanations for the significance of the club, its members, and its activities in shaping his school leadership. These explanations include the mentorship and modeling of practice the club provided, the collaborative discussion on curricular innovations, and the opportunities for research projects that could help leverage additional opportunities or facilities for black children. Always interconnected, these activities provided a professional web of development.

Unintended Spaces for Mentorship

Mentorship could be informal and was often dictated by the constraints of segregation, but mentorship was central in explaining how Byas learned to become a professor. Byas reports that, in traveling to and from the Association meetings and meetings within the state, he and other principals usually rode in a car in groups of three or four. Because of the segregation codes in the South that kept blacks out of many restaurants and hotels, black school leaders were bound together for hours on these trips. The injustice of not being able to break up a long trip, say from Richmond to Atlanta, a total of approximately ten hours of travel time, should never be overlooked. However, the carpooling created an environment in which the professors could begin to respond informally to ideas they had heard in the national settings and to speak frankly with one another about the possibilities and complications of implementing them in local settings. The importance of this intimate and productive setting should not be discounted.

As a younger professor, Byas particularly benefited from these trips. Because of his youth, he was valued as a driver by the older professors, and his services as chauffeur were unabashedly employed. However, the driving assistance he provided to the more seasoned professors was amply repaid by the opportunity to overhear, and to participate in, intimate conversations in which older principals continued, derided, or expanded upon the ideas discussed in national settings.

Byas's usual traveling partners included H. T. Edwards, principal of Athens High and Industrial School in Athens; J. S. Wilkerson, principal of Risley High School in Brunswick; and R. A. Bryant, principal of Cedar Hill High School in Cedartown, professors who were seasoned veterans of Association meetings. Edwards served on the Principals' Commission of the Association, one of its two governing bodies, and had access to knowledge about the thinking that informed the planning of its meetings that exceeded the knowledge of his companions. By 1957, he had been elected to the executive committee of the Association as well.[5] Wilkerson's school had been on the approved list since 1934, the year the Association first met at Spelman College in Atlanta and formalized itself as a body. The mood of that convention had been described by those in attendance as a "sense of education in exile, but not of defeat." The participants were deemed to have not "hung their harps on the willow trees of despair"; rather, they collectively embraced a vision for "bringing to pass things yet to be." During the long rides, Wilkerson could provide information about the initiatives of the Association over an extended period of years. Likewise, Bryant's school had been on the approved list since 1942.[6] Relating ideas from the national level to the local level was no new venture for these men.

Byas recognized a gem. "I had the good fortune to get with some of the older principals who had a good reputation as good school people," Byas recounts about these trips. His companions were fifteen to twenty years older than himself. "They wanted me to go because I could see and drive at night." However, Byas also affirms the significance of the conversations he heard in the car: "I learned a lot my first two or three years riding with those fellows."[7]

Intellectual Spaces for Collegial Exchange

The conversation in cars extended into the collegial exchange that occurred at School Masters Club meetings. Typically, members shared with other members any ideas from their schools that they believed to be working successfully and that they believed could be emulated in other settings. Byas reports that he used the meetings as "a professional sounding board . . . to get feedback from these people recognized as the top administrators in the state." One salient example of his use of the network in this way is in the presentation of his ideas about high school scheduling to the members of the School Masters Club. When he arrived at Fair Street in 1957, Byas had been unable to obtain scheduling information from his predecessor and concluded that no structure was apparently in place to determine how students should be placed in varied classes. In earlier years, high school scheduling in black schools was less problematic. Few black students were in high school, and the course offerings held few opportunities for selection. However, as Byas was expanding the curriculum, he needed to generate a structure for student placement, so he devoted himself to developing a rubric that could be used to plan a high school schedule. Byas maintained that, despite the need for all professors to engage in this activity, many professors did not, in fact, understand the myriad factors involved. He believed, moreover, that places like his alma mater, Columbia, taught that the school leader should make a high school schedule but that they did not tell the principal how to make that schedule.[8] The School Masters Club provided a forum to present his planning.

Using an overhead with two transparencies carefully taped together, Byas showed his colleagues the rationale and process he had developed for creating a high school schedule. His presentation was titled "Process Flow Chart of Necessary Steps for Developing [a] High School Schedule," and Byas used this chart to elucidate four phases in developing the schedule. He began with Phase I, which stressed the need to have all staff, pupils, and parents committed to being involved in the scheduling process. This phase included having a realistic evaluation of the school's current scheduling process, including its strengths and weaknesses. In Phase II, he stressed the need to determine the number of required courses and elective courses that needed to be offered, emphasizing that this determination should be made in accordance with state and local laws affecting course offerings and also by reviewing previous failures by subject. In this phase, he also provided meticulous detail on the administrative forms that needed to be developed and the kinds of staff and course evaluation necessary for a successful placement of students into various courses. Among other items, he described the development of registration forms, registration responsibility assignments across staff and feeder schools, dates, and tabulations needed for courses, study halls, space, and professional staff. In Phase III, Byas delineated procedures for schedule adjustments. These include having a developed procedure for conflict, schedule format, and roster completion and adjustments. He also included mechanisms to differentiate between new pupil registration and registrations for pupils who had previously failed. In the fourth and final phase, he pointed out the importance of making final adjustments that would balance loads, verify that all commission requirements were met, and provide copies of the schedule with all needed information to the students. In addition to his presentation using the overhead, Byas included hard copies of student registration forms and his tabulation sheets for course registration as handouts for participants.[9]

While the focus of Byas's presentation would appear to be on purely administrative detail, it also has caveats that helped address some of the difficulties professors faced when seeking to gain or maintain school approval. For example, Byas reports that the Southern Association had both quantitative and qualitative criteria for determining whether a school could be on the approved list. Some of the quantitative criteria, such as the number of books in the library or a commitment of additional expenditures per pupil for an allocated number of years, were fixed measures of school evaluation. Achieving these resources would require that the professor be able to generate support in a local school setting for financial resources. However, other, more qualitative measures required a professor to be creative within the school setting in his or her distribution of staff and students. For example, Byas reports that teachers could teach only one course outside their area of specialization and that superintendents sometimes raised questions about advanced courses with insufficient student enrollment. Meeting these qualitative standards could be challenging, especially for professors in smaller schools. By sharing with his colleagues a mechanism for reviewing course placement and teacher/student distribution, Byas was sharing process information that could be useful for a professor seeking to improve his or her school on these less easily measured variables by providing a structured mechanism to create the schedule. Byas reports that the School Masters Club members "almost unanimously thought it was an excellent idea" and that it contributed to advancing secondary education in the state.

Opportunities for Survey Research

A final significant activity of the School Masters Club is the information gathering and research reporting in which the members engaged. Among the reports of this activity that have survived is one submitted by the Committee on Research, a report compiled during the 1957–58 school year. The authors of the report, which was distributed on April 25, 1958, shortly after Byas had become a member of the club, had used a survey to gather data from nineteen of the club members' schools and report the findings to the membership. The report notes that responses from some schools came too late to be included and that some schools did not respond at all. Nonetheless, the authors believed the responses sufficient to compile the data and distribute the resulting report to all club members.[10]

Conducted during the same year as the curriculum survey at Byas's school, the survey assessed school support in four areas: custodial, clerical, budgeting, and guidance services. Results indicate that 95 percent of the schools had some form of janitorial assistance, but only one school reported full-time janitorial service; likewise, only one school had a part-time maid. The average age of janitors was forty-six, and average monthly salary paid was $161.00. Twelve of the schools had no other assistance available, and seven of them utilized other personnel to keep the schools clean. Almost half of the principals believed the janitorial help they received was inadequate.

Fifteen of the reporting schools affirmed the presence of clerical services; however, only nine of them had full-time clerks. Only two schools had secretaries with no college training, creating a salary range from $105 to $233.38, but on average, clerks had been available in the schools for only four years. Only four professors (21 percent) reported that they had sufficient clerical assistance. Approximately 25 percent of the professors' time was devoted to doing clerical tasks in some schools.

Both janitorial and clerical support would be significant needs in black schools. Insufficient support required professors and their staff to perform routine housekeeping and administrative functions that further diverted their attention from teaching, curriculum, and students. Although no record is provided of who washed windows, cleaned floors, and maintained school grounds, these and other tasks are ones that the professors would have had to perform themselves or for which they would have sought the aid of members of the staff or the community. Without a secretary, a professor was likewise handicapped in the typing of administrative letters, school reports, and faculty evaluations and in maintaining other forms of school and student records. In a segregated educational system, the lack of such support was another factor that diminished the quality of the educational product by increasing the noneducational responsibilities of the professor.

The writers of the report on black schools approved by the Association concluded that "most of the schools have inadequate custodial service," and they attributed this in part to the lack of concern of superintendents, who may have been using this area as a way to exercise fiscal economy, an action that, they believe, "is regrettable." They also argued that the salary level was too low "to attract younger and more energetic people to the occupation." They believed that, in comparison with the provision of janitorial service, there was "a greater degree of inadequacy in the provision for clerical service." They noted that while only one school had no janitorial service, several schools had no clerical service, although they acknowledged that the salaries of those employed were likely commensurate with the training most possessed. Their major concern about this area was that "most principals use a portion of their time doing some type of clerical work even though many of them have full time clerical assistance."

They also noted that almost half the professors (42 percent) failed to submit a budget to the superintendent for approval. Of those who did, 58 percent included no line item for professors' travel, teachers' salaries, clerks' salaries, athletics, or activities. Requests they most consistently made (58 percent) were for libraries. Other requests, such as repair and replacement of equipment, janitors' supplies, repair of buildings and grounds, graduation, and athletics, received a more even distribution of responses. No detail was provided that fully explicates the professors' focus on budgets. However, given the responsibility the black community traditionally assumed in supplying extracurricular needs for the school, a reasonable interpretation is that an examination of budgets was to be a catalyst to encourage professors to become more direct in their requests that the superintendent supply the material needs that allow the school to function. Byas, for example, is adamant that he was unwilling to allow his parents to assume major responsibility to supply school needs. The seed of this idea may have germinated from an increasing belief among black professors that the needs of their schools should be supplied by the superintendent, especially in the years following *Brown*. Encouraging professors to submit a budget would be one way to ensure that the requests for black schools were always in writing.

The report also focused on guidance services, an area of inquiry that had also been included in the curriculum survey completed during Byas's first year in Gainesville. In this category, 74 percent of the schools affirmed the presence of an organized guidance program, and 89 percent reported a guidance committee. However, most schools (74 percent) had no full-time counselor. Rather, teachers participated as counselors for students in 78 percent of cases, and teachers received in-service training programs to facilitate their capacity to understand the guidance needs of the student in 74 percent of the schools. Presumably, these teachers were the active participants in the levels of counseling services (68 percent), inventory service (68 percent), information service (89 percent), placement service (95 percent), and follow-up services (95 percent) that the report provides.

The writers of the report observed that cities had the capacity to offer an organized program but that smaller areas had difficulty in doing so, and they noted the different effects of these two circumstances. However, even in the smaller areas the authors noted the attention of the schools to areas such as record keeping for students and testing. They noted the absence of an occupational guidance course, commended the schools on excellent placement, and reproved them on the quality of follow-up services for graduates. The report's findings on counseling services are particularly instructive, especially the information on the training and utilization of teachers as agents to deliver guidance to the students. Indeed, this description may help explain some of the strong affective response of black students who consistently describe their principals and teachers as caring.[11] Additionally, however, the documentation of the lack of formal counseling services may simultaneously explain the significance of parental requests to have guidance counselors who could devote their full-time energy to the job of developing student post–high school success.

This report by the committee of the findings of its survey research serves an educative role for the club's members in its capacity to allow a professor to measure his or her own work against the standard of the activities of his or her peers. The authors concluded with the hope that their report would help all the organization "to see just what the status of [its] schools" is in the named areas. However, the report also serves the political purpose of providing documentation that could help individual professors pressure local school boards and superintendents to be certain that their black schools were performing in ways consistent with others in the state. For several decades, professors had been using the Evaluative Criteria, the standard evaluation system that was used by the Southern Association for both black and white schools to determine whether they would be on the list of approved schools, as a way to pressure school systems. As Cozart writes of the process in his history of the Association:

> The evaluative criteria of the Southern Association, when applied to high schools for Negroes precisely in the same way as applied to all other schools, proved to be the most effective means of generating and channeling the stimulation needed in local school boards and in attitudes of school superintendents in forcing State Committees and high school principals to see that their schools qualified for approval.
>
> It was common knowledge that most of the high schools for Negroes at this time fell far short of meeting some of the more important standards such as training of librarians, library facilities and science equipment. As a matter of fact, even if these schools had possessed the financial resources to pay for trained librarians, hardly enough were available to meet fifty per cent of the need. But let it be noted that within a period of three decades the improvement in schools defied all reasonable expectation.[12]

Cozart's point is a significant addendum to the historical portrait of agency in increasing facilities in black schools. More typically, the monetary increases from the late 1940s and into the late 1960s are linked to the attempt by state governments to forestall and later undermine the *Brown* decision. Cozart's point and the activity of professors in the School Masters Club suggest, however, that the receipt of money in local communities is also correlated with the active agency of professors in these school communities. Wilkinson, a member of the School Masters Club and the GTEA and riding partner of Byas, once challenged the educators to "not stand idly by" in planning for the availability of state funds. Rather, professors were to take active measures to be certain that the moneys found their way into black schools. In the case of the needs revealed by the School Masters Club survey, professors could utilize the rubric of the requirements of the Southern Association to pressure local systems to support their school.

The significance of this strategy is echoed in the insistence of the Association that black and white schools be measured by the same criteria. As noted previously, since the Association's inception, measurement by the same criteria was a clever political ploy to achieve equality, since the same criteria meant that black schools would need the same educational resources available to whites. The School Masters Club report, in its focus on the lack of services in three specified areas, served the external need of providing data that could be useful in the larger advocacy scheme. Using a research technique consistent with the activity of the Association, the club provided data that would be useful to pressure for facilities and support personnel. If successful in using these data as a negotiating ploy, the professor could more effectively serve as instructional leader, rather than having to devote substantial time to opening the building, typing letters, and providing college admission advice.

Though the report is not described as affiliated with, or influencing, the Dr. Jekyll and Mr. Hyde game Professor Byas was playing in his location through the use of the curriculum survey, several aspects of the activities correlate. Byas, for example, was a participant in the School Masters Club meetings and activity during the 1957–58 year, the same year in which the curriculum survey was being implemented. The strategy utilized, that of a survey, was consistent across both settings. The conclusions of Byas's survey with respect to guidance counselors also correlated with the focus on guidance in the Association and the conclusions of the School Masters Club report. Finally, the intent of both activities was consistent. Sufficient contradictions, however, prohibit concluding that the School Masters Club activity was the impetus for Byas's curriculum survey, particularly the timing of the beginning of the curriculum survey and the utilization of similar strategies by Byas in the years before he was a member of the School Masters Club. Nonetheless, the overlap in approach suggests the extent to which the Dr. Jekyll and Mr. Hyde game was played on multiple levels by black professionals. While the particulars of this survey may have not had a direct influence, the details of the game itself, no doubt modeled by other black professors, likely did have a direct influence.

No record exists of another survey of this magnitude produced by the School Masters Club. One document records the club's proposal to conduct an action research project that would provide twelve weeks of summer study to help selected students in the approved high school "attain a higher degree of performance as measured by national standards." Launched under the auspices of the Association, the program was to include sixty students who would represent each of the disciplinary subject areas. Thirty ninth-grade students would be selected. The following year, these students would return as tenth graders, and a new set of thirty ninth graders would begin. Annual reports were to be used to assess student progress. The ideology of the proposal focusing on improved performance is consistent with the state and national discourse about increasing the test scores of black children. However, no record exists of the club receiving the funding to initiate the program. With only the voluntary services that coordinated its activities and dues of five dollars per person, the School Masters Club never created major programs, but its capacity to allow members to learn from one another about strategies they might utilize in their own schools and to stay connected to national thinking cannot be dismissed.

Byas speaks directly about the importance of the information gathering in which he participated with the School Masters Club. "I thought it was significant," he recalls, "because if we were lacking some services in our individual schools, we could go to our superintendent and say, 'look, these other approved schools have got a janitor and we don't have anybody. You've got to know what the facts are and the facts can speak more forcefully than you can." [13]

The Umbrella of the Black Teachers' Network in the State: The Georgia Teachers and Education Association

Although the School Masters Club provided an information network for professors of approved schools, the GTEA was the larger, more comprehensive, and central conduit that connected national ideology to the mass of black educators. The GTEA identified as its purpose "to improve and extend educational services for the welfare of the entire community, and to improve the professional and economic conditions of the individual members of the profession." [14] For Byas and his colleagues, the GTEA was the framework that provided the overlapping opportunities for professional talk and growth that were at the root of state efforts to reinforce national ideology. As Byas notes emphatically, the GTEA was "where I felt free to express myself."

The back of the May 1958 edition of its quarterly publication, the *Herald*, then touted to have a circulation of ten thousand, provides a useful overview of the GTEA structure. According to this overview, the group organized the ten thousand black educators into city and county units, a total of 202 units. These unit groups were organized into eleven regions throughout the state, each with a "director" who represented one region on the board of directors. In addition to the eleven elected directors and one director at large, who was the retiring president, the board of directors consisted of a president, vice president, executive secretary, and treasurer and the chairman of the board of trustees. In 1957, the second of three executive secretaries managed the affairs of the group, L. H. Pitts. Through the executive secretary's office, planning for an annual state meeting, regional meetings, and varied departmental activities occurred. The executive office also coordinated departments that included higher education officials, principals, supervisors, guidance counselors, librarians, classroom teachers, state workers, and extension workers. In addition, affiliates, such as members of the Parent Teacher Association (PTA), bus drivers, clerks, and others were included in the umbrella organization.

The career of Byas's riding partner, J. S. Wilkerson, provides a lens through which to view the structure of the GTEA. Like the careers of many principals who ascended to assume leadership positions in the GTEA, Wilkerson's career models the ways in which a leader rose through the organizational structure. As chronicled in the May 1957 edition of the *Herald*, Wilkerson served as a local unit president, regional director, vice president, president, and director at large.[15] As president in 1952, Wilkerson had called attention to the problems facing black youth and prodded members to recognize the "tremendous responsibility and . . . grand opportunity" that the teaching profession offered, providing as points of reference his knowledge of the statistics regarding black teachers and his understanding of the position of the U.S. commissioner of education. Wilkerson was also president during the acquisition of a permanent headquarters for the GTEA in Atlanta on August 23, 1952, at a cost of thirty-five thousand dollars. Previously, the organization had been dependent upon the generosity of a black college for space in which to run its operations.

For his part in the "most progressive step [the] association had taken" in acquiring this fourteen-room, three-bathroom facility, with basement, three floors, and attic, Wilkerson had received many public accolades.[16]

Like Wilkerson, another of Byas's riding partners was also a seasoned veteran of the GTEA structure. H. T. Edwards was a former president of the GTEA, having assumed the leadership in 1951, when the legislature of Georgia had just approved the 3 percent sales tax that provided funding for the Minimum Foundation Education Program (MFEP), which had put the additional moneys into black schools. A leader who had the courage to speak openly about inequality, Edwards had used his position as president to alert members of the funding and to provide updates on the progress being made. He had noted his pleasure that the state had finally moved from the "talking level" to the "doing level" and that the new monetary appropriation would make available equipment and other forms of physical plant upgrade that had heretofore been unavailable. However, Edwards also believed strongly that the new acquisitions should provide ways of "exploring the many needs of our students, our schools, and our communities." Thus, new facilities and equipment were to be used to upgrade the educational program; they were not merely to be the expansion of physical fixtures.[17] Like the final riding partner, R. A. Bryant, who in 1956 was serving as a member of the four-member board of trustees of the GTEA, and like Byas's former principal, James Hawes Jr. from Elberton, who was serving as a member of the board of directors for Region Four in 1957, the men who composed an intimate professional circle for Byas were leaders long seasoned in advancing the race using the organizational structure of the black teachers' association.[18] The men must have mentored well. Before he would leave the professorship, Byas would advance in like manner, from involvement in local and regional activities to the elected president of the state group.

In its visual structure, the GTEA mirrored its white counterpart, the Georgia Education Association (GEA). Like the GTEA, the GEA also engaged in regional and annual meetings, published a monthly journal, and included a series of departmental affiliates. In addition, the white organization used its structure to disseminate national ideas about education. In practice, however, the GEA included in its membership white superintendents and state school leaders, all of whom were part of the white educational leadership that helped preserve a racial status quo by withholding resources from black schools. The two organizations thus differed substantially on issues of race and equality, with the GEA being, predictably, rather quiet. Moreover, the organizational structure of the GTEA served the very practical purpose of being a conduit through which issues affecting local black communities could be transmitted to black leadership throughout the state, and the black leadership could overtly seek to plan strategies that would influence the growth of black communities. The task of educating black children was deemed to be serious business by black educators, and their organizational structure was a means to elevate the status of the whole group. In 1957, as in the segregated years before and after, the capacity to get information to and from members was critical as a means of race elevation. Several layers undergirded this process: the annual meeting, the regional meetings, and the local meetings.

The GTEA Annual Meeting

As was the case every year, the 1957 annual GTEA meeting was well planned and well advertised. Horace Tate, the president of the GTEA in 1957, used his "President's Message" in the *Herald* as one way of alerting members throughout the state of the activities to expect at the annual meeting.[19] In anticipation of the annual meeting, Tate wrote to the membership: "As we approach another annual teachers meeting, we renew our efforts to the task of receiving inspirational . . . information." He noted the natural tendency of educators to "run down" as the year comes to an end, but he added that this was "good reason for attending such meetings." According to Tate, the State Program Planning Committee had "worked feverishly to employ for the teachers of [the] State outstanding educators of achievement, to guide us through out meeting to the end that we will derive aggressive educative skills that will aid us in our every day work after the meeting is over." He promised that the meeting would be "inspirational and motivational" and emphasized his belief that the "educational lot [of all would be] improved by attendance at this meeting." Concluding, he challenged the membership: "Let us come and share." Accompanying his article was an advertisement noting that the state convention would be in Macon April 10–12, as well as a two-page overview of the planned program.[20]

Of course, attending the meeting was not such a simple affair. Much as was the case with Association meetings, in the 1950s attendees were forced to confront the difficulties of segregation and the limited facilities that segregation imposed. Conventions were typically held in the larger cities of Georgia, a necessary venue because the annual convention needed a location sufficiently large to accommodate the several thousand people whom Byas remembers routinely attending meetings in later years. Although Atlanta was a favorite location, Savannah was another frequently used site. Both cities had a few black hotels and a sufficiently large black population to accommodate the overflow of attendees who would not be able to stay at the hotels. Staying in people's homes was more common than the use of hotels, and Byas reports that "people who came for overnight had to have somebody, know somebody's house that had extra room." The editor of the *Herald* spoke directly to the difficulties facing teachers who chose to attend the annual meeting. Noting the upcoming meeting in Albany, Georgia, a smaller location than Atlanta or Savannah, he reported: "The good people of Albany will do their best to make for your comfort and enjoyment." He was aware that the upcoming meeting was expected to "break all attendance records," so he advised the teachers: "You should hold in mind the limited facilities of the community to care for several thousand visitors. Secure your room assignment as early as possible; read the page on HOUSING elsewhere in this issue. Your full hearted cooperation and patience are requested in this mammoth job which your host community will face." The message acknowledges the need for appreciation and support of a black community that was providing a mechanism through which a teachers' meeting could be held while also implicitly acknowledging the constraints faced by teachers who chose to attend. He concludes: "If we assume this attitude, we shall make the best of crowded conditions and limited facilities."[21] In "making the best," attendees were confronted with the need, as Byas illuminates, to sometimes share "a bed with somebody you didn't even know."

Despite the housing difficulties, 1,000 teachers of the 5,500 members registered for the 1957 meeting. By the following year, the number of attendees would rise by 1,500 for a total of 2,500.[22] Byas explains attendance by invoking the black educator's perspective of teaching. "You thought of teaching as a profession," he explains. "[Attending meetings] was just the thing to do." His perception is affirmed in other secondary sources that demonstrate the validity of black teachers' perceptions of themselves in professional roles. However, the expectation of particular forms of professional activity by local black professors may also explain teacher attendance in large numbers. Professors often required their teachers to become members of the organization, and a 100 percent membership in the GTEA was elevated as a point of pride for local communities. Of course, being a member did not automatically ensure attendance; however, membership surely enhanced attendance.

During 1957, the GTEA board and varied committees planned, and delivered, a program hosted by Ballard-Hudson High School—a new school in Macon, Georgia, that had incorporated Byas's former high school. The format of this annual meeting was one that had been used for many years. Attendees and elected delegates filled the available space on the floor and were dressed in their finest attire, especially on the evening of the formal banquet. On the stage were rows of equally well-dressed and well-spoken state leaders, speakers, and local dignitaries, and draped above the dais on the background curtain was a banner naming the year's theme: "We Look at Our Schools—A Program of Evaluation in Action." Of the meeting's purpose, a *G.T.E.A. Newsletter* provides an apt summary: "Annual Meetings of the State Organization are held during which time renowned educators and other national personnel are presented to the members. These meetings are designed to broaden the educators' perspective."[23]

In 1957, as was typical for the annual gathering, the event involved varied meetings of the Executive Committee and board of directors on the morning before the general meeting began. Attendees registered throughout the afternoon, and dinner was served in the high school that evening. The meeting formally began with the first delegate assembly at 7:30 on Wednesday night in the auditorium with a program that included the president's address, adoption of minutes, and reports of standing committees and officers. This part of the meeting addressed broader advocacy issues upon which the organization was focusing. However, beginning Thursday morning and continuing through Friday night, attendees heard a series of speakers who addressed the theme in varied ways and met in small-group settings with other attendees who had similar interests or disciplinary backgrounds. This year, the president of Byas's former college, Fort Valley, was one of the guest speakers. C. V. Troup was the president who had sent Byas home for his actions on the Disciplinary Committee during his student years. At the Thursday afternoon session, in what was deemed to be his "usual manner" but "an unusual speech," Troup challenged teachers to be "dedicated . . . consecrated in the struggle for the mind of men." He urged attendees "to light the fire of truth in the minds of Negro youth which [would] make [them] free indeed." Later that evening, his speech would be followed by Columbia professor Roma Gans's keynote address. Obviously known by the crowd, since she was reported to have "stirred the audience as only Roma Gans can," she emphasized their need to think globally about educating young-sters who could counter the "Russian influence and save the future of the world." In a fashion reported to be "piping hot," she challenged attendees to a "new greatness," arguing that education had never before faced "the potential and obligation" as it did in that day.[24]

Speeches that elevated personal commitment to the task of education and that reflected educational trends were not particularly unusual. The annual meeting routinely involved local black presidents or local profes-sors who were part of the national intellectual or educational scene, as well as black educators who served as top academicians in their fields. For example, although W. E. B. DuBois's biographies focus on his activity with the National Association for the Advancement of Colored People (NAACP), teaching activity, and affiliation with Atlanta University, they typically fail to grasp his affiliation with black educators.[25] Yet DuBois served on the advisory board of the GTEA, spoke at local gatherings, and published in the *Herald*. Later, Horace Mann Bond rose to leadership in the GTEA as editor of the *Herald*. While his biographer captures his failure to produce scholarship during the period of his presidency at Fort Valley and notes the constraint his administrative responsibilities placed on his scholarly life, during these years, Bond wrote eloquently in the *Herald*.[26] In this capacity, he kept educators in the GTEA apprised of activities in other states and provided details on national matters that affected their livelihood. When he subsequently returned to Atlanta University, he re-sumed his affiliation with the GTEA, speaking frequently at meetings and serving on the committee that was writing the institutional history of the organization. Although others were not as intimately involved with GTEA organizational affairs, scholars such as Allison Davis, John W. Davis, and Mordecai Johnson were also among the many other black leaders and educators who populated various annual meetings in the state.[27]

Speeches given by the intellectual elite at state-level meetings enabled national ideology to be transmitted to the state level. These brief speeches, however, were not the only reason for the similarity in ideology at the state and national levels. Black educational leaders' connections with one another through institutional and social affiliations created a commu-nity of scholars who worked in varied settings to accomplish a consis-tent agenda. For example, R. J. Martin, principal of Ballard-Hudson, the location of the 1957 meeting, served as the master of ceremonies for the Thursday afternoon session and chairman of the GTEA trustee board.[28] However, Martin was sufficiently active in the American Teachers Association (ATA) that he would be elected its president in 1965. Just previous to Martin's leadership of the ATA, Lucius Pitts, who was executive secretary of the GTEA during the 1957 meeting, also served a term as ATA president. Ira Reid, sociologist at Haverford College and a convention speaker in 1961, was formerly of Morehouse College and Atlanta University. In particular, the presidents of black colleges in Georgia, such as Benjamin Mays, can be identified both at national meetings and at annual state meetings. The leaders at the state and national levels, then, were consistent in their ideology because they were often the same people operating in different venues. Indeed, an indication of the closeness of ties between the national scene and Georgia educators is the GTEA's hosting of the ATA national meeting the previous year, in 1956, and again in 1964. Between these years, in 1963, the ATA would move its offices to Atlanta, purchasing space on Ashby Street not very far from the GTEA headquarters building.[29]

According to GTEA protocol, some whites were invited to and attended the annual meeting. Particularly in the 1950s and 1960s when white educators accepted invitations to attend these meetings, their presence was consistent with the GTEA's desire that its members be aware of national educational ideas and be able to apply these to their own settings. White educators such as Roma Gans, who publicly discussed ideas permeating the language of white graduate schools, served the purpose of providing the rationale in a segregated world for applying the same concepts to black children. For the speakers, the inclusion of black children in the ideology may have been consistent with the national educational conversation, or at least with their own perspective on the conversation; however, the inclusion of black children in the ideology could also be inconsistent with the expectations white southern superintendents held for black children. Nonetheless, appropriating the educational argument of white educators in graduate schools of education was a way of convincing southern whites of the legitimacy of their advocacy for black children. The educational arguments served as important shields that allowed local black professors to lobby for black needs, coaching them in the language of education, while not attacking segregation directly.

In part, the visibility of the larger professional network of white educators during this period reflects the tenor of the sociopolitical climate of the years Byas was attending GTEA conventions. In the 1950s and 1960s, black educators could join the National Educational Association (NEA) and attend national meetings, an unthinkable possibility in previous decades. Within the state, institutions such as the University of Georgia and Georgia Tech began admitting black students.[30] Advertisements for the 1965 Summer School Session of Emory University appeared in the *Herald* along with travel advertisements for European study/travel. Particularly during the era in which Byas was a young professor and participating in professional development, black educators were increasingly aware of the opportunities that were possible in a desegregating society, and this new involvement is reflected in the literature of the GTEA as well as in its conferences.[31]

In addition to invited white speakers of national reputation, the annual convention included local white educational leaders or public figures. Although they were relegated to roles in which they provided a "welcome," or to similar salutary roles, local white mayors, superintendents, and other educational figures were invited to some of the assemblies and attended.[32] They may have served the purpose of mollifying local leaders with whom the GTEA had to work to create a successful program and provided a forum through which the GTEA members collectively convinced local white educators of their capacity as professional educators.

Throughout the meetings, panels and small-groups meetings were particularly significant in allowing attendees to engage the ideas presented by speakers and the theme of the annual meeting. No record of a panel session is available for the 1957 meeting. However, a detailed description of a 1952 meeting, with Orene Hall serving as a recording secretary, captures the moments that apparently typified the meetings. Miss Opal Dixon, the black Food Service training specialist for the Georgia State Department of Education who had initiated the Food Service Program and functioned as a teacher trainer and consultant since 1948, led the discussion titled "What Is Distributive Education." The account records that "several questions arose from the audience, faster than the Panel members could answer them." Among them were queries such as "on what levels is it offered?" and "what are its aims."[33]

An even more intense engagement apparently occurred during the meetings of various departments affiliated with the GTEA. These meetings included sessions for guidance counselors, classroom teachers, vocational teachers, extension workers, librarians, fine arts and music teachers, school lunch personnel, and others. They also included meetings designated for Jeanes teachers, the supervisors of black schools who initially were funded by Anna T. Jeanes in 1911. Each of these departments existed under the organizational umbrella of the GTEA, but each also had its own president and officers. Although the departments sometimes met independently of the state meeting "dependent upon the issues involved," the state meeting provided an annual meeting opportunity.[34] The meetings were designed to allow individual groups to discuss issues that influenced their work and to address the relationship of their departmental area to the theme of the meeting. In 1957, the groups met on Thursday morning, and other groups' discussions occurred on Friday afternoon. These small-group sessions were sufficiently significant in the program that "Briefing Sessions" were held for all consultants, leaders, and recorders who would serve to facilitate these groups. According to the report of the 1957 conference, "more than 150 leaders, consultants, coordinators, and reporters met in 40 groups to deal with the convention theme . . . 'We Look at Our Schools.'" Although records from the recorders of these groups are not available, the 1957 report of the conference notes that they were "the best Departmental and Affiliate meetings ever."[35]

The program also routinely included a speech by the teacher deemed to be the best black teacher in Georgia for that year. Since election of a teacher of the year was a job taken seriously by committee members and involved numerous applications from throughout the state, the teacher who was selected would be a model educator, and his or her speech at the meeting provided attendees with an opportunity to learn more about sound educational practices. In 1957, Mrs. Marie Hopson Dixon was the teacher of the year. According to records in Gainesville, she won by only a few points over a teacher at Byas's school, Miss Mattie Moon. Thus, Dixon delivered the speech at the Thursday evening banquet, along with a speech by the regional director of classroom teachers for the NEA.[36]

Striking is the replication of ideas across the varied convention speakers and the duplication of the ideas in the *Herald*. Participants ranged from faculty at local black colleges to teachers and principals from local schools, yet they often presented the same ideas. For example, Wiley S. Bolden, professor of psychology at Clark College (now Clark Atlanta University), spoke to convention members at a Teacher of the Year Banquet on the need to improve the academic performance of the black pupils. This emphasis on differences in achievement between black and white pupils was subsequently echoed by the president of the GTEA, who also extended his analysis to consider the difference in the average level and professional competence of black teachers and white teachers in Georgia. Consistent with the national talk on testing in the black network, articles on the same subject also appeared in the *Herald* twice in 1958 and again in 1961. Laura G. Johnson, a sixth-grade teacher at Milledgeville, re-ported difficulties with the dropout, foreshadowing a *Herald* article that appeared the next year, "Guidance for the DropOut."[37] This congruence in ideology is unsurprising given the centrality of the black college in pro-ducing many of the intellectual elite who delivered the speeches, the role of black faculty in leading the small-group sessions in which participants rehashed ideas, and the overlap of people and ideas within the state and nationally.

In reflecting on the interaction of the participants who populated the GTEA annual meetings, Byas reports the varied groups existing in a mutual relationship and respect. In particular, the relationship between black college presidents and faculty and local teachers was enhanced be-cause of the number of teachers who were enrolled in various black insti-tutions represented at the meetings. Since some teachers were earning up to nine hours a year while continuing to teach, many were familiar with the college faculty presenting at the state meetings. However, the inter-actions between practitioners and college faculty were not completely seamless. Some college professors were reportedly more enthusiastic in their attendance and their support of the profession than others, creating a scenario in which some college faculty were involved and well known by practitioners and others were less well known. Also, despite their famil-iarity with some of the faculty, teachers were more likely to be awed by college faculty and less inclined to treat them as colleagues.[38]

Surely to the joy of those attending, GTEA annual meetings were not all business. To see the professional world of the annual meeting as it existed for participants, an understanding of the ways in which the professional discussions were interspersed with efforts to reinforce cultural norms and broaden cultural horizons is also important. In a segregated world where attendance at concerts or participation in social affairs was lim-ited, especially in local rural communities, the GTEA structured its meet-ings so that the gatherings were not merely confined to business items. The program included choral selections, dance performances, and other cultural arts events that represented the talent of black youths in local high schools or colleges. Additionally, ministers from local churches or members of the GTEA offered invocations and inspirational songs, as the GTEA public rhetoric unabashedly included references to the Christian faith that linked most attendees during the period. As an opportunity to allow teachers to enjoy the meeting and the host city, the GTEA concluded its Friday sessions with a social event.

By Saturday morning, the formal meeting ended and most GTEA members returned to their respective homes across the state. The annual meeting had served the purpose of bringing to the forefront, in a very public way, the ideas that the board of directors deemed to be most important to address in black education in the state. However, the dissemination of ideology throughout the state through individuals left too much to happenstance. Therefore, the GTEA board also had other mechanisms to be certain the ideas were reinforced. In the GTEA history published in 1966, the authors note that the organization was deliberately structured so that ideas about instruction could be better disseminated to its varied constituents. The writers note that "the theme of the annual meeting of the association in April becomes the continuing theme of the local, county, and regional meetings in the fall, not only influencing the post-planning period at the end of the year but the pre-planning period at the beginning of another year as well."[39] This strategy made it likely that the ideas discussed at state meetings would be reintroduced at the local level.

The Replication of the Annual Meeting in Regional Meetings in the State

The annual meeting theme, according to GTEA leadership, was not merely a statement of intent but became an agenda for local activity. Themes were crafted by the board of directors and reflected the leadership's perceptions of both state and national needs as they related to black education. Indeed, the GTEA operated with the specific intent to "blueprint a course which brings the greatest gains." Typically, the "diagram for action" was most explicitly expressed in the theme selected for the year and was not expected to be mere "meaningless words."[40] In addition to addressing concerns specific to the state and to black needs, the theme could also blend a national idea with a local need. The theme thus was a central way to develop a plan of action for black educators for a particular year, and the regional meeting, in addition to the annual meeting, was a way to accomplish the plan.

The reports of two regional meetings in 1957 provide examples of the ways in which the annual theme was a program of action for a year across the state. For example, in 1957 Region Seven was reported to have 90 percent participation from the surrounding counties at "one of the most inspiring and stimulating" meetings the reporter believed the region had ever held. The panel discussion was coordinated by an Atlanta University professor, deemed to be "brilliant," and focused on the theme "Looking at Our School—A Program of Evaluation in Action." Likewise, Region Four reported the dissemination of the theme into the state at its regional meeting, which replicated the theme "We Look at Our Schools." The reporter records that "after a period of studying, planning and acting, and being cognizant of the existence of a number of newly erected modern facilities, it was obvious that the need to measure our progress toward desired goals was urgent." In particular, on January 25 at the meeting in Monticello, Georgia, the reporter noted that school workers in twenty-eight Georgia counties "looked at the schools in region four."[41]

Importantly, the replication of ideas is directly related to the responsibilities of the directors for the various GTEA regions. In Gainesville, Byas's teacher who had lost teacher of the year by a few points, Miss Mattie Moon, was the first female to be elected to lead a region, having been elected during Byas's first year as professor and during the same month he attended his first Association meeting. However, her activities enable us to understand the role of the all directors in facilitating the dissemination of the theme into the regions.[42] In the capacity of director, Moon attended regular meetings at the GTEA office with other regional directors from across the state and met regularly with the executive director to help generate an agenda for black education. She was centrally involved in all state initiatives and assumed the primary leadership responsibility for facilitating the development of all the teachers and principals within her region. Without the work of the directors, the business of information transfer into geographic regions could not have occurred.

Though a complete set of reports of regional meetings is not available for 1957, the reports of the previous year illustrate the dissemination of a theme through regional meetings. For example, the theme in 1956, "Curricular Framework for Georgia Schools," continued a two-year focus on that topic. During these years, one *Herald* writer reports, "many of us set out to restudy and revise our local program staying within the boundary of this state pattern." Health was a critical issue in the state's curricular framework; moreover, inadequate sanitary facilities continuing at many rural black schools and the decades-long focus of the GTEA on addressing critical health concerns in the black community made this a salient area for inquiry among black educators in the state. A regional reporter captures this need: "Knowing that physical and mental fitness is a most persistent problem for Georgia and for the nation, last year we undertook to implement The Curriculum Framework in the area of health and physical education."[43] The reports of varied regions demonstrate the prevalence of the stated theme throughout the regional meetings, and they highlight the ways educators engaged the theme in regional settings. For example, two regional reports in the *Herald* are identical. The others reflect only slight variation. Throughout the state, the evidence demonstrates that the conversation in regional meetings reflected the ideas proposed as significant for discussion that year from their board of directors.[44]

As internal documents demonstrate, the replication of the same theme throughout a year was no accident. To facilitate the dissemination of ideas related to the theme and the organization of the regional and local programs, the GTEA provided a "Suggested Outline for Regional Programs." This outline provided the exact date that each regional meeting was to be held, with the dates spanning from late September to early November. Moreover, it detailed by time and topic the structure of the regional/district meeting from 8:00 A.M. until 3:45 P.M., when the meeting was to be dismissed. Most significant for this discussion, the outline included the recognition of invited consultants, followed by the panel presentation from 10:15 to 11:10 A.M. and the discussion groups, which continued until 12:50 P.M., lunch to be served thereafter. The directions regarding the plan include: "One main speaker and/or panel of not more than five persons followed by Buzz Groups in the Auditorium, Small Groups in separate rooms or questions from the floor, based on issues set forth by the speaker or panel on the theme." Among the administrative and procedural guidelines provided was a suggested calendar in which local associations were urged "to use the GTEA theme and objectives as the foundation of their programs." Similar instructions on the format of the regional meeting are also reflected in "A Suggestive Program for Regional Meetings G.T.E.A.," published in the *Herald*. This program addressed such details of the meetings as placement of local talent, invocation by a local minister, presentation by the regional director or the director's appointee, and announcements. Regional meetings were taken very seriously by planners, and everyone across the state was expected to be exposed to a similar program.[45]

Regional reports in the *Herald* demonstrate the extent to which this outline was followed. Region Five describes the "rich panel discussion" that occurred on the theme of health and physical education. It then notes that "all persons in attendance including bus drivers and citizens were assigned to a group for an intensive study of the theme." After presenting detailed information on the people and activities throughout the day, the writer concludes: "Thus, the Regional meeting came to a close with everyone in attendance having gained much valuable information." In Region Six, "the afternoon session was arranged to provide for the individual interests" of the teachers. Eight groups composed of a consultant and a recorder met in separate rooms to discuss various phases of the health program. Afterward, a general assembly was held for everyone to report and discuss the findings of the group meetings. Region Eight follows the same pattern: "The consultants and group leaders were situated in various rooms in the schools; there they helped their specific groups to become sensitive to the total health program for Georgia schools. The interest shown in the group meetings by the teachers indicated that they were extremely interested in securing information and 'know how' in promoting and developing the total health program."[46] Interestingly, the reports from the different regions are consistent, despite GTEA membership varying across these regions from 80 percent in Region Five to 95 percent in Region Eight.[47] Although data on regional involvement are not consistently available, the format of regional meetings appears to be consistent over time.

In 1958, the year after Byas's arrival in Gainesville, the pattern was consistent with that of previous years. An unnamed author in the *Herald* writes that the Regional Directors and Planning Committee "have done an unusual job providing for the one day professional meeting." The eleven regions affected by the planned program included more than eight thousand teachers, all of whom engaged in a program that focused on improving instruction in the middle grades and the implications of the testing program in Georgia. Among the speakers in the varied regions were Horace Mann Bond, then at Atlanta University, who presented at two regional meetings. Morehouse, Paine College, and Fort Valley were also represented, as was the state department and Oglethorpe.[48]

To be sure, the extent to which the activities reported in the *Herald* were engaged by educators across the state, especially in more rural areas, cannot be determined. However, other reports demonstrate the ways in which some educators in local settings were exposed to the same ideas. Local county teachers' meetings among black educators were routine in the organizational structure of the GTEA. Frequently reported in the *Herald* are examples of the nature of engagement that occurred among local educators in county meetings throughout the state. In 1957, an apt example was the Turner County Teachers Association, which met prior to the beginning of the school year to outline its planned program for the school year. The report describes the activities of the program committee, whose members "worked diligently" to construct plans for the year based on "an analysis of the education field . . . they felt would aid the group most in their immediate environment." Among the topics to be discussed were health and personal hygiene. In November, the group discussed a film, "Safe As You Think." Both the discussion topics and the nature of the film are consistent with the state's earlier focus on health. During this period, the *Herald* also provided local reports from Barrow County, Madison County, Cornelia High School, Fulton County, and Decatur County.[49] Unlike the agendas of the regional meetings, those of the county meetings do not reflect the same consistency in format or ideas. Rather, local county meetings appear to be a blend of the state theme and local needs. However, the appearance of the annual theme at the local educational level is consistent across reported local activities.[50]

The result of the GTEA structure may be interpreted as an information dissemination mechanism that consistently linked people and ideas nationally believed to influence the development of children with the needs of black children within Georgia. Simultaneously, the structure provided a mechanism through which issues of the difficulties in educational settings could be channeled through the local and regional levels to become part of the conversation that would shape an agenda for educating black children. This dissemination happened primarily through the election of regional officers who were in touch with regional needs and held valuable decision-making roles at the state level. In turn, the eleven regional directors, in concert with the GTEA staff and administration, utilized their corporate knowledge to make decisions about the kind of information that would be useful for black education throughout the state. This bi-directionality of information gathering and information dissemination kept black educators throughout the state aware of the planned agenda for black schools.[51]

The Professor in the GTEA Structure

Professors operated within the structure of GTEA in two ways. Importantly, they served as the visible leaders of the group, which was otherwise composed of the teachers. With few exceptions, professors served as presidents, regional directors, and local leaders. Hidden from the questioning eyes of local white superintendents by the structure of the organization and its visible focus on general educational issues, professors used the GTEA to quietly craft an agenda born of an understanding of local needs and informed by the best thinking nationally. That agenda was subsequently disseminated into local communities through the systematic structure of the organization.[52] The importance of the professors' role in this system is captured in the *Herald* by editor Aaron Brown:

> Principals are playing their role with efficiency and dispatch. They are the professional leaders of their schools and in many cases the recognized race leader of the community. They face many and varied experiences and receive very little thanks from those whom they serve. The Principals have carried the major burden of the Association, here I mean the parent association, the GTEA. They deserve a great deal of gratitude for what they are doing. . . . We must not permit ourselves to ignore the fine contributions being made by our principals.[53]

Brown's accolades capture the productivity of the professors in the system during the 1950s. Their significant role would continue throughout the life of the association.[54] Though ostensibly a teachers' organization, the GTEA was primarily led by professors. Thus the organization provided a mechanism through which professors exercised collective leadership in shaping a vision for black education throughout the state. Important to note, the professors providing this leadership were primarily male. Although women are described or photographed in some leadership roles in the structure, their presence is minuscule compared to their numbers in the population of classroom teachers. The gender inequality observable in this hierarchical structure is not addressed directly in the *Herald*, although when women are present, their activities and beliefs appear to parallel those of their male counterparts.[55]

One of Byas's more visible roles in this structure was as a member of the Resolutions Committee. The Resolutions Committee was a particularly challenging committee on which to serve, as its members were responsible for defining the problems confronting black children in the state and, often, critiquing the behavior of superintendents and boards of education. Byas recalls that recruiting members was often difficult because of the scrutiny many professors suffered when they returned to their local districts and were asked by their superintendents to discuss the stance the association had taken on varied issues related to school integration. In the years in Georgia following the *Brown* decision, professors were reportedly pressured by superintendents to disavow the GTEA's endorsement of *Brown* in one of its resolutions. This pressure sometimes required professors to sign a form saying they disagreed with the position of the group. The period of this activity was one in which the Sibley Commission was actively seeking the opinions of citizens about desegregation in order to determine Georgia's response to *Brown*, and some superintendents actively sought to shape the opinions of their black subordinates. Under such circumstances, many professors were understandably concerned about being a member of the Resolutions Committee of the GTEA.

Byas, however, was not merely a member of the committee but its chairman for many of the years he was in Gainesville. Although he was also questioned by his superintendent about the GTEA's position on desegregation and faced the same kind of repercussions as his colleagues across the state, Byas resorted to the dual persona that served him well in leadership. In an offhanded rather than direct manner, when the superintendent reportedly sought to solicit Byas's opinion about putting black and white children together in school, Byas dodged the setup. He blithely noted that the superintendent and the board had always made decisions about pupil placement and that he had heretofore never been involved in the decision making. "And, if it is all right with you," Byas continued, "I would rather not get into it now." He also explained to the superintendent that he did not feel comfortable discussing with a nonmember the policies of his association.[56] How the superintendent interpreted Byas's demeanor is unknown, but Byas did not lose his job as a result of his statements; nor did he sign any papers saying he did not agree with school desegregation. In fact, his work on the Resolutions Committee continued with such visibility that in later years Byas would also run for, and be elected to, the vice presidency of the GTEA, a level of participation that further confirms Brown's report that professors were central in the leadership of the GTEA.

The second way professors operated within the structure of the GTEA was as providers of support in the area of principals' professional development. The Elementary and High School Principals' groups of the GTEA worked to help the principals better administer their schools. Professors reportedly varied in their educational knowledge and in their commitment to using education to elevate the needs of the race. As Byas notes, "blacks are not superior. You have some who are good and some who are not." Although professors received professional development support from other sources, notably the Principals' Workshop hosted yearly by Atlanta University, the GTEA's Principals' groups constituted the most direct support structure and one that encompassed all professors.

During annual meetings, professors met under the auspices of the Elementary and High School Principals' groups. With their own presidents, these groups were two of the small groups that always met at annual meetings and discussed topics of significance to principals. Byas was once simultaneously president of both groups. He reports that in this capacity he deemed it his responsibility to be sure that professors whose schools were not on the Southern Association's "approved" list had the information they needed to begin the preparatory process at their schools, particularly that they had the information to address the nuanced qualitative standards. Remembering his own experience as the principal of a non-approved school at Hutchenson, he notes that many of these professors were anxious to understand the standards so they could apply them to their settings and one day become members of the School Masters Club. As part of his activities in the area of professional development support, Byas repeated his presentation on the high school schedule. The idea was considered so innovative during its era that it was subsequently published in the *Herald* in a five-page article titled "Our Georgia Schools: Together We Attack Our Problem." The article provided a comprehensive assessment of the Gainesville context and the measures that were developed in this context. Complete with charts and chronology of how changes were made, this article represents one of the more comprehensive pieces written by a principal to disseminate practical ideas in the *Herald*.[57]

Byas's activity with this group is also revealed in a meeting he chaired at the GTEA headquarters. Called a "Mid-Winter Professional Program of the Georgia Secondary School Principals," the meeting took place on Saturday, December 11, 1965. The group of professors in attendance engaged in an information session that lasted from 9:30 A.M. to 1:30 P.M. Preliminary statements and introductions were minimal, with most of the session being devoted to two speakers, both discussing topics related to federal initiatives and their possible influence on schools. The professors took a forty-five-minute "Coke Break" and concluded with a business session.[58]

According one of Byas's colleagues, meetings of professors at the GTEA headquarters covered any topic the GTEA leadership believed was critical to be discussed. Many of these meetings took place on Friday evenings. Brown explains:

We would leave our schools. It depended upon the activities [as to what was discussed]. If it was an athletic program, then we came and talked

about the athletic programs. . . . We had representatives for each classification [of athletic schools] who met. . . . They would come here and
get directions from the state athletic association, and then we implemented [those directions] on the district level. . . . We met here and
decided where the tournaments were going to be, what we were going
to do with illegal players, who would be judges for fine arts festivals.
The trophy folk would be here to sell trophies.

Significantly, Brown notes that most of the work was "a work of heart,"
since participants received compensation for travel and food but not direct payment. However, he adds that these meetings allowed professors to
be highly organized in how they implemented activities within their districts and individual schools. Byas echoes the sentiment. "All of us were
volunteers: We didn't get paid for any stuff, except for professional sat-
isfaction." Of the meetings, he and another professor recall: "We would
come up here and argue all night sometimes." The sessions, while collegial, were not always ones that initially generated uniformity of opinion.
Conflicts flared and subsided. But in the end, decisions were made that
governed the behaviors of activities in black schools.[59]

Some professors also continued their conversations by hosting a Principals' Conference in regional and local settings. Records from these meetings are more sparse and span a variety of years, but together they provide
a glimpse of local activity.[60] In 1955, for example, the *Herald* records the
program of the Region Six principals' meeting, noting that the gathering,
which included group meetings, was "largely attended." In 1963, a photo
caption describes the principals and supervisors in Region Four: "It is
nothing unprecedented to find the principals and supervisors of Region
Four discussing educational matters . . . on a given afternoon." The caption also notes that the "council meets each quarter or as regular as necessary."[61]

County principals' meetings also extended the ideas of the Principals'
Conference and the GTEA annual and regional meetings. A 1955 issue of
the *Herald* provides a report of the activities that may have been part of interim principals' meetings as they were structured on the county level. The
writer reports that the "principals of Dekalb [County] are organized and
meet monthly to discuss problems on the administrative level." The topics reported as having been discussed include maintenance and scheduling. The writer reports that "each month we aim to discuss problems and

state how they have been met in schools that had similar ones."[62] Not surprisingly, Byas can be documented as a participant and leader in these extended GTEA activities as well. He was the president of the Ninth District Principals and Curriculum Organization, and, although the documents do not illuminate these activities further, he would have been intimately involved in planning professional development for other professors while fulfilling this role.

A final professional development activity in which Byas participated, though one that was less central in his discussions about development, was the annual Principals' Conference. Sponsored by the GTEA and the Division of Negro Education and in later years held in concert with other significant local leaders, the Jeanes teachers, the annual Principals' Conference was another means of promoting similar ideas among professors about how to educate black children. On the significance of the conference to the students, one participant records: "There was no holiday for the pupils of Georgia when the principals of the Negro schools went to Albany on November 18th for their twelfth annual meeting." He notes that "the teachers and the pupils conducted their respective schools as usual. In some schools most of them knew that the professors had gone to the annual meeting. Those who knew did not expect that their schools would be any different from what they were before the professors left for the conference. In fact, probably very few stopped to think about the occasion." For the professors and consultants, in contrast, the meetings were "an experimental demonstration of the democratic process at work in education under the guidance of an effective leader." The writer notes that principals can quickly memorize the information about education taught in colleges and universities but that information is "put into practice at a rate that is often discouraging." He mentions the much quoted saying "As is the principal, so is the school" and argues that the day represented an opportunity for principals to gain a "new view" of that statement.[63]

A review of the Principals' Conference through the years provides an understanding of how it functioned in professional development. For example, in earlier years when Byas was still in graduate school and the principals who would later be his mentors were participants in the session, the professors' deliberations focused on their role in curriculum development, the child-centered school, and the community-centered school. The character of the meeting is best captured in the minutes. According to the reporter, the morning's events unfolded as follows:

As the principals assembled to consider their subject "The Role of the Principal in Curriculum Development," they began to plan their work. A small group assembled early to do some pre-planning. At that session they developed the atmosphere and preliminary plans for the conference. Matters pertaining to grouping, group meetings, general sessions, reports, findings, evaluation and consultants were discussed informally and definitely agreed upon by the planning group. At the opening meeting, which might as well have been a regular faculty meeting in a school, a keynote address was brought by an outstanding educator in the field of the special topic. This might have been the principal of another school, the superintendent, a college professor, or any other individual possessing special abilities in the area to be considered.

After "the keynoter" had set the stage and lifted the horizon, the groups were formed. In general, individuals working in similar situations and possessing common problems went by choice into a group. If a group happened to be too large or too small, adjustments were made so that the group could be small enough to provide opportunity for individual participation. With every group went one or more consultants who had been drawn by invitation from the nine institutions of higher learning throughout the state and from the various departments of the state.

The minutes then summarize the points of view expressed by attendees at the conference. These observations include the need for consultant services; the relationship between school size and student services; the importance of individual school self-studies; the significance of involving all available resources (human, social, and natural) in solving major school problems and planning programs; the importance of planning a curriculum that would support democratic living; and the need to sponsor a curriculum that would address real subject matter but also place emphasis on "activities that occur apart from the classrooms." The minutes conclude with a summation of the significance of the event: "If the twelfth annual conference of principals of Negro schools had accomplished no more than its demonstration of how the democratic process operates in developing a school, it would have made an enduring contribution to education in the state. The needs discovered and the methods of attacking problems provided each participant with something definite to do when returning to his respective school." The minutes note the "enthusiasm developed and the mental rush to return to their schools" but also affirm "the recognition of the principals' need for constant critical analysis and continuous evaluation."[64]

The following year's meeting focused on improving human relations. Together, the professors considered questions such as how the professor could do an effective job at public relations, how to get started with delivering extended school services, how principals could get children in school and keep them there, and how to develop a workable budget. In a climate in which the MFEP was introducing expanded funding into black schools, being sure black educators understood the extended school services available was deemed to be important if the services were to be delivered into black communities. Attendees were reportedly brought up to date on political developments in the state by Robert Cousins, the director of the Division of Negro Education; they engaged in joint conversation in eleven group meetings with consultants supplied from state colleges, listened to the address of M. T. Puryear of the National Urban League, and engaged in conversations about the use of audiovisual aids and the school lunch program. At the root of these activities was that the professors would be "reminded to be aware of many changes going on around them."[65] Among other topics discussed during these years were "Public Relations and Educational Statesmanship" and "Improving Human Relations through Creative Administration and Supervision." The child-centered school and the community-centered school also appear among topics of the principals' concern.[66]

The cycle of professional development for professors within the state began at the state annual meetings, continued as information was disseminated into regions and local communities, was reinforced at the Principals' Conference, and came full circle when individual principals reconvened at the headquarters of the GTEA for additional meetings to be apprised of the state of black education. Together with the School Masters Club, professors were thus creators of and recipients of multiple layers of professional development within the Georgia black professional network. In addition to attending the annual meetings and the regional meetings of teachers, they engaged in their own sessions at the annual meetings and convened their own regional meetings. They gathered, when necessary, at the GTEA building with the executive director of the association to discuss other matters pertinent to running their schools. Moreover, they engaged in these activities during the evenings and weekends, as well as during school hours, which meant that their work for the day needed to be completed when they returned. For these activities, whether the professors were leaders or participants, they received no pay or reimbursement for expenses. However, they did receive a variety of ideas that might be implemented in their individual schools.

No comprehensive record has been uncovered that demonstrates the ways in which myriad professors utilized the support of these meetings to influence school policy.[67] Horace Tate, executive director of the GTEA from 1961 until 1970, recalls that, as a young student, he was aware that his principal "used to go to meetings. He used to talk to me about meetings. . . . You know, I wasn't big enough to know, but later on I began to see . . . where he got some of [his] talk from." Perhaps it is true that the impact of the professional development activities that the professors participated in during their meetings can be best understood by observing the professors' successes in their schools. But it must be remembered that it was in the meetings that the professors often learned the strategies that allowed them to be successful. Byas reports that it was "not only what I learned [at the GTEA meetings]. It was also what I carried, the ideas I thought I needed to do at my school."[68] His assessment is correct. Together with the national network and the cultural and educational experiences he brought to the equation, Byas had access to all the tools he needed to circumvent the strategy of a superintendent to provide less than quality education for black children in Gainesville. In addition to explaining how the curricular survey happened, the ideas in this professional world also reappear and inform the activities of his school in subsequent years.

5

Whatever Is in the Best Interest of Kids

At thirty-three, I was at the glass ceiling among principals. What am I going to do for the next thirty years? Then I started trying to innovate. I needed to ask a question about everything we are doing: How can we do this better—curriculum, in-service, student achievement, cleanliness —everything we were doing. How could we do it better?

—Ulysses Byas

Byas's school, Fair Street—now rebuilt as E. E. Butler High School—was the site of the regional GTEA meeting in 1962. The new school was named for the recently deceased prominent black physician and school board member Emmett E. Butler Jr. and was several miles from the original Fair Street campus. Students were enamored with their new building, calling it "one of the most beautiful schools in Georgia for Negro high school students." The new structure held twelve general classrooms and more than seventeen auxiliary rooms, including a gymnasium, a language lab, and a band room.[1] Using different versions of the Dr. Jekyll and Mr. Hyde approach, the professor had exploited the state and local coffers controlled by school board members all-too-willing in the early 1960s to provide money to black schools, especially if additional money could prevent integration. In this climate, with the specter of integration looming, Byas managed to outfit the school handsomely. "Almost anything I asked for, if they were planning an addition, they put it in," he remembers. Unlike in 1957, when attaining resources was more difficult, by the early 1960s the "board had the pocketbook of the community open to try to circumvent desegregation." The new Butler boasted a sunken library with a glass front, cozy orange carpet and blue shelving, and a classroom opening to the back of the library. Among black schools, the facility was striking.[2]

Photos of the GTEA event held at Butler show a gymnasium, converted for the event to an auditorium, filled with rows of well-dressed teachers. According to the article in the school newspaper, "more than five hundred teachers, principals, councilors, curriculum directors, retired teachers, lay citizens and other interested persons" attended the meeting. The professional conversation during the meeting centered on the emphasis being placed on guidance at the state level. In panel presentations followed by group discussions where teachers "might have an opportunity to seek some solutions to some of their problems, attendees engaged concerns about guidance in black schools throughout the morning sessions. The event was so well organized by Miss Mattie Moon, a teacher at Butler and the first female director of Region Four, that Butler and Miss Moon were commended by the president of GTEA, Horace Edward Tate, who noted the "superb program" and the ways in which "all aspects of the program were excellently carried out." In some ways, the accolades are unsurprising. Byas's school boasted 100 percent membership in GTEA, and Byas served as the treasurer for the local teachers' group. With Miss Moon as a regional director, he and his teachers were continuously aware of the professional conversations at the state level and could easily be commended for their "warm hospitality" in hosting other teachers in their region.[3]

Teachers and principals engaging in conversations on teaching and challenging themselves to excellence in the delivery of instruction was a centerpiece of GTEA ideology. A "President's Message" in the *Herald* the year Byas first went to Gainesville captures eloquently a vision of the responsibility of black teachers shared by many. Wrote Tate, "The Negro teacher in the south, even in Georgia, faces, today, the greatest challenge of any leader of this century. To inspire and inform . . . the minds of today's children . . . We cannot erase the past nor present inadequacies but we can and will influence the future by our present dedication to the task at hand." Tate's emphasis on the importance of the teacher in black education was still a significant component of the professional talk of GTEA during the time Butler hosted the Region Four meeting. For example, at the state gathering the year before, C. V. Troup, president of Fort Valley, emphasized the importance of black teachers addressing the intellectual and cultural background of the students being taught. In keeping with how Byas viewed his challenges as a professor, Troup emphasized that black educators needed to keep abreast of trends in education through travel, advanced study, and wide reading. His speech noted that teachers had also been "deprived of so many of the finer things of life," and he encouraged teachers to identify with the poor economic backgrounds of their students. At the next year's annual meeting, Horace Mann Bond would sound a similar note. In his keynote address, "Teaching: A Calling to Fulfill," Bond would argue vehemently that the "Negro child has been, and is, the victim of a colossal wickedness." Similarly to Tate's remarks in the *Herald*, Bond's address would call upon teachers to eradicate the injustices, despite the fact that they were not responsible for those injustices. Repeated articles in the *Herald* also focus on teaching, including detailed articles on teaching practices for particular disciplinary areas.[4]

Association meetings also provide a context for focus on teaching at the regional meeting. According to Cozart, author of the Association history, the "pressure" of standards from the Southern Association "forced much attention upon the planning for growth among teachers and administrators of the Association." Noting that the Association understood "superior academic and professional performance on the part of teachers as the key to improved performance on the part of students," he emphasized that "the professional-growth concept [was expected to] filter down to the individual campus."[5] Cozart reports that the Association devoted much attention to issues related to teaching; his contentions are, moreover, supported by Association proceedings in which speakers typically emphasized the importance of "quality teaching" as a factor in "improving education and its product."[6]

The emphasis on teaching in the state and national conversation provides an ongoing context for the regional meeting at Butler. It suggests that discussions of teaching *should* be present in conversations among teachers in local settings. However, the ongoing contextual talk about teaching did not have to filter into local schools despite the Association and the GTEA's hope that it would. In the confines of their own school setting, black teachers did not have to embrace the ideology of their professional meeting. Yet, records of teacher activity at Butler suggest strongly that the national talk did filter into the school's professional talk and practices, and that, not unexpectedly, at the center of these activities was the professor.

In his first year at Fair Street, Byas had led a curriculum survey that necessitated a full year of additional work hours for teachers, despite no additional pay and with no reported repercussions for failure to participate. In 1962 at the new Butler High School, faculty continued to engage in extensive site-based school projects. What professional activities explain the behaviors of the teachers? To be sure, part of the explanation is aligned with the perspectives teachers brought to the teaching act. Black teachers viewed themselves as professionals; as participants in regional, state, and national activities such as the GTEA and ATA they heard first-hand about the importance of their role. However, the extent to which these ideas were repeated and put into practice can only be understood through an examination of the ways professional development occurred in the local school setting.

A detailed look at Byas and the faculty at Butler uncovers the ongoing professional development that occurred at a local school and the ways the ideology of the network informed the practices in a local school setting. Byas's school-level interactions with faculty, for example, provide examples of the tensions between democratic and directed leadership. The activities demonstrate the ways in which ongoing concerns about the needs confronting black children helped to generate innovative schooling structures for the students. They also reveal the ways the professor modeled collaboration, even in the form of assessment of his leadership, and demonstrate the repercussions when a teacher refused to conform to agreed-upon expectations for professional behavior. Because of the beginning of desegregation in Gainesville by the mid-1960s, the examination of this professor and faculty professional engagement necessarily also includes Byas's challenges in introducing two white teachers to the professional norms of the black school.

Directed and Democratic Faculty Professional Development

Faculty meetings at Butler High School were routinely professional development seminars.[7] In fact, Byas says that continuing professional development for teachers was "the point" of his meetings. His perspective is consistent with the GTEA language on the role of the professor in the development of teachers. Quoting a National Association of Secondary School Principals (NASSP) bulletin from 1960, a *Herald* article emphasizes that as teachers were to develop students, beginning wherever students were, so the principal was expected to develop teachers, beginning wherever they were and molding them to "their maximum capacity." Indeed, to be effective, the professor was expected to raise the capacity of his or her teaching staff.[8]

Faculty meetings were the most visible form of increasing the capacity of the staff. Byas explains that as the school faced problems, the faculty meeting was the place where the problems were solved. He reports that the meetings might be led by him or by the teachers. "If we had a topic where I was the person most able to lead it," Byas reports, "then I led it and we discussed it and tried to come to some conclusion [about how to address the idea in the school setting]." More frequently, however, teachers led the topical discussions. "You see," he explains, "you try to determine where a teacher's strength was and try to get that teacher to share that with others."[9] The topics varied, but the format was consistent. Typically, three teachers formed a committee and presented the information to the rest of the faculty, with the principal functioning as observer. These professional development conversations dominated faculty meeting talk, typically accounting for two of the three sessions scheduled for a month. Moreover, the solutions to problems the faculty generated in these settings became official school policy. As Byas notes, "We always put [ideas] in writing. We had teachers participate in . . . establishing a local school policy on everything that we did."[10]

Byas's description of the utilization of faculty meetings as collaborative sessions to generate policy ideas is affirmed in the self-study compiled by the faculty during preparation for a reevaluation visit by the approval committee of the Association. The faculty's philosophy notes that the school believes "in cooperative planning between administration and faculty."[11] The philosophy reads: "The administration, consisting of an adequately trained staff, should work together in a cooperative spirit where each member feels a keen responsibility for the success or failure of the total school program and is free to make suggestions and participate in the improvement of the educational program according to his ability." The note subsequently appended reinforces the philosophy. In a statement to his teachers, Byas writes: "At the time of the evaluation this philosophy was adopted by the School. Please study this and if you have some recommended changes, we will consider them at the next meeting."[12] Repeatedly and consistently, Byas strove to be a leader who would exercise a democratic style of engagement with professional ideas.

Two factors are significant in deconstructing Byas's policy-building activity in the school. The first is the relationship between professor as leader and teacher as collaborator. To understand the facets of this relationship, consider an ongoing faculty discussion about the importance of teacher planning in enhancing student performance. One back-to-school memo written by Byas captures directive leadership as he addresses specifically his expectations on the matter of teacher planning:

To: All Teachers
In my remarks during the week of preplanning I stressed the impor-

tance of the teacher planning for every minute of time so as to make the utmost of the students' time and to stimulate and create interest.

Your success in teaching depends directly upon your ability to plan successfully for your many activities. Do some reading about planning and plan very carefully as possible for each responsibility. (See our official school policy on lesson planning.)

Byas then delineates five basic steps in lesson planning and concludes by reminding teachers that these steps are essential, whether they are planning a classroom lesson, meeting with parents, supervising a club or committee, or planning a unit of work for the week. The memo concludes, in capital letters: "NONE OF THIS WILL HELP YOU UNLESS YOU CONSCIENTIOUSLY PRACTICE DAY BY DAY TO IMPROVE YOUR SKILLS IN PLANNING."[13]

As a solo document, the memo suggests that Byas's leadership style is more dictatorial and less democratic, a conclusion that contradicts the black professional network's embracing of democratic principles and Byas's statement about the importance of collaboration among teachers as a foundation for generating school policy. However, when the memo is contextualized by reviewing the *Policy Statements Handbook*, to which it refers, the democratic orientation is more evident. The *Policy Statements Handbook*, published in-house at the school, was a ten-page legal-paper-sized document available to all teachers that covered a plethora of administrative, curricular, and philosophical ideas about teaching. Statements of policy are referred to as "releases." On page 1, for example, under the first "release," the professor notes that a series of releases will be forms through which the faculty might collectively evolve a "written statement of internal school policy." According to the statement, this plan was "in keeping with [the teachers'] request." This first release covered administrative details on procedures for exams, grading papers, grade sheets, student report cards, honor roll lists, and permanent records. More instructive for understanding teacher planning is the second item, called "Release # 2: Subject-Teacher's Lesson Plans." This overview is consistent with the tenor of Byas's memo, although the release provides more elaborate details. It begins: "The major object of this release is to state succinctly our conclusion relative to this subject as derived in our faculty meeting on October 24, 1960 and to state that this is our *official school policy* concerning lesson plans." Before the release provides the details of the policy, the introduction emphasizes: "We agreed upon the following principles." Among the principles identified was the importance of all teachers planning their lessons and leaving plans when they are absent. It also notes the importance of all teachers planning in ways that reflect school objectives as approved in the most recent evaluation and that are consistent with the official course of study. Finally, details on the format of the plan are provided, as well as a reminder that the school would issue teachers' planning books.[14]

Together, the back-to-school memo and supplementary materials in the *Policy Handbook* suggest a leadership style that is organizationally directive and simultaneously communitarian and democratic. The memo captures Byas as the primary instructional coordinator within the school. He reminds teachers of previous conversations and refers them to other materials that provide more detail on the topic. His comments allude to the beginning of school year activity common in schools and sometimes featured in the *Herald*, especially during the earlier years when pre-planning was a time when professors and teachers engaged in joint activities to plan the instructional program for the year. In reminding teachers of the results of their pre-planning discussions, Byas positions himself as the instructional leader of the school, a responsibility that extends beyond the idea of a professor as being merely the coordinator of buses or janitors or other administrative tasks.

In positioning himself as a professional leader, Byas also echoes GTEA values on the importance of the professor in the life of the school. An article in the *Herald* reports that the professor is expected to work with teachers to develop school policy and "once identified, these problems become problems of the staff and are studied and acted upon under the leadership of the principal."[15] Another article exemplifies the *Herald*'s emphasis on the valued characteristics of an effective professor. In addition to stimulating community, which Byas had effectively accomplished with the curriculum survey, an effective professor had four other in-school characteristics that defined how he or she should relate to teachers. The valued professor within the segregated school was to be the leader but not "a boss." He or she was to apply the democratic method, recognize good teaching, encourage the development of specific talents, and maintain high morale.[16]

However, both the memo and policy statement at Butler also recognize the importance of teacher initiative if the mutually agreed upon program would be actually implemented by teachers. This idea reflects the GTEA's emphasis on democratic participation and teacher ownership. In another article in the *Herald*, writer W. F. Crawl comments on the need for the professor to relate to the superintendent, to teachers, and to the community. A similar article on administration in the *Herald* points out that the "principal has the responsibility to motivate the teacher—the attitudes he/she should show toward the students is the attitude the principal should show toward the teacher."[17] In other words, the professor should lead but motivate rather than merely dictate. Moreover, the language of the article posits that teachers have a responsibility to respond to the professor's leadership. Crawl, for example, writes that the principal must have teachers "who are anxious and willing to grow professionally."[18] His perspective is consistent with the closing line of Byas's memo, which notes that unless teachers plan to be full participants in professional activity, none of the agreed upon principles would be helpful. The idea of democratic leadership buttressed by receptivity is consistent with Byas's general beliefs about teaching: he is emphatic that as a teacher he has the responsibility to "do the best planning that I knew how . . . in the interests of my students." However, he also recognizes that the students "had an obligation to try to realize it . . . and to work hard." In like manner, Principals' Conferences organized professional development but challenged professors to develop their own professional attitudes. In each setting, leadership coupled with individual reciprocity results in a relationship of mutual responsibility and respect in generating a professional plan for school operations.

The second significant factor in deconstructing Byas's policy-building activity in the school is understanding the relationship between Byas's specific actions as the leader of his teachers and his general philosophy of education for black children. As the professional leader in the school, Byas had one central concern with regard to his teachers' professional development: that all school activities were in the best interests of the children they served. Byas is emphatic that all educational decisions should be influenced by the needs of children. "You do what is in the best interests of kids," he repeatedly emphasizes. On his own role in the process, he is equally clear: "My job, number one, is to know what's happening in the field of education." The national, state, regional, and local meetings in which he participated as learner and as teacher provide evidence of the seriousness with which he assumed his "number one" job. As professor, however, he also had a number two job. On his role with teachers, he explains, "You see, I've got to inspire my people." Despite the limitations of the segregated setting, he argues that "the setting they are in can be as rich as they want it to be." In fact, he is adamant that when you have excellent teachers, you have most of what you need to run an exemplary school.[19]

Intertwined with Byas's philosophy is the belief that merely meeting the same standards that white educators met was insufficient. To the contrary, his goal was to exceed the standards of white schools. Of this idea, Byas recalls, "It was not enough to find out what the others were doing and do that. You were always behind. Part of your obligation [was to] find out where the others ought to go and leap frog them [so that] you get there before they get there." If they functioned as imitators, black schools would be in a perpetual state of trying to "catch up." His desire was to be the creator and to enable his school to surpass the goals whites had for black education and also the goals they had for white education. He wanted blacks to be at the forefront.

This general philosophy—that black schools should exceed white standards, rather than imitate them—is evident in several of Byas's actions. One example is an episode with the typing class while the students were still at Fair Street. One year after the typing class was added to the school's curriculum, in the wake of the funding that had come as a result of the curriculum survey, an advanced typing class was begun for students able to type a minimum of thirty-five words per minute. Together with the typing teacher, Byas sought to find a way to make the advanced class a meaningful experience for students. Their collective decision was to approach the nonprofit agencies in the community that needed to send form letters and ask whether the letters could be given to the school to be used as assignments for the students. Students then typed the letters for the agencies, including adding their own initials at the bottom as the person who had typed the letter. The experience created an authentic learning opportunity for students and was, reportedly, so successful that the neighboring white high school began to imitate the practice. In fact, Byas reports that, once the white high school offered the same service, his own students "couldn't get any more letters after that" and the initiative ended at the black school. Importantly, however, the practice had begun at the black school.[20]

Byas sought to make sure his school was ahead of the local white high school in other areas, also. Butler was the first local high school to offer the SAT. Byas scheduled it four times a year, once in the summer. The local college gave it only three times a year and the white high school not at all. Thus, anyone wanting to take the SAT in the summer was forced to come to the black high school. Moreover, when many people had never heard of being able to get college credit for a course, Butler also led the area by being one of the first schools to obtain College Board approval for an advanced placement program. Since Byas had many faculty members with master's degrees, the school was able to offer advanced placement in both chemistry and history. It was reportedly also the first school in the state to teach a course in physiology. At the time, the state did not even have an identified physiology textbook.

Byas's desire, in his words, to "leapfrog" the white schools in innovative student support can be seen even in his early years as a professor. At Hutchenson, in Douglas County, Byas was the first leader of any school to accept the national telephone company's offer to connect students who were ill and confined to bed with their school classes via wire. Byas had learned of the program at Columbia, but the idea was so new that the local telephone company had to consult the parent company before it could implement it. By the next year, the white high school was also using the same program for one of its students.[21]

Each of these activities provides illustration of the aspect of Byas's leadership that compelled him to not merely keep up but to excel. This vision must be melded with the challenge of the national and state teachers' meetings to build the capacity of teachers. Using democratic engagement as a form of interaction and creating a school environment superior to that of area white schools are both examples that provide the foundation for the professional development activities in which he engaged with his staff.

Collaborative Professional Development in Action

Several examples elucidate the process and result of collaboration between professor and teachers. An example of process is the activity and discussion among the faculty regarding teacher-made tests. Byas reports that little attention was paid to teacher-made tests in his education courses. He remembered only one professor at Fort Valley mentioning them; the professor had said that "many times a teacher would ask the wrong question looking for the right answer and then fault the student because he didn't get it." Byas reports that, as a result of lack of attention to this area, he convened a committee of teachers to explore the subject, with him serving ex officio as its leader. The committee examined teacher-made tests, considering such issues as how to write a multiple-choice question or a true/false question. He notes that the committee reported to the faculty, at which point discussions ensued, and, with modifications, the report eventually became school policy.[22] In a "Report of Committee on Testing," recorded in the *Policy Handbook*, the text confirms the belief of the testing committee that teachers are aware of "the necessity of better teacher-made tests." The progress of the committee on testing was discussed at a faculty meeting, and the administrative details of the test format were agreed upon by the faculty. These included, as uniform format for all tests, details such as name of test, date given, and teacher's name and grade level. The document also includes macroformat suggestions—for example, that test items "be grouped according to point value" and that the tests utilize the two-part format of semester tests.

Importantly, the report also provides a glimpse of the dimension of human difference that surely challenged the collective statement of position that characterizes most releases. The report notes that a lengthy discussion was necessary in order to reach the conclusion that all semester and six-week tests should be typed. Moreover, the question of whether to put all easy questions at the beginning of the test was one that was deemed to be "an argumentative point finally agreed upon." After disagreement, the teachers finally concluded that they would put easy questions first, as these "would build up the confidence of the students." Other issues discussed that became part of policy included providing a minimum of two subtests during each marking period and using these subtests to form the foundation of materials for the final test; including essay questions on each test and assigning a minimum of ten points for this section; and counting spelling as an evaluative component of all tests, with individual teachers determining the amount of points that would be affiliated with this section.

The result of the discussion on teacher-made tests reflects the collaboration in the faculty meeting but also demonstrates the influence of educational scholarship. For example, the suggestions in the *Policy Handbook* about how to improve teacher-made tests, including constructing objectives, simple recall and completion items, alternate response items, choice items, and matching exercises, are a summary of material from a measurement and evaluation text by Greene, Jergensen, and Gerberich published in 1945. Byas was familiar with these authors, noting that they had "done a lot on teacher-made tests." However, the faculty handout, "Constructing Test Items," is neither a direct replication of the measurement text nor a direct reflection of the policy statement. Rather, the multiple forms of documentation on teacher tests suggest the extensiveness of the faculty conversation and reflect the multiple materials available for teachers as they sought to improve the quality of their own tests.[23]

As an example of the ways the professor and his professional colleagues held the teachers accountable for their decisions, Byas reports that "for each six weeks of semester tests, everybody gave me a copy of their test. And then I had a committee of two or three people sit with me and . . . pull out a test and critique it." At the end of the committee process, the group reported at a faculty meeting. "We wouldn't identify whose test it was, but [we might say] now here is a test made out by a teacher on our faculty and here's the sort of questions."[24] The process created open accountability for the implementation of mutually agreed upon ideas, since "people knew" their work would be evaluated by their peers and the principal and could be used to generate discussion at a faculty meeting. Teachers also understood that the professor received copies of all of their tests and that he would sometimes take the time to review one or more of the tests submitted. In articulating his perception of teacher response to this practice, Byas reports that teachers were "open and good."

Perhaps one of the most highly visible collaborative faculty projects was the implementation of the college-type schedule, an idea Byas describes that is not evident in any GTEA or Association materials. In fact, this idea was one Byas deliberated with some of the colleagues with whom he was most impressed at Association meetings as a way of gaining the input of peers he respected. In the annual meeting report of the Association in 1963, H. T. Edwards, Byas's riding companion, mentor, and friend, reported to the School Masters Club about Byas's sharing his implementation of the college-type schedule at the Association meeting. He noted: "Byas of our state cited the schedule changes in E. E. Butler High School. This generated much discussion. Many of you are already aware of innovation in scheduling. There might be those who might want to talk to Mr. Byas relative to this."[25]

While no record remains of these conversations at the Association, the result of Byas's thinking is evident in the Butler materials. In the college-type schedule, all courses were scheduled to meet three times per week, one for an hour on Monday and the remaining two for two hours each. Every Monday, students met all five classes. In the words of the report: "For two of the remaining four days, students and teachers meet three classes per day. The other two days they meet two classes and one study period." In implementing this idea, the *Policy Handbook* notes that this schedule resulted from the faculty belief that student achievement could be improved if the faculty decreased the number of daily preparations for faculty and students. In the policy statements, Byas provides a detailed description of the conversation and beliefs that led to the innovation in scheduling:

> Soon after moving into the new structure in the month of October, 1957 [the renovation of Fair Street that occurred during the first semester of Byas's leadership as principal], we learned that the building was inadequate to house our growing school population and talk was started about an addition or a completely new high school at another location.
>
> During the school year 1961–62, in contemplation of this new school, our faculty once again decided in a series of faculty meetings to take another look at the program with the idea of adding depth; we felt that our course offering and the coming physical plant offered challenges and opportunities never before dreamed.
>
> One subject of discussion in faculty meeting was the scheduling of classes. After talks with students, parents, and the superintendent, the proposal was to organize our high school on what we call, the college type schedule—[as a means of improving student achievement].
>
> After some five months of discussions [with approval of the superintendent, if the proposal was approved by the accreditation commission], we received permission from the Secretary of the Accrediting Commission to try this type of schedule on an experimental [basis] for this school year. We are now operating under such a schedule.[26]

The report is important in that it provides additional affirmation of the corporate nature of faculty meetings. In particular, by noting that five months ensued before a decision was made, it gives some sense of the amount of time devoted to the collaborative process.

However, the report does not provide a comprehensive portrayal of the innovation of the idea or the other creative endeavors that were spawned from it. The incorporation of the college-type schedule also led to another idea practiced within the school: the group study hall. In this plan, the goal was to have students "really use this time" and to give them "some techniques which would be conducive to developing sound habits of study." In this newly revised plan, instead of scheduling several study periods in different rooms, the professor assigned two to five teachers, typically representing different disciplinary backgrounds, to supervise one large study hall per period held in the cafeteria. The number of students supervised ranged from 60 to 120. The idea was to utilize a team approach in which teachers would give students instructions on how to study utilizing three different publications by Science Research Associates and McGraw-Hill—*Learn How to Study, How to Study and How to Be a Better Student*, and *How to Study*. All students were required to purchase assignment books, and teachers in each class were responsible for being sure that assignments were actually recorded by students. Just before the bell, Byas reports, teachers had students enter the assignments into the assignment book. In the study hall, teachers were expected to check assignments and to determine whether students were working toward the school objectives.[27]

According to their assessment of the new policy, the students at Butler were very pleased with the new schedule. The policy statement conclusion in the teachers' handbook noted that "the reception and enthusiasm on the part of the students toward this type of schedule has far exceeded any of our expectations."[28] Moreover, student newspapers extended the description. In the student newspaper the *Clarion*, a December 1962 front-page article was titled "How Do You Like Our New Schedule: A Tabulation from the Student Body Survey of the New School Schedule." According to the article, students were asked to consider whether the new schedule had helped or hindered their work. The results indicated that 263 of the students believed the schedule had helped them, 71 preferred the old schedule, and 5 of the votes were voided for unnamed reasons. The article then provided photos and commentary from four students and two teachers. The comments were apparently chosen for their diversity. Two students liked the schedule and believed it gave more time to complete assignments and that it might enable more students to be placed on the honor roll. Another student did not like the classes for two hours but enjoyed the study hall and lunch period. In contrast, the third, a young woman, liked the two-hour classes but not the study hall. "If I don't have anything to study," she complained, "I am made to get some sort of book and read it. Then I am wasting two hours." She also noted that the class on Mondays confused her. Both teachers were supportive, although one noted that the schedule had its advantages and disadvantages.[29]

In addition to being able to give their opinion on the new schedule, students had the opportunity to respond to the new study halls. The responses demonstrate the extent to which surveying members of the school community and publicizing results, even challenging ones, were staple ingredients in the school climate. In an article reported in the school newspaper, the *Clarion*, in April 1965, "Should We Have Study Halls?" the students responded to faculty discussion. Student writer Angelina Hughey reported that "a question arose among the faculty members as to whether we should or should not have study halls included in the school schedule." She quoted the teachers as saying that many of the students did not "make use of the time that [was] set aside for them to study" and posited that the goal of the *Clarion* staff was "to make a survey around the campus and get the opinions of the students and faculty members." The article then provided the response of six members of the school community. All six responses raised concerns about the study hall that mirrored the initial points posed by faculty. Though some noted its import for some students, all agreed that the program was being inconsistently used by the students. For one student, the misuse was especially problematic, as she saw the time as one in which the students could be earning another unit of credit, a need she viewed as particularly important since the state increased the number of units for graduation during that year.[30] This solicitation and publication of student responses to initiatives suggest a collaboration in which student opinions could be voiced without fear of reprisal.

These examples uncover the activity of the black school as a program developed by black faculty in concert with the school professor. Their thinking directly mirrors the talk of their professional associations but applies the ideology directly to their setting in a process of collective ownership of the product. Although the detail and breadth of activity at Butler may reflect the particular energy of this particular school professor and his training and professional networks, the idea of professional development as a focus of faculty meetings in black schools is substantiated in other accounts.

The Professor Models Leadership

Byas had the responsibility of orchestrating leadership and spurring teachers to embrace professional tasks. However, the professor's credibility in these tasks was amplified because of his willingness to model the values he espoused. Thus, as the professor reminded teachers of their responsibilities as teachers, so he sought to solicit teacher input on his professional responsibilities. Likewise, he modeled for them the importance of being lifelong learners and dressing as professional educators. He even took the lead in supporting teacher development as desegregation policies placed two white teachers in his school.

The first of his series of modeling-related activities was his use of the survey method to formulate the faculty's image of an effective leader. As evidenced by the curriculum survey and the School Masters Club report, the survey was clearly a tool utilized in black school settings as a way of understanding the expectations and activities of a constituency. In relationship to professional development, the survey was also a tool for encouraging reflection among the faculty. As part of professional development, Byas used the survey to encourage faculty to examine both his leadership and their professional beliefs.

In the first of two surveys Byas distributed to his faculty, he sought to learn their perspective on a variety of professional ideas, some of which linked directly to topics discussed at professional meetings in the state. The survey began with the note: "I believe that, in so far as possible, the administrator should know his faculty. Because of this, and other reasons, I made this form to help me in this quest. You need not sign your name, but please give a response to all items." He then solicited the teachers' ideas on topics such as membership in professional organizations, human relations, curriculum, extracurricular activities, teacher roles in the classroom, and teacher orientation toward students. For example, he asked for responses to statements such as "Teachers should discuss classroom problems with other teachers; [teachers should] concern themselves only with students in their homerooms, [teachers should] be concerned with motives of mis-behavior; teachers can be helped in dealing with students by having insights of student's home." He also included statements that would generate responses based on the principal's role. These included: "The faculty should strive to carry out the principal's program; the faculty meeting belongs to the principal." In all, the survey sought responses to 27 statements and asked teachers to respond in one of seven ways: "1) necessary in all cases, 2) necessary in some cases, 3) un-necessary in any case, 4) necessary, but impractical in some cases, 5) necessary, but impractical in any case, 6) yes, 7) no." No data are available on the teachers' responses.

In another, shorter survey, Byas probed more deeply their perceptions of the professor's role. Based upon its instructions, this survey was one utilized during a faculty meeting session in order to prompt conversation.

In small groups, teachers were to decide whether their group "agreed" or "disagreed" with the statements. He encouraged them to attempt to come up with a unanimous answer. However, they were also encouraged to "try especially to discover reasons for disagreement." If a group could not achieve consensus based on the questions as worded, they were told to "change the wording in any statement enough to promote unanimity." Three of the questions the teachers discussed were whether the professor should be a skillful teacher and be able to instruct other teachers, whether the professor makes decisions about teacher responsibility or teachers, or whether the professor should assume personal responsibility for student achievement. In the fourth question, he sought to know whether he would be a more effective professor if the group answered "agree" to each of the three above-mentioned statements.

The survey on the school leader can be viewed as a way of inviting public reflection. That is, while Byas assumed the leadership in promoting the professional development of teachers, he also invited their evaluation of his responsibilities as professor. By initiating conversation on his role as a leader, Byas allowed himself and his staff to generate a shared belief about the relationship between the professor's role, teacher evaluation, and student achievement. Although Byas never directly addresses the effect of this process in soliciting faculty engagement on other professional issues, the vulnerability expressed in open evaluation and discussion surely helped unify varied perceptions of his role into a single vision and likely helped create a climate conducive to the open discussion of other topics. In his utilization of the survey as a way to gather information from his faculty, Byas's ideas are consistent with a National Educational Association (NEA) reprint published in the *Herald*, "How Professional Am I?" The article mirrors the format of the survey instrument for principals developed in a book Byas owns, *The Principal's Profile*. Consistent with both, Byas utilizes the survey in his work with teachers as a mechanism for more fully understanding their professional beliefs.[31]

Interestingly, however, his work does not appear to be generated from the NEA material, as his survey was conducted in 1961 while neither the *Herald* publication nor the *Principal's Profile* appeared until 1963. His idea is more likely linked to one of the Principals' Workshops hosted yearly. During the summer of 1959, for example, the leader of the workshop worked with black professors across the state on survey evaluation instruments. Though Byas did not attend the session, a copy of the instrument was mailed to him by the director of Negro Education, T. A. Carmichael.

Carmichael writes: "I recommend this instrument to you and hope you will see fit to let your teachers evaluate you."[32] As in his expectations for teacher knowledge that reflected professional ideas, so Byas held himself to similar standards in his use of the survey instrument to evaluate his performance.

As the school leader, Byas also intentionally placed himself in the role of learner, thus modeling that learning could be a lifelong process and was not limited merely to the students. A classic example of his assumption of the role as learner occurred when Byas was placed in the uncomfortable position of needing to authorize teacher purchases for science equipment that were based on the superintendent's allotment. To allow teachers to order solely whatever they wanted violated his sense of professional responsibility and gave him no leverage with which to argue with the superintendent that they needed more money. In the particular instance he describes, the superintendent had approved only two hundred dollars to fill a science lab. Byas knew he needed more money than that, since he had "more equipment than that in his kitchen," but without the content knowledge, he believed he had few ways to mount a cogent rebuttal. In response to the need for additional knowledge, Byas enrolled in school. Of this episode, he recalls that "when Sputnik went up and everybody was talking about increasing science—I was a social studies major. I felt that I had to go back to school. I had never taken a course in chemistry in my life, and I didn't know the difference between a beaker and a Bunsen burner."

To provide better leadership in his setting, Byas went to Atlanta University and registered for courses in college chemistry and in genetics. Without the background and in class with science majors, he found he had to locate some high school science books and read. In fact, he reports that he was reading chemistry seven or eight hours a day just to bring himself up to the level of the other students in the class. "I never worked so hard in my life to make a C," he reports. However, when he returned to his school and was able to interact with his science teachers in a more content-knowledgeable way, he garnered their respect.[33] Eventually, he also earned a second certification in science. In the post-Sputnik era when science instruction was increasingly visible in the *Herald*, the additional certification enhanced his leadership capacity.[34]

In addition to placing himself in the role of learner, Byas helped other professors do the same. One example of the training he provided other professors in their role as learners was that of teaching them about lunchroom portions. Some of his colleagues did not see this skill as an administrative necessity. However, Byas explains:

> I had to teach principals who were responsible for running a lunchroom how to get that lunchroom out of debt. They had no idea how many weenies were in a pound or how many peach halves were in a gallon. And when I set with the principal . . . he wanted to know what the number of weenies in a pound [had] to do with [him] going in the hole. When his lunchroom people out there would tell him he needed 40 pounds of weenies and they'd serve 18 pounds, the rest of them they'd carry them home after work. . . . I showed [the principals] why they needed to know how many servings they could get. . . . And when they did that, the lunchroom got out of the hole.[35]

Since he had been an officer's cook in the navy, Byas had a clear understanding of food portions, and this he shared with other professors, who were subsequently able to balance their lunchroom budgets. This orientation, of being sure he had some basic knowledge about the components involved in running his school, explains a central tenet of his leadership style. As the leader, he was unwilling to rely solely on others to access appropriate expenditures for the school. He concludes: "If you are a leader out front and you are trying to tell other people what they ought to do, then you've got to be able to do it."

Other examples of his perspective on the professor as learner are captured during his years as a leader at Butler as well. In 1964, Byas was one of two Georgia educators awarded the John Hay Fellowship for summer study. With receipt of this award, which included travel, tuition, and a three-hundred-dollar stipend, he joined 173 teachers and 85 administrators for summer study. "At these institutes," Byas's report reads, "participants read and discuss significant books, take courses in philosophy, literature, history, attend special lectures in music and art, and have time for much reflection and informal talk." In describing this opportunity in the school newspaper, Byas noted that during the previous six months, he had visited Detroit, Canada, New York State, and then Bennington, Vermont, where he spent the month of July studying at Bennington College as part of the John Hay Fellowship program. He refers to himself a "fellow student" and, along with his visit to the World's Fair, counts his participation in the program as "an experience of a lifetime."[36] Unsurprisingly, the leadership of the professor as a learner can also be correlated with teachers' involvement as learners. As reported in the school newspaper, the *Clarion*, nine of the teachers also attended various workshops, professional conferences, or conferences with students during the previous school year.[37] They attended these conferences in addition to the usual meetings at the GTEA, which was just considered the "professional" thing to do.

In a final example of modeling leadership, Byas also embraces the professional dress that has come to be associated with black teachers. He expected for himself and for them that they would come to school "looking the part," which he maintains is equally as important as "playing the part." "If you don't look it," he explains, "the folk are not going to be impressed with it." The expectation was not one always held by the black community. Indeed, parents told him that it was not important that he always be formally dressed, especially in Georgia, when fall and winter temperatures could be soaring. Even in the hottest of weather, Byas was notorious for his bowtie, and he never removed his jacket even during the day. As far as Byas was concerned, the formality had a pedagogic purpose. He explains that dress was important as a modeling tool for black students. "Our kids see 100 percent of the informal," he explained. "They never see the formal. And I feel that it is inclusive of my duties to let them know there is something besides the informal that they see. I wanted to be an example to them." While his teachers did not have to maintain the formality he maintained, they were expected to "look the part," and they complied.

Dress codes among black professionals were significant for another reason. The formal dress that is so prevalent in portraits of black teachers and administrators during the era also reflects accommodation to the norms of segregation. Black educators understood that a black person dressed like a maid or chauffeur would be treated in like manner by southern whites. In contrast, a black person with a shirt and tie on was more likely to command a modicum of respect. The importance of dress for the black teacher can be better understood as a black professional value by contrasting it with the dress of white teachers. Byas's first white teacher at Butler, Jerry Hollingsworth, was reportedly stunned by the dress expectations at the black school. Arriving at Butler as a teacher new to the system straight from Reform, Alabama, and believed by the superintendent to share white visions of preserving segregation, Hollingsworth inexplicably embraced the black system of dress and dourly observed "Boss, I got to buy me some more clothes." He said, "You all dress up over here." In Byas's estimation, teachers at white schools were not held in the same kind of esteem as were teachers at black schools, and they apparently did not have the same need to dress as professionals. Of course, whites also did not have the need to "prove" to anyone that they were worthy of being full citizens.

Black professionals also believed that dressing was a way of modeling for students how to move beyond some of the restrictions of segregation through the status of education. The *Herald* reinforces this extended view of black teachers and their dress. "Let 'T' stand for touching. The teacher must touch the lives of the pupils," the president of the GTEA wrote in 1963. "The teacher's conduct must always be exemplary for the students are at their most impressionable stage when they are in school. And they often adopt the attitudes, dress, mannerisms, and idiosyncrasies of their teachers." His comments are deeply situated in an understanding that the home environment of the child may not provide aspirations but that the child was capable of success "in spite of his environment which by all odds should destroy him." However, the role of the teacher was to represent "a goal to be attained."[38] Thus, the dress of black teachers recognizes the realities of white-imposed restrictions and simultaneously models their beliefs about the norms that would be necessary to have their children participate in an integrated world. Of course, dressing did not make a good teacher or principal, as Byas quips about the dress of his fellow principals: "We had a good group of principals by and large, and those who were not good looked good."

In making easily visible the importance of self-reflection and modeling the expected professional behaviors, Byas set a tone that complemented the collaborative approach he sought to attain with teachers to develop a school program. He created space that allowed his leadership to be evaluated by teachers and modeled ways of making himself one with them in development of the school. In each of these examples, he constructed his leadership as one that publicly minimized authority and encouraged collective exchange. However, his authority in the setting was no less present because he chose not to create public display.

Contested Terrain

In a family-compiled book that contains memories former colleagues have of his leadership, selected teachers praise Byas's style as a professor. Although the book is biased because of its intended audience, some teacher commentary provides additional perspective on how Byas's actions may have been viewed by teachers. Several teachers capture some of the specifics that correlate with Byas's own descriptions of himself. One teacher talks about his value of students: "So strong was his belief in his students that it overflowed and was absorbed by all of us. He made us feel that we could be whatever we set out to accomplish. . . . He glorified and praised us when we did well. . . . His pride in us was genuine and heartfelt." Another example picks up his orientation also, noting the "splendid job" he did "coaching and working with teachers."

This limited feedback could paint a romantic portrait of faculty meetings and his leadership were it not for Byas's report of the difficulties incurred. The process of engagement with an intellectual idea necessarily invited disagreement and exposed human foibles. Although Byas says that he did not see deliberate attempts on the part of teachers to ignore faculty conversations, he also emphasizes that the diversity of personalities made consensus challenging: "You get a group of people and you get some folk that are lazy in that group. You are going to get some who don't want to do anything except what they have been accustomed to doing. If that's a little bit, they still want to do that little bit. But you had on the other hand some people who wanted to be outstanding in their professions and anything they could innovate and learn and encourage their kids, they wanted to do it. So we had the whole gamut." Thus, to have a collaborative faculty meeting required some management skills and finesse on the part of the principal to lead the group through disagreement to consensus. Like many of the other plans for the school, Byas approached this task with a deliberate strategy.

> I learned early in my career that there are some people in every group who are leaders. They don't have the position, but they are leaders. If anything comes up, [some other people] will watch and see how they react. If you say, "Show your hands" [to vote for an idea], some people won't put hands up until they know what [someone else] says.

> I had to pay attention to this in all my settings. You wait long enough to see who the people are that folk will follow. When you learn who those folk are, you have a conference with them one on one to get their permission on an idea before you present it to the whole group. That's the only way you can get things done. If you go in there because you are hot on this idea without getting permission from your trend setters, if they say they are against it, that solidifies your opposition.[39]

In this description, collaboration required carefully concealed strategies that would lead to consensus. It suggests, moreover, that collaboration was the form of engagement but that the professor also brought some definite ideas he sought to have implemented.

The dance of generating agreement among the staff for the implementation of new ideas required intentional observational and management skills on the part of the professor. This skill is addressed directly in a *Herald* article, "Tips to the Beginning School Principal." In the article, author T. U. Ryals writes of the major role of the principal in creating the school and helping it to operate smoothly.

> Like other executives, the principal often wonders about the most effective way to exert leadership in a school. How democratic should I be? Which decisions should I make myself and which should be discussed with the teachers and other staff members? Is it better to be viewed as a strong, decisive leader, or as a permissive democratic executive?
>
> Very often, a principal is puzzled over these questions. He wants to be democratic—but he also wants to be decisive and effective. He wants to create an open and permissive atmosphere for his staff—but he also wants to keep things under control.[40]

The challenge for the professor was to examine the educational philosophy that informed beliefs about leadership, then to behave in ways that conformed to the philosophy. He could "decide and tell," "make a tentative decision and test it," "decide and sell," "consult the group," or "join the group in deciding."

In adopting several of these possible approaches, Byas fulfilled the mandate in another article in the *Herald* about the principal, to be "a catalytic agent behind the scenes" to help ensure student success.[41] Byas's desire to implement a program whereby music would be played on the intercom throughout the school day is one example of the "decide and sell" strategy. Drawing upon his reading of classic studies in psychology, Byas reasoned that if playing music in a henhouse produced more eggs, then creating an inviting, soothing background might also positively influence student achievement, especially since some students were not interested in the teachers' comments and could be counted on to create distractions. By playing music all day, he thought these students might listen to the music and stop creating disruptions.

Byas presented the idea for faculty discussion, but teachers were divided on its potential usefulness. "Just try it. I want everybody to just try it," the professor requested. However, to preserve options in his request, he told those teachers opposed to the idea that they could turn the intercom off in their classroom. Although this program was not implemented long enough to be evaluated to determine its effect on student behavior and achievement, teachers and students embraced it, despite the fact that one of the leaders among the teachers never switched her intercom to the "on" position to receive the music.[42]

Of course, facilitating open conversations in faculty meetings created certain risks and required temperance on Byas's part when he believed a teacher had violated the protocol of engagement for faculty meetings. When a confrontation occurred between himself and a faculty member in a meeting, he was in a particularly difficult position. Practically speaking, the situation did not have to be difficult. Because black schools were typically ignored by white superintendents, the professor had almost complete autonomy to hire and fire teachers. However, for Byas to embrace his authority in the setting of the faculty meeting would undermine his efforts to create a collaborative community. Thus the delicate balance of providing leadership while creating collaboration could be easily upset if a public challenge forced an authoritarian response.

The report of one such confrontation captures the essence of his leadership style. Although vested with the authority to be directive and dictatorial, Byas intentionally chose a strategy that disentangled the two in the public setting. The teacher involved in the incident was new to the school and a recent college graduate. She was still not acclimated to the professional protocol of faculty meetings and was also not experienced enough to be aware of the way she may have been used as a pawn by some discontented faculty members. According to Byas, in one particular faculty meeting, some older faculty members who did not themselves want to protest an idea urged the young teacher to be the person who would speak openly about a difference of opinion. The older faculty members would have been aware that disagreement with an idea could be discussed, but they would have also understood the professionalism that was expected to accompany disagreement. That is, an idea could be debated, but disagreement with an idea should not descend to personal attacks.

However, the new teacher was unaware of the unwritten rules governing discourse in the faculty meetings. Rising to make herself well heard, the new teacher used the setting of the meeting to berate the professor publicly. As Byas remembers, she admonished him by stating that she "was not going to tolerate [his behaviors]." Although her statements raise questions about the behaviors she deemed inappropriate on the part of the professor, from Byas's position, the new teacher was "real disrespect-ful." By "disrespectful," he implies the violation of modes of interaction that encouraged collegial talk but nonetheless maintained an unstated authority on the part of the leader. On the violation of these unwritten rules, Byas reports that his faculty expected that he would reprimand her, or "light into her" as the language would have been during the era. How-ever, Byas reports that he "diplomatically shifted the conversation and went on with the meeting." Perhaps to allow himself time to put aside personal offense, he waited until the next afternoon to ask her to stop by his office.

Behind closed doors, Byas reports an action that unmasks the un-spoken authority but that is also consistent with his belief that teachers should be assisted to become the best instructors they could become. Of his conversation with her, he reports that he explained to her:

> I was in a better position to embarrass you than you were to embarrass me, but that's not our game. I don't want to embarrass you. I hope you wouldn't want to embarrass mc because I know that I am the leader. You don't have to tell me that; I know that. Here's what I want you to do. . . . If you need any help in it, come back and we'll discuss it. Be-cause my job is to help you be a good teacher, as I understand a good teacher should be. . . . It's not my job to get back at you. It's my job to help you.

He reports that his response generated tears but that she turned out to be "excellent" as a teacher. Of his beliefs about himself as leader, he points out that "you can't be so right that everything folk say you strike out and you have to tell them you are the principal." Indeed, he explains, "If you have to tell them you are the principal then you are not."[43]

The interaction provides a poignant example of the tension between democratic collaborative decision making and the cultural norms of au-thority in the black community. As many historians have documented, in the black community the position of teacher commanded respect. Even more than the teacher, the professor was one deemed to be a community leader and was extended the respect his extensive training accorded him. Thus, the professor operated between a community norm that accorded hierarchical status based on education and respect and a professional norm that encouraged democracy and collaboration. While Byas did not overtly utilize the power accorded him by his hierarchical status in the faculty meeting, he was aware, as his comments suggest, that he had the power in the school to make decisions that affected the livelihood of his staff. Despite his activity to encourage collaboration, his teachers no doubt understood this power as well, although the extent to which the authority impeded collaboration is unknown.

The faculty meeting confrontation and the private conversation that followed dispel any suppositions that the professor existed without challenge to his authority as school leader or that efforts at collaborative interaction always met with success. Difficulties arose, even in a cooperative environment. When they did occur, however, the private conversation was intended to produce teacher behavior consistent with faculty beliefs within the school derived through consensus and black professional norms. In general, Byas worked from the assumption that if people did not understand a point being made, the responsibility was his to be sure that the point was made more clearly. However, if the efforts were unsuccessful, the formal evaluation was a means of openly acknowledging difficulties that could result in termination.[44]

The Professor in Formal Evaluation

While Byas embraced democratic participation as a method of policy development, he held high expectations that individual faculty members would always adhere to agreed-upon policies and that they would challenge themselves to standards of excellence. In his interactions with individual teachers during evaluations, the authority vested in his position is evident. As the school leader, he believed that his job was not merely to applaud teacher strengths but also to identify weaknesses, with the goal of helping the teacher eliminate the weakness. His belief was that teaching needed to be improved so that student learning could be improved. Even more, Byas believed even the best teacher could be better.[45]

The formal evaluation of teachers was as consistently a part of faculty development as professional faculty meetings. In a memo to his teachers noting that "during this season of the year it is a part of the annual ritual to examine our concepts of teaching and to evaluate teaching personnel," Byas devotes two pages to providing what he regards as important information for teachers. In one paragraph, he quotes from Emerson in the *American Scholar*, focusing on the importance of being well read, noting that reading was "quite indispensable to a wise man." In the second paragraph and continuing to the end of the document, he summarizes a recent article in the *Harvard Educational Review* and delineates some of the assumptions the author makes regarding essential characteristics teachers should have. Byas writes that "as we look at teacher evaluation it is well that we review some of these assumptions." His summary focuses on teaching as a behavior that is complex and often developed in situations other than classroom teaching. However, he notes that the behavior is subject to analysis, change, and improvement and that teachers can themselves engage in these activities.

In additional preparation for his evaluation, Byas reviews the details of the types of behavior crucial for teaching, among them good classroom management and organization of instruction.[46] Although the ideas were obtained from a recent edition of the *Harvard Educational Review*, they are extensions of the perspectives discussed by black teachers since Byas entered the profession. In 1951, the *Herald* reported a local GTEA unit in which the professors proposed evaluating teachers based on preparation, representation, and personality. The practices of teachers, the engagement of students, and the physical conditions of the room were also important areas to observe according to the director of instruction in the Rochester Public Schools, who wrote an article titled "When the Principal Visits the Classroom" for the *Herald*.[47] Byas's description can thus be correlated with both the ideas put forth by northern graduate school publications and the ideas of the local black professional community.

Byas notes that, in preparing for faculty evaluations, he might "pop [into a teacher's classroom] any time." His goal was not to "embarrass" teachers but rather to examine the relationship between professional talk in faculty meetings and actual practice. This level of accountability in the school was typical among expectations. For example, in private files, Byas maintained records of the final grades for all classes by subject matter, noting both the total number of students enrolled and the number of failures. He also maintained the same data broken down by individual teachers within the varied departments. This analysis allowed him to compare, at a glance, a teacher's number of classroom failures relative to the failures of others within the department or within the school.[48] The degree of his awareness of individual behaviors and how these behaviors compared with school standards is evident in his evaluations.

Not surprising, given his earlier communication style with black parents, an individual letter to each teacher constituted the yearly evaluation. Although letters are excerpted to maintain anonymity, the selections below demonstrate the diversity of expectations held by the principal for his teachers. Even the best of his teachers could expect to be challenged to be better. And poor teachers were, well, not tolerated. To one excellent teacher he writes, "During the past six years I have constantly ranked you among our top teachers." After elaboration of the positive points, he names two areas in which he believes improvement can be made, both relating to the extension of curricular ideas. He ends: "I know that you will make improvement in these areas. . . . You are among the best."

Another praiseworthy teacher also receives the combination of praise and challenge. "We have no other person on the faculty with as much ability and skills in several areas as you have." He offers the observation that the teacher's "interest level is below your potentiality" but notes that the teacher is "still a credit to this school." Byas offers some suggestions, noting that if the teacher would apply these ideas the result "would very easily make you the top person" on the staff. After encouraging pursuit of the master's degree, he ends by noting: "I believe that you have what it takes to be our top teacher."

Both letters to exemplary teachers illustrate Byas's willingness to praise good performance. However, even with his strongest teachers, Byas pointed to areas of suggested improvement, and he utilized the evaluation as a mechanism for always holding high standards for all of the teachers. The emphasis on the master's degree was of particular importance and occurs in several letters. As desegregation approached, black teachers were increasingly encouraged to obtain higher training. In some quarters, this training was thought to protect black teachers from being fired, as some anticipated would occur.

Not all teachers were so fortunate as to receive positive evaluations. Where problems were greater, Byas offered additional recommendations, even while he maintained a tone of encouragement. Some teachers were challenged to work more consistently with their ability; others were encouraged to work on applying their natural ability to solve school problems. Where a teacher was deemed to be "average," Byas's assessments were frank about the performance, while simultaneously noting that he believed the teacher's abilities were above average. Where necessary, he solicited additional work on the teacher's part in classroom management and in taking a more active role in faculty meeting discussions. However, in each case, he concluded with an affirmation: "You are a credit to our school and community, and my job is made easier when people of your character and ability apply themselves toward solutions of our common educational problems."

In more dire circumstances, the professor enumerated difficulties, and the letter or other supplementary documents indicated times the principal met with the teacher to resolve matters. In one case, Byas reminded a teacher that the school had a "100 percent professional group of teachers," and he reprimanded her for her outburst during a meeting. He noted that "faculty meetings are for professional devotion to problems at our school and the development of students; not for arguments." He also enumerated other specific areas of concerns, among them using commentary that berates students and engaging in personality clashes with other teachers. He was abrupt in sending a direct message that continued behavior not in line with that of the rest of the faculty would result in termination and asked that the teacher "understand this clearly." He concluded: "You and all teachers should be thinking people who have ideas and opinions and should be able to express themselves in a professional manner using accepted educational terminology. In my capacity as principal, I expect this and have tried to have an atmosphere in which self expression is the expected and the rule." However, his directness— "please understand this clearly"—sent a message that communicated his unwillingness to compromise on any of the points he raised.

In a case in which a decision for dismissal appears to have been already made, the file provides the documentation of the teacher's noncompliant behavior throughout the school year. Reminiscent of his observing and recording the behaviors of his students while still a seventh-grade teacher, Byas maintains six pages of handwritten notes that document repeated instances of the teacher's difficulties with her colleagues, as reported to him by other staff. The teacher allegedly destroyed the project a student was completing in another class, in the presence of her own students, and "totally disregarded" another teacher "as a fellow faculty member" in a particular activity with students. The result was "quite a degree of confusion in the presence of students." The notes also record disregard for the procedures of a school-sponsored event. When Byas assigned her and another teacher the task of meeting to outline the program of study in a particular content area for the next year, the collaboration was unsuccessful because the teacher reportedly insisted that "she already knows what she is going to teach." In other infractions, the teacher violated the school's policy on selling items during the school day and spent some time on the school phone when the professor was away from the office.

Additionally, some of this teacher's actions in faculty meetings were deemed "extremely unprofessional and in bad taste."[49] Byas's conclusion was that her "actions and in-actions" were creating "disunity, upset[ting] the peace and general psychological well-being of faculty." Although he noted that the teacher appeared to be "not conscious of the seriousness" of her actions, his conclusion was that she could no longer be a productive member of the faculty.

The teacher whose actions were denounced does not appear in subsequent principals' reports that list faculty, demonstrating vividly that violations of the rules governing black teachers' behavior were not allowed. Byas was not new to this process, having terminated three teachers at his earlier position at Hutchenson. However, the termination of a teacher was also not an action Byas took without thought or without having offered support. In handwritten notes that appear to be the draft of a subsequent letter regarding this teacher, he wrote: "When a principal does not recommend a teacher for re-employment, I am sure that there should not be any doubt whatsoever in his own mind. He, to satisfy his conscience, must do everything in his own power to first bring a person into acceptable practices of procedures; however, if in spite of his actions, this cannot be done, he has no other recourse except to recommend a change in personnel." He continued by noting the person's stellar qualifications from an "academic and experience point of view" and reported that he made extra efforts to provide support. These included having a talk with the teacher at the beginning of the year and seeking assistance from the Jeanes curriculum director. But when his actions were deemed to generate an insufficient response, Byas did terminate the teacher.[50]

In earlier years, when the professor had less authority to hire and fire, the dismissal of teachers required some strategy. For Byas, the strategy had been to merely leave off the names of the teachers he wished to terminate when providing the superintendent with the list of teachers he wished to rehire. Board approval of the list was tantamount to Byas's having elected to fire the teachers whose names were not included.[51] Byas reports that the three teachers who were dismissed while he was a professor at Hutchenson circulated a petition to have their jobs reinstated. Although they were unsuccessful, their efforts depict the extent to which the teachers believed they had been unjustly treated. In later years, the professor ostensibly had more authority to terminate if there was sufficient documentation of teacher incompetence, at least as perceived by the principal. The paper trail of infractions for one teacher and the letters, written apart from the annual evaluations, for another teacher served the purpose of documenting incompetence. As before, however, no data are available that provide the teachers' perspectives on their perceived failures.

Reprimand letters capture a definite authoritarian mode that contrasts strongly with the collaborative approach Byas reportedly embraced during faculty meetings. The letters document vividly that Byas, taking his responsibility as leader seriously, held clear expectations about his areas of responsibility and entertained no disagreement on some matters. For example, pupil assignment was principal-driven and completed in consultation with teachers; a teacher not directly involved with a particular student or assignment was not welcomed into the process. Moreover, in a departure from his views as a college student, he deemed a (male) teacher leaving campus without permission problematic. The departure violated school policy, and, more important, it left students unsupervised. His tone in these letters sends clear messages about his sense of authority in handling violations. Where a violation was sufficiently problematic, the teacher was told that the letter would be retained in the professor's file and in that of the superintendent, a clear indication that the teacher was considered to be on probation in the matter.

Termination seems to be consistently sparked by violation of at least two of three critical areas Byas deemed important for teacher performance. In the three documented cases of dismissal, teachers had been consistently reprimanded for similar difficulties. They were uncooperative with other teachers, thereby creating an unprofessional climate that jeopardized collaborative efforts that would generate ideas to help children. Whether in faculty meetings or in individual groups, negative interactions among peers were deemed to be unproductive for a positive school climate. A second area that elicited reprimand was violation of school policies, such as leaving school without notification. Finally, any violation that created difficulties for students, either leaving them unsupervised or placing them in awkward or embarrassing situations, seemed to spark particular ire. Teaching, he maintained strongly, was supposed to support the students. A poor teacher could not develop children, and without the development of children, the black system could not operate.

The evaluative activity of the professor when contrasted with the professional development mode of faculty meetings suggests an unspoken complexity in the leadership role. In developing rules for faculty behavior, the professor invited professional decision making. Even when he generated the ideas, they were presented to the faculty as suggestions for discussion and approval. In this mode of policy development, the leadership practices reflected democratic principles. However, in assessing compliance, the professor adopted an authoritarian mode. His practice was one that consistently evaluated teacher behavior against the policy developed by faculty. When violations occurred, the professor exercised his authority in assisting faculty to develop behaviors consistent with the predetermined norm or initiated documentation that facilitated the dismissal of a noncompliant teacher; in some cases he did both. Because of the respect many black teachers reportedly had for their professors, this tension may not have negatively influenced the day-to-day operations of the school. Indeed, the combination of solicitation of ownership of the faculty through collaborative planning and the authoritarian enforcement of policy through directive leadership may have helped generate the dissemination of teaching values that were consistent across many segregated school environments. This consistency would not be unexpected, as it represents the similar values of those teachers who remained in the environment and does not account for those disgruntled teachers who were forced to leave.

Unwritten Rules and Practices

The formal school documents and individual letters were one way Byas's expectations were formalized for faculty. However, Byas also had other unwritten rules not captured in any of the documents. In one example, Byas reports he was adamant that male teachers refrain from any social involvement with the high school girls. He reports that he "insisted that faculty members not take advantage of any of the girls. And if they did, if they tried to court, they didn't stay long." Byas attributes his adamancy on this point to his own former principal and mentor, James Hawes, when he first began teaching. Hawes reportedly was equally emphatic that male teachers at his school remain uninvolved with students. When Byas became a professor, he enforced a similar rule. "We had to set the moral tone," he explains. "And we had to look the part of the leader, and I insisted on that."[52] Although he understood that some of the girls had been late starting school and were, therefore, in an appropriate age range for a young male faculty member, he insisted that "professional" interactions be maintained at all times.[53] Another belief Byas held was that the best teachers were certified in more than one area. Because of the school's status as "approved," Byas did not want to assign teachers to content areas in which they did not have some certification. Yet as the number and variety of courses offered were increasing in black schools, he also wanted to widen the array of courses from which students could select. His autonomy on the matter of curriculum was sufficient, as far as the superintendent was concerned, that "the only people I had to convince would be my faculty," he explains about new course offerings. This desire to increase offerings influenced hiring decisions. He explains that he began hiring people who had at least a major and a minor and preferably two majors. "I wanted somebody who could do two or three things," he points out. "That would multiply the number of courses I could offer and still be approved, and not have teachers teaching out of field." Although teachers who did not comply with this preference did not receive a negative evaluation for faculty performance, his perspective may help explain some of his support of teachers' continued training and acquisition of degrees. It also reflects the concerns of a math teacher who argued in a *Herald* article that the push in the 1960s to include more math and science courses in the curricular offerings in black schools should not result in professors offering courses that staff may not be trained to teach. The writer encouraged professors instead to use the expertise of the staff as the key to developing new courses.[54] Byas deflects the writer's concern with his effort to hire teachers with dual certifications. In doing so, he could increase his curricular offerings without compromising his commitment to training.

As the 1960s progressed and desegregation of students loomed, Byas's unwritten beliefs also capture some of the surprises and difficulties a professor could confront when the superintendent transferred white teachers to black schools. In anticipation of his first white teacher, Jerry Hollingsworth, Byas reports that he prepared "an elaborate outline" that he expected to use "to break Jerry in." He is adamant that he did not want the new teacher "feeling sorry for our kids." Rather, he wanted the teacher to hold high standards and "push them where they needed to be pushed." Although Hollingsworth would later become one of the favored teachers in the school community and express his enthusiasm for Byas's leadership, in the beginning Byas was not "sure he knew how to do it" and prepared himself to offer the support he perceived the new teacher would require. However, to Byas's surprise, Hollingsworth entered Butler with a desire to adapt to the cultural and educational norms of the black community. Within three months he had proved to the professor that he would behave in ways consonant with the others on the all-black teaching staff, and he became an integral part of life at Butler. An example of his adoption of the dress norms that had earlier baffled him is evident in a photograph of the coaching staff, which depicts four well-dressed black men, with suit and ties, and Jerry Hollingsworth standing with them, also in suit and tie.[55]

In appreciation for Hollingsworth's successful performance, Byas laid aside his plans for teaching the culture and climate of the school to incoming white faculty. However, his attribution of the capacity to teach black children exhibited by Hollingsworth to the second white teacher was premature. Byas reports that the new white teacher's classroom was filled with "chaos and confusion" and that students were trying to "literally tear up the place." The teacher's solution was to distance herself from the responsibility of solving the problems in her classroom by threatening to send the students to the principal's office, a response that did nothing to encourage student cooperation. In frustration, Byas allowed the exasperated white teacher to listen on the intercom to what was happening in the classroom of a neighboring black teacher, where the same students who were uncooperative in her class were behaving in a cooperative manner with that teacher. He then posed the question: "Why is it that these same students can behave as students in her room and come to you five minutes later and tear up the place?" Consistent with his beliefs about teacher development, he explained to the teacher new to working with black students that "when you have to threaten students by having to bring in an outside person, you have lost control yourself." Because the new white teacher was a more experienced teacher than Hollingsworth had been, Byas was blindsided by the amount of support she required to be taught to function in the previously all-black environment.[56]

Although insisting on high moral standards for male teachers and encouraging additional professional training were signatures of his unwritten policies, Byas would not remain at Butler long enough to have a fully formulated policy for helping white teachers think about how to inspire and educate black children. As the protests of the 1960s inspired blacks to reject openly the constraints that had suppressed their possibilities as citizens, so the 1960s environment also prompted the resurrection of the forthright Byas who had been carefully concealed as a professor during the years when direct confrontation did not help black schools but merely cost a job. Very soon, the old Byas would reemerge, first in his leadership of a community and then in a career-changing confrontation with the superintendent. In the mid-1960s, however, Byas still had several more years to be a professor before the final eruption occurred.

6

Not without
Partnering
with the
Community

*The time I was a school
administrator was real
turbulent times in the
country. We probably had
more changes in our society
than any other time.*
—*Ulysses Byas*

The black community was changing tremendously in the mid- to late 1960s as the segregation that had defined downtown Gainesville and black life in general was gradually being dismantled. The changes that were occurring resulted in more open social and professional interactions between blacks and whites. To be sure, Gainesville's established black business icons remained. The Roxy Theater was still a popular spot for family entertainment, as was the American Legion for those who enjoyed evening entertainment by frequent performers such as James Brown and the Famous Flames. Black-owned restaurants commanded a thriving clientele. Black taxis continued to pick up patrons, and the businesses in the Odd Fellow Building—the funeral home, barber shop, and drug store—maintained a loyal customer base. To these older establishments were added new ones. In 1964, black proprietor Grady Cheeks owned a modern Texaco Station on Athens Street; not far away on the same street was the Central Record Mart.

With these restaurants and other businesses continuing to prosper, the black community retained a sense of familiarity for its members. In the background, however, was an increasingly desegregating world. As though exemplifying the wider changes, President Lyndon Johnson visited the home store of a black couple, the Reverend and Mrs. Alvertus Butler, in Gainesville in May 1964.[1] The president's visit came the year after John F. Kennedy's assassination in Dallas and the electrifying speech of dreams delivered by Georgia native Martin Luther King during the March on Washington. The Civil Rights Act of 1964, which finally protected black citizens from discrimination and segregation in voting and education, had just been passed; the Economic Opportunity Act would pass later that year and the Voting Rights Act the following year, in 1965. The era was a season in which a "war on poverty" seemed a real federal initiative, though perhaps not as real as the war on the streets. The assassinations of Malcolm X, Martin Luther King, and Robert Kennedy prompted multiple race riots—forty-three in 1966 and sixty in 1968 after King's death. The era was one of unparalleled hope coupled with increasing anger and disillusionment.[2]

This period in the evolution of the black community generated particular demands on the black professor. In some ways, the community activities of the professor paralleled traditional roles, particularly the responsibility of the professor to seek and sustain relationships with the black community. These relationships had never been coincidental or cursory; rather, they were intentionally courted and maintained by professors who understood that the mission to build a school could be accomplished only by supporting and building the black community. However, in other ways, the synergy of the period propelled the black professor into new roles. Adam Fairclough argues that on the eve of desegregation black principals could not continue their traditional roles as community leaders because of the strong pressure placed upon them to halt civil rights activity. His interpretation accurately describes the pressure some professors confronted from white superintendents during the period.[3] However, it does little to elucidate the varied forms of leadership the professor did exercise in leading communities during the period. Byas exemplifies a black professor who both continued traditional methods of involvement in the black community and served as a mediator between the black and white communities in ways designed to smooth the community's transition to an integrated one.

The Professor and His Relationship to Black Communities

Traditionally, the professor lived in a world where the black community both bequeathed liberation and expected accountability. The interaction between the black educator and parents was liberating because black parents typically allowed educators to function in loco parentis. As other literature on segregated schools has captured, black parents put a tremendous amount of trust in the teachers who instructed their children, with the most frequent affirmation from parents being that students would be held accountable at home for any reported misbehavior at school. Since the educational levels of the parents were typically low and supporting their children required experiences many had not themselves had, parents relied upon the support of black teachers and principals to help their children succeed in school.

However, the relationship between parent and the black educator also required accountability on the part of the black educator. Although no documentation exists of parents verbally demanding accountability, the professor understood that the educational leader had to seek the approval of the parents in the community and that the two groups had to work successfully together. One way in which black teachers remained accountable to, and worked with, parents was through the historical collaboration and shared agenda of black professional educational organizations and parent-teacher organizations. For example, American Teachers Association (ATA) meetings were held in the same city and on overlapping dates as the national black Parent Teacher Association (PTA). Likewise, within the state of Georgia, the annual Georgia Teachers and Education Association (GTEA) meeting was regularly scheduled to overlap with the state PTA meeting. The overlap of meetings captures the infrastructure that symbolically and practically facilitated the shaping of a shared agenda for black educators and parents, allowing the two groups to function in different arenas but toward the same ends.

In addition to participating in formalized structures that undergirded accountability, the professor also understood that, in local settings, the approval of the black parents in the community would have to be sought on the community's own terms if the school was to function successfully. If a professor ignored the cultural norms, parental support would be reduced, which in turn would jeopardize the school's success. Horace Mann Bond discovered this truth the hard way when, in the caption for a photo in the *Herald*, he called several well-known educators in Georgia "Big Shots." Although he had used the phrase casually and without much thought, the phrase suggested that these educators stood apart from the plight of most black Americans. Immediately reprimanded, Bond apologized publicly in a subsequent issue of the *Herald* for his error in elevating some members of the black community over others. Such a distancing by educated blacks did not bode well for community building. Indeed, members of the black community held disdain for, and recounted jokes about, the educated ones among them who lost connection with the established community norms. To gain local black parents' support, the professor had to abide by the norms the black community valued.[4]

Ignoring the necessity of accountability to parents could jeopardize the professor's autonomy within the school and even his or her job. For example, a routine question a superintendent might ask professors was "What are your parents going to say?" As Byas notes, the white superintendent cared little for the actions within a black school as long as the parents did not complain. "White folk didn't bother us. Anything I wanted to innovate, so long as my parents went along with it and I didn't ask permission, it was alright because folk didn't come over there and bother us." In the early years, when neglect was the norm, the superintendent would send the black school "some coal," Byas remembers, and "that was about the size of it. So long as you didn't kill somebody or beat somebody across the head unmercifully where people complained against you, you could do anything you wanted at the local black school." Although superintendents became increasingly interested in providing resources to black schools as states sought to equalize the facilities of black schools rather than integrate the black and white systems of schooling, the autonomy experienced by black principals with regard to actions in their bosses' schools never significantly changed. In fact, as Byas recounts, "The black high school principal under segregation was perceived as the black superintendent, and your white bosses left you alone."[5]

The neglect on the part of the superintendent may be attributed to his overarching concern with parental views, a concern born perhaps less out of a sense of responsibility for their children's educational needs than out of a desire to maintain the status quo. If the parents in the local black community liked their professor and did not complain, the superintendent could absolve himself of responsibility for the school and retreat into a world that upheld white superiority. He was not likely to interfere with the black school unless parents were unhappy. This reality made parental complaints a constraining influence on an environment that was otherwise one the principal could almost unilaterally direct. If parents were not pleased with the leadership of the professor, they might choose to complain to the superintendent. Complaints resulted in inquiries into the affairs of the school and could result in dismissal or reprimand. Thus, the capacity of the professor to continue innovation in the school was inextricably linked to pleasing his constituents, the black parents.

Professors of the era understood that they needed the support of the community, practically and psychologically, to preserve their autonomy within and ensure the success of the school system. As a result, school leaders had to be very deliberate in constructing ways of delivering services to the black community. The services they delivered addressed individual student needs and community needs. More important, professors also addressed the need to create a collective support for the school that would aid in educating the community's children. However, the ways in which they accomplished these goals differed as the 1960s evolved.

The Professor in Traditional Interactions
with Individual Black Families

Traditionally, the professor used community visits, religious participation, and language as mechanisms for developing bonds with the black community. The importance of language use and church attendance has been noted already in other segregated school literature. In part, the literature suggests that professors implicitly understood and valued the norms of the black community because they were products of the community. However, the extent to which the professors' norms may have been inconsistent with those of the black community and may therefore have required adjustment has remained ground untilled. Some differences did exist, and they suggest that the professor, though sharing the black community's cultural heritage, did not automatically share its cultural norms.

One example of the divergence between professors and community can be located in their differing beliefs about black educators' professional responsibility for student behavior. Byas describes conversations with parents that made him aware of these differences and that ultimately taught him a valuable lesson about the expectations of black parents. As a graduate student fresh from Columbia who understood professional expectations for parental participation and its importance for student success, Byas sought the assistance of a parent whose child was performing poorly in his academic studies. Byas expected the parent to assist by assuming responsibility and assuring him that the child's academic performance would improve. However, to Byas's surprise, the parent was less concerned about the behavior of the child and more dumbfounded by the behavior of the educator.

"Why are you coming to me with that, professor?" the parent reportedly asked. The question was one of incredulity. "You handle that boy the way you think best." The parent's bafflement depicts the extent to which black parents trusted black educators to act in the child's best interest. However, the follow-up question also demonstrates the extent to which the parent's perspective about the role of the educator and the role of the parent differed, despite the fact that the professor and the parent shared an ethnic identity. The parent further queried, "Didn't you go to school for that?" In other words, did Byas not have the educational training to know how to make a child behave while under his supervision at school? Byas explains that the parent would "look at me as though I were not doing my job."[6] From the parent's perspective, a master's degree from Columbia should have given Byas the strategies he needed to cope with school problems. The parent deemed it to be the educator's job, not the parent's job, to be sure that the child behaved while in school. As this example suggests, embracing this cultural norm of the black community sometimes required readjustments on the part of the professor so that he could align his behavior with the community's expectations.

The differing norms between professor and community can also be located in matters of visits to black homes. Arriving at a home where the family gathered on the porch, without chairs, Byas reports that he might hear the command that a younger member of the family "go and get the 'fessor' a chair." Upon reaching the porch and greeting the family, the professor was faced with a dilemma that required choosing the culturally appropriate norm. He could accept the hastily retrieved chair, thus non-verbally assuming a stance that elevated him above the other members of the family seated on the porch. Or he could refuse the chair, saying that he "would just sit with you all." In the black community, the appropriate norm of the era would have been to sit on the floor of the porch, an action that indicated a reduction of educational stature and a willingness to identify with the needs of the community. As Byas termed it, the community would then deem the professor to be "all right." However, the extent to which this behavior was a community-accepted norm that required revisionist behavior on the part of the black professor is captured in Byas's point that he quickly learned to wear "old clothes" so that he could be seated anywhere.

The divergence in the professor's norms and the community's norms can also be evidenced in religious settings. In many instances, attending church with members of the community would not have created undue difficulties for the professor, as the dominant black religious practices were either Baptist or Methodist, and most black leaders were familiar with both of these denominations. However, the black professor needed to extend the same courtesy of attendance to black congregations outside the better-understood communities of faith and sometimes outside the professor's personal comfort level. Seeking not to offend those who had divergent beliefs, Byas sometimes reported himself to be "nondenominational," explaining that if "everybody [was] praising God, that was all [he] needed." The language is significant in that it captures a shared value of the era—a common belief in God—while sidestepping denominational differences. In many instances, the utilization of this common language would be sufficient; however, in a different religious setting, the professor might also be required to invent new language to negotiate differences between himself and the community on religious matters while simultaneously maintaining an appearance of similarity.

One example of the divergence in community and professor views in matters of the practice of religion is captured in an episode early in Byas's career. Byas reports accepting an invitation to visit a particular congregation that worshiped in a small facility and practiced its faith with loud music and physical forms of exuberant praise. Indeed, the worship service was so deafening that he reports the difficulty he and his wife had keeping their young daughter from becoming frightened. By this time, Byas had married a former colleague who had taught with him under James Hawes in Elberton, Annamozel, and the couple were the proud parents of one baby girl. "They had a great big loud speaker set up and microphones and all that stuff," he remembers. "And they did such screaming and hollering like you never heard before, and it scared our daughter." In fact, like the congregation, the child had begun "screaming furious," Byas remembers. He explains that he whispered to his wife to take the baby outside until the worship service was over. He, of course, remained, waiting for the obligatory moment when the professor would be called upon to speak and wondering what he would say in a setting that had been of such discomfort to him and to his family. At black churches, acknowledging the professor and asking him or her to "say a few words" was standard protocol.

> Well, I said to myself, "You can't tell a lie in church. But, I've got to say something that the people can relate to." So, I said, when they finally called on me—"The new professor is here." They asked me to say some words. And, I said, "Those of you who saw me when I came in you may have noticed that I was sitting on that edge of the pew [pointing to the entrance point of the pew from the aisle; only he, his wife, and child were seated on that particular pew]. And I said now that you called on me, I'm almost to this edge of the pew [pointing to the other side]." And I said, "I want you to know, something moved me here tonight." And the crowd went wild.

In adopting language that said he had been "moved," Byas was deliberately imitating the expressions of the congregation. For them, the movement to which he referred implied a spiritual response; for Byas, the movement was physical in that he was attempting to escape the noise. However, because Byas deliberately chose ambiguous language, he was able to imply a similarity of religious response without criticizing them for a worship style unlike his own. Failing to grasp the nuances of his response, the crowd responded with the affirmation that the new professor "was all right."

His public persona aside, Byas admits privately:

> I never could tell them [what moved me]. They just assumed that [the Spirit] moved me. But it was that big amplifier. That loud speaker that was sitting over there next to me and had scared the baby. "What happened to your wife?" they asked me. I said, "Well, the baby got to crying and we didn't want to interrupt the service, so she carried the baby [out to the car]." They said, "Crying babies don't interrupt us. She could have stayed here with us." But I wanted to tell them, "You scared the hell out of her." But that wouldn't have gone over real well.[7]

The diplomacy in his public response to the black community was not unlike that used with the white superintendent. Much as he had to shield his true feelings from the superintendent for the good of the school, so he was sometimes required to refrain from expressing his true feelings to the community as well for the good of the school. Where unveiled personal response would damage the capacity to achieve good public high schools for blacks, the professor kept personal response to himself.

Traditionally, the intentional sharing of language, in this case religious language, helped establish commonality, even when the professor and the community did not share the same cultural norms. The fact that cultural norms within the black community varied meant that, even though he was a member of the community, the professor could not effortlessly continue the practices of his youth; rather, creating affinity with the community was sometimes an intentional act on the part of the professor. In reflecting upon this challenge, Byas explains the willingness of the professor to adapt to the language of the community. In particular, he notes that the use of language was a deliberate way to bridge the differences between himself and members of the community, with the end result being to create increased parental interest in school.

When you get in a setting where people know [how to speak with an expansive vocabulary], if you are meeting with college presidents, then you've got one speech. But, if you are meeting with citizens who live out in the rural [areas], who themselves have never been to school and many of the kids were in high school for the first time in the family, I can't be going out there as an authority and they're trying to listen to me and I'm putting all the "ly's" and all of the syllables in a speech — saying "pro-bab-ly" instead of "probly" because some folk won't know what you're talking about.

Byas believed that "his work required" the ability to "establish quick rapport . . . because you don't have too many visits." He explains that "people have got to have a good first impression of the 'fessor.'" He explains that the professor is not required to "go overboard" with the interaction but to do "just enough to be sure you have communicated with them." Importantly, Byas views it as the job of the professor to meet the community at the community's level, rather than expecting the community to meet him on his level.

The intentionality of this language use in the community when used with individuals is enhanced when contrasted with the language use the community expected of its professor in public settings. In church, at school, or in a public setting, the black community valued the professor speaking the language of the "educated" person. Publicly, to speak with the expansive language members of the black intellectual elite utilized was a point of pride, whereas in an individual setting with someone with less education, it would be considered talking down to and would invite estimations of arrogance or pride. Professors had to understand and utilize these distinctions in community norms and adjust their actions accordingly.

Byas's willingness to negotiate tedious paths of cultural norms, some familiar from his childhood but others different from his own educational and social experiences, is a characteristic displayed by other principals in Georgia. One of his colleagues also reports visiting different churches in the community on a rotating basis so that he would provide equal attention to people of varied faiths. Laughingly, he notes that "he even went to a church where they wash feet." The activity was not embraced in his own religious affiliation; he notes that "I had never seen that before." However, his participation endeared him to the community members.

The professor also adds that he went and "stood on the corner where the fellars talked trash," in spite of the fact that one of his teachers told him that he should not be "down on the corner with those folk." For the professor, however, these interactions helped him know "who was doing what in the community," which provided useful information should he need it.

Byas explains the ways in which the rapport with the community and the fellows on the street corner or in the pool hall could net dividends for the school in the form of useful information. "I had good rapport with people who owned pool rooms and all that stuff," he explains. When his students skipped school, the community members would call him. "Professor, if you come down here and come in the side door, you're gonna catch all of them." Consistent with accounts in segregated school literature, in which the students marvel that their professor seemed to have been "everywhere," Byas notes how his students wondered how he could possibly have known where they were.

> One day, on the day of a big ball game, some kids decided they were
> going to stay out of school and where they were going to meet and
> everything. And somebody called me. . . . Professor, they gonna be at
> such and such house. And the kids would wonder how in the world I
> would pop up. . . . If people saw three or four kids walking down the
> street during school hours, they'd call. "Say, I saw them going down
> the end of such and such things. I think they're going to such and such
> house." And I would just pop up there. They said I was everywhere.

The students, of course, were not aware that the professor received "all sorts of calls [like] that." In effect, when they felt comfortable with the professor, the black community could serve as a hidden observation system that reduced truancy because of its unpaid and self-regulating reporting mechanism.

Strikingly, the parents did not themselves confront the students and tell them to return to school. As owners of pool halls and, more important, as parents of the children, they surely had the authority to send the children back to school. Literature on the black parenting style is littered with references to the authority black parents are likely to utilize and the ways they flavor their interactions with children with authority. Moreover, the black community typically operated in a communal mode that would have made it acceptable to send other people's children back to school, as well as their own. However, the failure of these black parents to do so, instead calling the professor to function as a local truancy officer, provides further evidence of the distinct line they drew in relegating issues of schooling to the authority of educators. The educator was responsible for the student. As the earlier parent's quote noted, the educator had attended school to learn how to manage students. The parent's job was to provide the support.

In more serious cases, the rapport established with the community also had a direct effect on the whole school and not merely the behavior of individual students. When his school was vandalized and the student body was visibly upset that their new facility had been damaged, the chief of police asked the professor to "stay alert." Having witnessed the level of student dismay over the occurrence, he expected that the community might confide in the principal in ways it may not have chosen to do directly with a police officer. Byas had to wait only two days. On the second day, he received an anonymous call that gave him five names and information about where certain stolen items could be found. Byas passed the information on to the chief of police, and four of the five offenders received five-year prison sentences. Because members of the community trusted the professor, the information could be given to him, and the rest of the community need never know its source.[8]

Unmasking the difference between black community norms and those of the black professor is significant to demonstrate that the black professor was not merely an accepted member of the community because he shared an ethnic heritage. Indeed, geography, religion, and personal preferences could create cultural norms for the black professor that differed from those in the local black school community. Significantly, however, the professor assumed that it was his professional responsibility to mitigate the differences and seek common ground for the good of the school. In important ways, the professor deliberately chose to meet the community at its cultural location rather than expecting the community to meet him on his.

The Professor Supporting the Needs of the Black Community

The willingness of the professor to engage the cultural norms of the community was traditionally an effective tool through which he established rapport. However, the professor also had the responsibility to help instill in parents a deep concern for advancing the potential of their children. This concern could be expressed through individual interactions with particular parents about the needs of a child, or it could be expressed through school programming that addressed the needs of a group of children. Although these messages would assume new forms as money and opportunity became available in the later 1960s, the traditional value of communicating individual and corporate messages was a staple in the professor-school relationship. In particular, the interaction between professor and parents demonstrates the willingness of parents to subordinate their beliefs and accommodate to the ideology of the professor. They conceded this authority when they were convinced that the professor had the best interests of the children at heart.

As an example, Byas recounts an incident in which a parent initially disagreed with him about what was best for his son but later capitulated after understanding the professor's motivations. Byas had placed a young man he and the faculty perceived to have potential into the Algebra I class, much to the student's dismay. Byas explains that the faculty did not give students choices about taking advanced classes. "We picked [the classes for] them," he recalls. The practice of course placement was embraced because he and the faculty believed that students who were "academically able" should receive the best education available. Typically, this practice was supported by students and parents. However, in this case the parent and the student disagreed with the course selection. The student complained to the school and to his father, arguing that he would not be able to pass the course. Shortly thereafter, the father, equally as angry as the son, arrived at the school. In hot contestation, the father emphatically argued, "You have electives here. What are you doing electing for [my son]?"

Characteristic of the patience ascribed to other professors, Byas reports that he listened until the parent finished, and then he asked the parent if it was his intent to send the child to college. The irate father reportedly replied that it was but that he did not see what that had to do with the conversation at hand. Byas responded by emphasizing the importance of the class as preparation for college. Through this explanation, the professor was able to get the parent to view him differently: initially seeing the professor as someone who was trying to hurt his son by placing him in a course he might fail, thereby jeopardizing his college chances, the father came to see Byas as a person who sought to help his son by being sure he had the prerequisite courses that would help him fulfill the family dream. Possibly, in recognition that he no longer needed to fight to protect his son because the son was not being hurt, the father's interaction shifted from anger to inquiry. "You think he can pass it?" Giving his honest assessment, the professor replied, "I wouldn't have put him in there if I didn't think he could. But we need your backing so that he'll know that you're backing us up. Rather than coming in here and trying to argue for us to take him out, you need to go back home and tell him you are convinced that he needs to be back in that course." Byas reports that, apparently convinced that the professor was seeking the best for his son, the father complied. With support from school and home, the student both performed well in the course and subsequently attended college.[9]

In this episode, the father let go of his anger and deferred to the expertise of the professor. A likely explanation for the father's shift in demeanor is that the professor's patience, language, sincerity, and knowledge helped convince the parent that the school had the best interests of the child in mind in making the assignment. By pointing out to the father the need for Algebra I as a prerequisite for college, the professor provided information to the parent that was previously unavailable. While the parent had a desire for the son to attend college, he was not sufficiently familiar with college requirements to understand the relationship between college and the current course. By supplying this information, Byas demonstrated his willingness to help the son attain the dream the father held for him. Moreover, by expressing confidence in the son's ability, he affirmed his belief in the student's potential. Providing new information and communicating to the parent a belief in the child's success subdued the parent's anger and resulted in his acquiescing to the plan of the professor. Such an action would have been impossible without the parent's belief that the professor was interested in his son.

A second example demonstrates the willingness of the community to respond positively to a collective message, even when the message is initially at odds with community values. Shortly after Byas arrived in Gainesville, he modified the policy for eligibility for the football team, insisting that players maintain a passing average in their courses if they wished to play football. In doing so, he disrupted the winning record of the football team in a community where the school was generally considered the "rallying point" for the community. A colleague of Byas's notes of black high schools and communities, in general, that "everything centered around the school and the activities that were going on in the school. [The activities of the school] held communities together."[10] Thus, to disrupt a winning football team could have repercussions throughout the community. For the new professor, however, academic excellence was more important, and he was willing to jeopardize tradition to uphold academic integrity. "We had professional football players when I went up there. They'd come during football season and play football and then you wouldn't see them anymore until the next year."[11] Byas decided this behavior by the players was unacceptable and announced that a failing student could not play, even if it meant creating a failing team.

> I announced at the end of my first year that those students who did not pass the majority of their courses at the end of the semester prior to participation would not be eligible to participate the following semester. At the next game, we were losing and the coach wanted to put in [one of the students who did not meet the criteria]. I told him, if you put [the student] in, I'm going to forfeit the game. And I stuck to it. Well, we lost the game.

His behavior in dismissing valued players predictably generated anger among his coaches and star players. Some players even threatened to turn in their uniforms. However, the professor was undeterred, responding that they should "turn them in." He was convinced that either the students would perform well academically or they would not play.[12] In choosing to disregard the preferences of a local black community that valued its winning football team, Byas placed himself at odds with the community's norms and values. However, his rationale for this decision—the importance of academic competence—also surely conveyed to the community the extent to which he was unwilling to allow the students' education be compromised because of sports. In refusing to bend on this issue, he communicated to the community a deep interest in the welfare of its children. In this particular instance, the outcome was eventually positive. Byas reports that the following year, with the same rules in place, the school was in the finals for the state championship. This achievement must have also communicated to parents that academic excellence and athletic skill could coexist.

Both reported episodes represent divergence in ideology between parent and school about the most appropriate strategies to promote student success, but they also capture the trust vested in the school and the willingness to accommodate the leader if parents believed the leader was acting in the best interests of their children. In the first example, the professor, in seeking the best for children, pushed the student to achieve an academic success that neither the student nor the father believed was possible. Although the father had the technical "right" to remove his son from the class, he chose not to do so, primarily because of the trust he had in the professor and in the professor's perspective. In the conflict between community and professor over athletics, the response is similarly positive. Although the community could have collectively resisted the rule, no evidence exists that it did so. In both cases, the community and individual parent were willing to accept the professor as working for the collective good and were willing to reverse their own opinions when they believed in his efforts on behalf of their children. Although all interactions surely did not end so positively, the selected examples capture the community and school trust partnership working successfully.

Importantly, as he raised the academic standards of the school, Byas was careful to allow all members of the school community to remain psychologically connected to its success. For example, during the first year the students moved into the new Butler High School, they hosted the annual homecoming with a different flair. In previous years, when they were at the old Fair Street building, which was centered in the black community, an annual parade had been held. This year, the new school was physically distant from the black community, but the event was intentionally inclusive. The newspaper article, "Butler High's First Home Coming," reports that the band and cheerleaders traveled to the Fair Street School, then an elementary school, and had a pep rally with the students on the front lawn. However, after the pep rally, "the cheerleaders and fans marched to the housing projects. There they gathered for a pep session." Unsurprisingly, and possibly linked to the ways the school had intentionally invited the community's presence by remaining visible within the community, when it came time for the game to be played, "a large number of fans turned out for the occasion."[13]

In meeting black community members and garnering their support of the schools, Byas smoothly utilized the norms of the community while simultaneously using school structures to convince parents of the extent to which their trust in the school was deserved. By publicizing the activities of successful students, as the school frequently did in its newspaper, Byas was able to show the community that its students were excelling, just as the community had hoped. However, these traditional forms of leadership, themselves time consuming, assumed new and expanded forms in response to the activity swirling around the Gainesville community in the 1960s.

Programmatic Features That Help Parents Develop
Their Children in a Changing World

In the 1960s, blacks were hoping for an integrated world, but no one could have predicted the form that world would take. As the federal government finally enacted a series of laws allowing blacks to participate fully as citizens, the community faced a conundrum. In many instances the values of the lawmakers in Washington had not yet disseminated into rural communities and towns throughout the South.[14] The slowness with which these values were embraced in some southern settings meant that for most members of the black school community segregation was still a familiar setting. In fact, the continuation of the segregated Butler High School, despite court expectations, provides one example of the ways local politics and patterns disregarded the visionary federal world. Simultaneously, however, increasing opportunities for full participation meant that educational and economic doors were now open to blacks that had heretofore been shut. Entering this new world of opportunity required different forms of engagement, but there were often no guideposts that might be helpful to those blacks still used to segregated norms. In anticipation of integration, while saddled with continued segregation, the black professor was vested with the responsibility of interpreting the norms of a new world and providing support and modeling that would help members be able to participate in this world.

Byas accomplished the challenge of this era through several identifiable activities. He used the school in public and visible ways to address the educational needs of the black community, those of both the students and their parents. In addition to creating visibility for the school and its programs in ways that would build the community's pride in its offspring, the school also provided specific types of programming that were central in helping black parents who needed additional support to allow their children to take advantage of expanding opportunities. These programs consistently addressed the collective needs of the community to propel its students forward, such as students wanting to attend college, as well as the needs of students who were on the fringe of the student population, such as those who were in danger of dropping out of school. Moreover, Byas also sought to infuse an understanding of the meaning of democracy so that students could assume their responsibilities as citizens. Participating in democratic practices in school, in ways they could not yet learn from their parents outside school, was also a direct form of preparing the youth for a new integrating society.

Understanding the ways the school supported these collective needs of students in a changing world begins with an understanding of the professor's objectives for the school newspaper. In addition to providing journalistic experiences for students, the school newspaper was a deliberate way the professor sought to build rapport with the community and convince it that the children's best interests were being maintained. Just as Byas had utilized the newspaper to forward information to parents about the curriculum survey when he first arrived in Gainesville in 1957, he continued to use the newspaper in the intervening years to create particular perceptions about the school among the parents. "It was my contention," he explains, "that we could not compete with the local media." As a result, he believed that the school newspaper was a way of getting good publicity for the school in the community. Byas thus viewed the school newspaper as a central form of communication to black parents, one in which the news he wanted published about the black school could be accessible to the community that needed it. Byas notes that he wrote an article for each paper and that the newspaper was mailed to every household in the community.[15] Of his purpose, Byas notes that he was "trying to encourage folk and let them know about the school."

Byas also links the school newspaper to the reports students would give their parents about school when they were home. He explains that every day the student left the school and went into the home, he or she provided an impression of the school, either good, bad, or indifferent. In recognition of this silent power of influence, Byas points out that the school, in part through its newspaper, overtly sought to give the students something about which they could be excited. Myriad forms of student activity appear in the school newspaper, documenting the ways in which student art, opinions, and other forms of expression were integrated throughout the school life. Of these various reports, one that Byas believes attracted a good deal of parental attention was the perfect attendance list. He notes that perfect attendance was a goal that any student could seek to reach and that the individual names of students with perfect attendance were highly publicized. He explains: "Because if the students think well of the school and what's happening, they go home and they talk about it. They go to churches and talk about it." One 1964 document is a carefully maintained list of students with perfect attendance. Byas believed that the publication of the list in the newspaper netted positive returns for the school: pride on the part of the students and support for the school by the parents.[16]

An equally important way the school supported the vision of the community to educate its children was by championing students' academic success. Newspaper accounts provided high visibility to students who had high academic averages. In December 1957, only eleven students, seven of whom were males, had academic averages above an 85. However, these students appeared on the front page of the paper, with names and photograph. Additionally, the paper regularly featured inductees into the National Honor Society and included a series of editorials and articles aimed at increasing student success. Among these is an article written by a student, "Why Don't Fair Street Students Earn Better Grades?" The student offers as explanations students perhaps being insufficiently encouraged or being distracted by extracurricular activities. However, he also acknowledges the "fairly recent" incentives that had been offered by teachers to encourage students to learn. Since the editorial was published in December 1957, the new teacher initiatives can reasonably be linked to Byas's move to the school. Other articles include titles such as "It's Stylish to Study," "The Car Causes Drop in Grades," "Importance of School Records," and "The ABC's of Daily Success." Several statements embedded in other articles capture some of the collective sentiment among students that the school was becoming a place where studying was expected to be taken seriously. Under the eleventh-grade news, the student reporter records that the class has "improved greatly" and is "becoming more concerned and we are studying." In another article, "Around the Campus," student writer Johnny Robertson writes that the smiles some students had for pictures disappeared when report cards were distributed. He encouraged students who were disappointed to "do better next time" and all those who did well to "keep up the good hard work."[17]

In a very visible way, the service delivered by the newspaper was to depict the education of the community's children in ways that made members of the community proud of the local school and the students who populated it. Importantly, Byas presented these activities to the community, intentionally seeking their positive assessment of the school's program. Moreover, he explains that happy students, who grow accustomed to seeing themselves and their friends heralded in the school news, help enlist positive community support, as happy students would report to parents a positive view of the school.

In addition to the school newspaper, a second programmatic feature that served black parental needs by supporting the development of their children was College Night. Aimed specifically at the parents of the most successful students, this school-sponsored event was particularly important in the life of a black community in which so few parents had themselves been to college. Without the support of the school, parents would have had great difficulty getting their children enrolled in college. In March 1963, the newspaper reports that the "College Program Night" hosted five representatives from black colleges. Other colleges were invited but were reportedly unable to attend. However, the parents and students were given the opportunity to meet in three sessions with the college representatives of their choice. In these sessions, students and parents discussed issues such as requirements to enter college, the cost of books, room and board, tuition, and so forth. On the response of parents to the school-sponsored program, the student newspaper records: "The consensus of opinion was that the organization was good and that the program was commended for the large turnout of parents." One year later, the number of colleges represented at College Night had increased to seven.[18]

College Night can be adequately contextualized and interpreted only if it is viewed as an activity that was possible directly because of the professor's professional network. One editorial by Byas in the *Clarion* captures the connection between his participation in this network and College Night. He began by noting some of his professional activities, including recent trips to the state principals' meeting and upcoming travel to Kentucky and California. Instructive for interpreting College Night, he also gave the number of organizations with which he was affiliated.

> (1) Our Local Teacher's Organization; (2) Regional Teacher's Organization; (3) State Teacher's Organization; (4) National Teacher's Organization; (5) Regional Principal's Organization; (6) State Principal's Council; (7) State School Master's Club; (8) National Principal's Organization; (9 State Accrediting Commission; and (10) The Regional Accrediting Commission. This is by no means all. . . . For if one is to stay abreast so that our schools and our children will get a fair change then we must meet the challenge of the time.

After explaining the point of varied affiliations and Butler's history with the Association, he depicted the direct relationship between his activity and the support he was able to provide students: "In addition to the very rich personal experiences gained through attendance at the Annual Meetings [of the Association], I get the opportunity to meet and know personally College Presidents, Admission Officers of Colleges and Administrative Deans of Colleges. This has helped in a number of instances where we were trying to get some help for our deserving graduates."[19] This direct reference to his relationships in professional settings is important in helping to explain the ability of his school to sponsor College Night and in explaining the varied assemblies the school hosted, which included such speakers as college presidents, Benjamin Mays among them.

Within the school, Byas also supported college-aspiring students by being adamant that they be given a clear measure of their success. He believed that, by showing them how their education ranked with that of other students, he was further equipping them to be able to compete in college. For Byas, this measurement utilized standardized testing, an area of discussion that had dominated the agenda of his first Association meeting and continued to be discussed at other meetings of black educators. As a way of measuring student progress, Byas added the National Merit Scholastic Examination as a regular component of testing for the eleventh-grade students in his school. The students knew they were taking advanced placement courses, but Byas was determined to use national testing to help them understand that "they would have to study." He explained that he "wanted the top students at Butler to know that even though you were tops [at our school], when you get in competition with tops from other places, you still have a lot of work to do, and that's what we used the exam for."[20] Although student scores remained below the national average, records show an increase in student scores over the seven-year period when testing was implemented under Byas. For example, the number of correct answers for English usage increased from 371 in 1961 to 831 in 1963. Math increased similarly, from 348 to 875, as did social studies, science, and word usage.[21] Of note, these increases correlate with increased resources and faculty training.

Providing support for student and parental aspirations for college, including using his personal networks and sponsoring standardized testing, was one way the school addressed the needs of the black community. These avenues of support are particularly salient because they represent examples of ways the community could not have supported itself and needed the school to address directly its aspirations for the children. Butler, however, did not serve only the purpose of supporting parents who wanted to get their children admitted to college. In an equally important program, Butler also focused on ways to prevent dropouts by changing school habits at an early age. This program provided parental support for students on the opposite end of the college spectrum. Since fewer than 25 percent of blacks in Gainesville had a high school diploma in the late 1950s, supporting parents in their desire to keep children in school was essential. Moreover, as indicated by their desire for a truancy officer and as revealed in the results of the curriculum survey, parents were already themselves concerned about receiving this support.[22]

Butler's Dropout Prevention Program for students in seventh and eighth grades was one way Byas programmatically encouraged students to remain in school. The professor requested financial support for the program from the superintendent, who referred him to the board of education. As a result of his request, Byas reportedly received five thousand dollars to buy uniforms for the students. Byas explains that the period was one in which superintendents were "scared" not to provide monetary support for black schools. "The white people wanted to preserve segregation, and I could perceive they had their pocketbooks open. Anywhere I could justify a program, I went to them for the money," he explains. He adds also that he received only part of the money he wanted. However, even with this support, the school was able to initiate its program. According to Byas, the students enrolled were "at the bottom of the school list, who had never done anything positive." He reports that teachers volunteered their time and that students arrived for the program at 6:30 in the morning. The program included a military drill, which was later performed for the whole school in assembly and enthusiastically received by the students who were the peers of those students in the Dropout Prevention Program. The home economics teacher and students prepared breakfast at no cost to the students. After school, the students spent approximately another hour, and teachers helped them review their assignments for the next day. Prior to going home, the staff fed the students dinner. Although most of the students were from homes where parents needed the economic support, Byas preserved family pride by allowing parents to believe they were doing the school a favor by letting the children participate. He saw this face-saving strategy as an important part of the advertisement for the program, as he did not want to make parents think they were receiving a handout. To generate additional student interest, he reports that they sometimes had a bonfire at night and that one teacher would come and play the guitar.[23]

The school's effort to address the concerns of parents about dropouts is amplified in Byas's Principal's Messages in the newspaper. Writing in

March 1967, he emphasized the significance of the *Brown* decision and the importance of students getting a good education. He noted that by the time most Butler High School students had reached seventh grade, they had "obtained more formal education than their parents." He used this fact, however, to argue that students must begin to think about what is possible for them.

> There are many excuses parents and students give for educational denial by choice. Some had to go to work, keep the children, pay a bill, wash some clothes, stayed up late, went out of town, went to the doctor, overslept, had nothing to wear, had no ride to school or were looking for a job. Others were cleaning up, stayed home with someone sick, had no lunch money, thought they were expelled. . . .
>
> We hear many other excuses for educational denial by choice—it was raining, feeling bad, dislike of school, to go out of town, failing grades, no one cooked.

In the editorial, Byas explained that in the previous year eighty-five students at Butler were not promoted to the next grade, and he emphasized that these students were absent a total of 2,160 days. "That's an average of twenty-five days absent per student," he pointed out, adding that at the date of the writing "some fifteen or twenty of them have dropped out of school completely." The problem, as Byas viewed it, was that black children were "denying themselves, by choice, of their right to a basic education." He ended by delineating some of the ways students got off track, such as being late or absent or getting behind in class work, and challenged students to consider the extent to which they had used any of the excuses named. "Do you possess any of these characteristics? Do you come to school regularly? If you cannot answer these questions in the affirmative, the net article on dropouts will include you," he warned.[24] Like black professors before him reportedly were, Byas was direct and honest in his appraisal of student behavior. In this case, by visibly elevating the need to stay in school, Byas's editorial championed the desire of black parents to help their children attain high school diplomas.

Together with College Night, the Dropout Prevention Program demonstrates tangible ways of providing support for the parents whose children were most on the fringe in the school. By providing support for parents whose students were excelling, the school performed a direct service to the community by elevating the DuBoisian idea of the talented tenth. Likewise, by assisting parents with helping their children stay in school, the school was also providing a direct service to the community by increasing the number of black children who would be eligible for jobs requiring a high school diploma. This act would reduce the number who would have to be employed as maids or in industry work. In one Principal's Message, in fact, Byas noted the students "who are concerned about entering the employment market immediately" and devoted the remainder of the message to naming specific local companies seeking employees, sometimes providing the name of the person the student should seek in applying.[25] Whether the school was supporting college admission or employment, parents could have read its actions as direct interventions on their own behalf.

Byas's plan to teach students about democracy was a final programmatic feature employed to propel the community forward. In effect, his goal was to use the school to prepare black students to assume their places as full participants in American democracy. The concept was not a new one for him in Gainesville. As a teacher, he had begun to promote education in democracy, motivated by the denials for full participation in his own life, the thrust of his professional organizations, and, presumably, the graduate training under Harold Rugg that helped supply him with the educational jargon with which to hide his beliefs. As a young professor at Hutchenson, he continued to believe in the importance of training for citizenship and took measures to implement it. Shortly after taking the new position, he had challenged the status quo of rural Georgia by introducing black students to civics education. The southern black turnout rate in the recent presidential election had been only 13 percent. Of those blacks who voted, 57 percent had a college education, a statistic that to some degree correlated higher education with civic participation. Byas already believed that the students needed to be introduced to their responsibilities as citizens of the United States and that education was a mechanism through which black democratic participation could be spawned.[26] Thus, within a year of his arrival, he had determined to register his students to vote. Leaving behind a reluctant social studies teacher, the new professor had escorted thirty-eight to forty of the students to the courthouse in Douglasville to register. Shortly thereafter, he invited the thirty-three white candidates running for office to present an assembly at the black school.[27] Although he been accused the previous year of potentially being an "integrationist" (a word that could cause a professor to lose his job in the 1950s) by a white ring salesman miffed that the black professor had denied him the ring contract and used a black representative instead, Byas had adopted a concealing demeanor with the members of the white community who questioned him, maintained his position, and was not openly challenged in his voter registration effort. Had the white community objected to his civic education plan, he intended to use the prescribed state curriculum as a shield. According to that curriculum, part of his job was to teach citizenship. Veiled to the white community would be the ways he was intentionally implementing the political rhetoric that dominated the discussions in black educational associations about civics and education during the period. He knew that the professional world of black educators expected him to assume responsibility to "help students become effective members of democratic society."[28] However, the white community did not. Thus, Byas was slyly exploiting the curricular mandates in ways that served the needs of the black community while appearing to be merely acting as a benign, cooperative educator.[29]

Civic education assumed a more visible position in Gainesville as the unfolding events of the 1960s created openings for black participation that had been overtly rejected in the previous decade. As a leader in the community, however, Byas assumed an equally visible and distinctly straightforward manner in discussing the ways the new opportunities for civic participation should be embraced by blacks. Echoing his behavior at Hutchenson, Byas believed that if the students were to function as citizens in a democracy in the larger world, they must begin to practice these behaviors in school.

Teachers considered one of his in-school proposals to teach the students democratic participation a bit radical when he initially posed the idea for their review. He had brought to the faculty the suggestion that honor students be allowed to engage in a democratic study hall. The idea was so alien that teachers initially balked. Indeed, he reports that this idea was one he had to "fight for" to have it considered seriously. When the idea finally received reluctant approval from the faculty, the democratic study hall began. The most important feature was that, in this study hall, the students were self-supervising. Byas explains that "we are teaching students how to be self-directed, and yet all up through the twelfth grade, they are always under the supervision of a teacher." His argument was that eleventh- and twelfth-grade students who made the honor role the previous semester should be assigned to a different type of study hall.

The faculty placed several requirements on the participants. One rule required the approximately twenty-five to thirty students in the democratic study hall to select a leader of that study hall. The selected leader assumed responsibility for setting other rules. This leadership component reflects the structure Byas utilized for his seventh-grade students at Elberton and his own seminar experience with Rugg as a graduate student at Teachers College. The other rule the faculty imposed was that no more than three students could leave the classroom at any point and that the student leaving was required to write his or her name on the board. Of the experiment, Byas notes that students did self-regulate, especially when a student could not leave because three other students exceeded the agreed-upon time limit. Reflecting upon the experiment in democratic training, Byas recounts: "Students would chastise one another. Some teachers observed some students sleep, and some teachers were upset. I said, 'So long as he is not disturbing the class, let him sleep. He may have a job working at night, and he may need sleep.'" Byas reports that this study hall was in place for the final three years prior to systemwide desegregation. In that climate of anticipated integration, the study hall provided a very important exercise in democratic self-responsibility for emergent citizens.[30]

The problem with the study hall experiment was that it influenced the behavior of only a select number of students, those most academically able. Byas's goal, however, was to teach the entire school community about citizenship. For this purpose, he consistently utilized the school newspaper. His editorials more typically challenged students to value education and to use their lives in productive ways. He described a rewarding life and the need to make good choices in order to attain this life. He pointed to the "rapid progress" made in the new space age and challenged students to be sure they would "measure up in this ever increasing competitive democratic society." The repetitiveness with which he emphasized the importance of education in his editorials suggests strongly that education was to be the means through which black children would be able to begin to participate as full citizens in this new chapter of U.S. history.[31] One editorial, focused on the problem of school dropouts nationally, directly challenged black parents to assist their children in becoming full citizens:

It is the responsibility of the parents to see that the child acquires, through schooling and otherwise, the tools which are necessary to live a good life. This is his basic-civil right. If the parent does not insist that he get this right and get it now, he will not be able to claim other rights throughout his entire life. There ought to be a march of students, pushed by parents, to the school each day. Their song could very well be, "We march and study today in order to enjoy the fullness of citizenship tomorrow."[32]

Byas's description of these editorials makes explicit links between education and democratic living. In reflecting on these messages, Byas reiterates his admonishments to children to stay in school. He remembers emphasizing to black children that they should be prepared so that they would not be denied positions because of lack of preparation. He explains that he taught students that "you have been swindled, economically swindled because folk worked you and didn't pay you. . . . This is a democracy; you have a right to go to school."

As at Hutchenson, Byas also had arguments prepared for anyone who might challenge his editorials and other communications with students. He vehemently argued, "I'm teaching citizenship and I'm teaching American history."

> I'm telling them what happened because those people who are ignorant of the past may be doomed to repeat it. They had to know that they had been educationally cheated, economically swindled, and socially ostracized. My thing was that descriptive terms . . . would make the victim feel guilty and responsible for whatever the deprivation is. I said on many occasions that we need to use terms that suggest that somebody has done something to them or withheld something from them. If I tell you you had been cheated, you are a bit embarrassed because someone external to you had to tell you you've been cheated. But when you come to your sense, you want to know what did they take and who did it? Now you are on the mental offensive.

His emphasis on the last point is explained in his conceptualization of the school leader. Byas explains that he "went into the principalship thinking [he] could make things better for the kids by trying to make them understand that the system had denied the people who looked like them and some people were still trying to deny them. And it was up to the student to get as much education as they could." By being sure black students received an education, Byas was upholding the long history of American education—to prepare students to become citizens in the democracy.

In sum, the school served the direct needs of the community by adopting programmatic structures and messages that directly prepared children for lives different from the lives of their parents. Through his use of the school newspaper, Byas imparted to the black community specific ideas about democracy and about the importance of education if children were to be prepared to function in the democracy. By opening college doors for students interested in college and by keeping broader employment opportunities open for students in danger of dropping out, the school sent a powerful message to the community about the role its children were expected to play in a changing world. For parents unsure what this world might look like and caught between expectations for change and continuing impediments, the professor's leadership was important. As the professor had led them in their efforts to achieve equality, so the professor was central in developing new programs and ideas in this changing era.

The Professor's Direct Support for Adults in a Changing World

In ways not fully documented in the segregated school literature, the professor also provided other services for the community that increased the economic and educational levels of its citizens during these years of the civil rights movement. Consistent with a 1959 meeting of the Association, which focused on adult education, and consistent with his experiences at Fort Valley in adult education, the professor provided direct support to adults as a way of serving the community. This programming addressed the specific needs of its adults, apart from the ways the children were supported, and often served as a model for both parents and children during this time of emerging integration by enabling adults to participate in a variety of integrated activities.

Byas's facilitation of the hiring of black policemen is one example of his direct support of the black community. During the 1960s, Gainesville provided increasing opportunities for blacks to fill positions that had heretofore been unavailable to them. One area of employment that became open to blacks was the police force. The problem, however, was that blacks consistently failed the test. They passed the academic portion of the test but failed the aptitude section. Frustrated in its efforts, the police department sought the help of the black professor. Could the professor take old copies of the test and coach potential applicants?

Byas agreed to perform this service, especially since it would serve the purpose of allowing the community to hire more black policemen. He reviewed the tests and reports, noting quickly that he understood "right away why blacks were flunking." He explained, "They had questions like 'When dealing with a suspect, the policeman should be a) mean, b) kind,

c) hostile, d) firm, e) indifferent. . . . Invariably, the black would answer from their experience with police officers. It was always hostile, mean, or at best, indifferent. They never would put 'firm.'" In his evaluation of the difficulties black applicants were having with the exam, Byas is alluding to black communities' beliefs about the brutality of white policemen. Indeed, a painting by Jeff Donaldson during the era, *Aunt Jemima and the Pillsbury Doughboy*, used familiar American icons to capture police brutality toward blacks by depicting the black Aunt Jemima as being attacked by a policeman, represented by the Doughboy.[33] After identifying the difference in perspective that was prohibiting blacks from being hired, Byas used a class setting to make explicit to the applicants the differing norms. He explained, indeed "drilled into them," that they should "forget about what happened to you." He identified with their experiences, explaining that he too had to confront the same kinds of episodes in his life as a black man. However, the nine students were coached to "forget about that and think about what he [the policeman in the test question] ought to do." Challenging the imagination, Byas insisted that "when he stops you, he ought to be firm and he ought to be fair." His students apparently grasped the expectations with the principal serving as cultural mediator. Eight of the nine passed the test, and black policemen were hired. Although Byas challenged the police department about the fairness of its exam, noting specifically that some "folk answer out of their experience" and that the department should not expect positive responses when the people live in areas where "policemen are mean, hostile and indifferent," his primary service was to the community in that his coaching facilitated the presence of blacks on the police force.[34]

In this changing climate in which new opportunities were opening for blacks, the professor also created an adult evening school as another mechanism for increasing the community's educational, economic, and political strength. Supporting the development of adults was an interest that had been with him since Fort Valley and into his first years as a professor, when he had offered adult evening classes at Hutchenson. At Butler, the practice expanded. Parents who had not completed their own high school degrees could elect to take classes Monday through Thursday during the school week. Each evening, one set of class offerings began at 6:15 and the second at 8:30. Classes ended at 10:30. Among the classes offered were English, General Math, Elementary Math, Typing, Home Economics, Business Math, Elementary Social Studies, Elementary Science, General Science, American and World History, Biology, and World Geography. The adult education program at Butler was referenced in the 1964 edition of the school newspaper. Byas wrote that he had begun working on the Adult Education Program when he returned from summer travel. He described it as a program "which our community so badly needs." He also reported that adult high school graduates from the evening program were recognized at graduation ceremonies.[35]

Not all of his support for parents and members of the community was so easily identifiable as the matriculation of adults in the evening education program. One area that was less visible, but no less appreciated by the recipient and those people the recipient might have told, was Byas's treatment of the school's head custodian. Because of his participation in the School Masters Club survey, Byas was aware of the difficulties confronted by black schools throughout the state in obtaining custodial help and the difficulty of providing them adequate compensation. Although superintendents during this period were more amenable to providing monetary support to black schools, Byas did not wait for the superintendent's support. Instead, he used his own ingenuity.

Without an insider perspective, Byas appeared to be a fortunate professor who managed to employ a particularly faithful custodian. "Many folks wondered why [the custodian] would come up to the school after a basketball game and clean up," Byas remembers. "They wondered why my lead janitor worked all the time." The attentiveness of the custodian, however was directly related to Byas's willingness to create a supplement to the custodian's salary. Byas explains that he kept a vending machine with sodas at school. Students could not make purchases during the day, but they could go to the machine after school hours. Byas allowed the custodian to keep all the profit the machine generated. "Whatever he got out of the machine was his business," Byas explains. Since the custodian was a ninth-grade school dropout and the father of seven or more children, the gesture directly increased his household income and thereby generated good will and loyalty to Byas. Moreover, Byas's actions provided a way of solving a problem still vexing black schools. "Where there is a will, there is a way," Byas explains of his efforts. Although he never upholds the injustice of having to use ingenuity to address school resource needs, he laments when the leaders of schools do not take this kind of interest in helping members of the community.[36]

Beyond his efforts within the school, Byas sought to provide adult support within the community through the physical development of the community. Recalling his earliest skill, that of a carpenter, Byas decided, with his brother, to engage in sponsoring community development by initiating a subdivision for blacks. The project, named "Morningside Hills," had homes beginning as low as $10,000 on lots of 80 × 150 or larger. The homes had three bedrooms or more, with ceramic tile baths, maple floors, built-in cabinets, and paved drive and walkway. They were also either all electric or all gas. At the time that Byas initiated the project, only three black families lived in brick homes in Gainesville/Hall County, and he, as principal, was renting a house where he says the heat was piped in through one central spot on the hallway floor. He felt he needed an adequate place for his family and that he could help the community as well. In an effort to interest the community, he sponsored an open house, including having the local furniture company decorate the home for the day. Byas reports, however, that despite the interest, ultimately only four people were able to purchase homes. At the time, local banks in Gainesville were loaning blacks only $5,000 to buy a frame house.[37] A brick house at $10,000 may have been ahead of its time.

Byas asserts that he "didn't go into [the project] to make money," especially since he "couldn't afford to lose any money because I wasn't making that much." Under the original plans, the former carpenter set out to make a 6 percent margin of profit, which is an extraordinarily low amount. Though Byas did not complete the project, he points out that the initiative eventually convinced white contractors that there was a viable market in the black community for more modern housing. However, when the white developers came in, the minimum house price rose to $16,000.[38]

In providing community housing for single, female teachers in the community Byas was more successful. Historically, black teachers who came to work in small rural areas were required to board with a family in the community. As a young teacher at Elberton, Byas himself had to live in a family home where he shared meals with the owner of the house. Although his situation had been an amiable one, even after he married and brought a wife to live with him, Byas was aware of the lack of privacy a teacher had who was forced to live with a family. In some ways, the restrictions were greater if the teacher was female. As Byas recalls, "People would always put the teachers' business in the street. If they stayed up late at night, [people talked about it]." He decided he would call some other members of the community together and see if they could jointly build a facility that could be rented to teachers. His action to provide housing for teachers is consistent with that of some other black leaders during the period.[39] The result was an eight-bedroom home with four complete baths. It had a common area and a kitchen area.

As with the subdivision, part of the effort was business and netted a financial gain for Byas and the other community members who invested in the $12,000 project.[40] With a steady supply of teachers, Byas and other participants could be assured of full occupancy, which was generally the case. However, the investment also served a direct need within the community. The teachers' home charged less rent than a teacher would have paid individually in the home of a community member, and it created a space where teachers could have much more of the privacy due an adult.[41]

Byas's activity can be interpreted as solely a business interest, or it can be contextualized by viewing it as one manifestation of his effort to address the economic needs of blacks in Gainesville. Byas was a member, for example, of the Citizens' Advisory Committee, serving as chairman of the Public Information, Model House, and Program Planning Committee. In its by-laws, this group notes as its primary functions the desire "to concern themselves with the full range of housing and community development activities in Gainesville, to learn about the nature and extent of deficiencies of these activities and the means of remedying them, to make recommendations for improvement, and to help inform other citizens and groups as to the need for the improvement and thus develop united community understanding of this need." As a member of the committee, Byas functioned in an advisory capacity with the city commissioners and became widely involved in issues such as housing codes, public facilities, urban renewal, and housing and planning for the elderly.[42] Because of these activities, he was alerted to community needs in broad ways, and he served as a model for community members of modes of interaction in an increasingly less segregated world.

In other arenas, the professor also served as the model for the black community in the climate of changing race relations. For example, white leaders in Gainesville elected Byas to serve as the only black participant when Gainesville became one of the finalists for the fifty-five All-American Cities. This coveted position provided exceptional visibility to Gainesville, as it was in competition to be one of the best cities in which to live in the United States. Byas functioned as a mouthpiece for the city, including picking up the visitors who were evaluating the city in the final round of competition and flying with three others to San Francisco to "talk about what they were doing." Although including a black in such a visible role may have served the purpose for the white community of increasing Gainesville's likelihood of selection by distinguishing itself as a town that had moved beyond the restricted environments of many southern cities, the selection of Byas also served a need of the black community. As evidence of the extent to which Byas's selection represented the whole community, the school sponsored a surprise "send-off" program in his honor. The program was held in the school's gymnasium and included gifts such as an "E. E. Butler High School Personalized Pillow for his comfort" on the "non-stop jet." In a period when few blacks were included in airline travel, having their professor participate in the city delegation apparently generated major news for the school community. In the picture of the delegates, featured prominently in the top right corner of the *Clarion*, the caption reads: "Principal Byas and other delegates at Gainesville Courthouse."[43] The omission of the names of the white delegates may reflect an editorial omission, or it may suggest the extent to which the school community was singularly focused on the pride it had in its own member.

In interactions between blacks and whites during this period, modeling the pattern for addressing one another is another example of the leadership of the professor. Byas describes never liking the practice of whites calling blacks by their first names while reserving titles for themselves and other white peers. In earlier periods, as Leon Litwack has noted, part of racial etiquette demanded that blacks use titles when speaking to whites, as visible demonstration of their deference and respect, despite the fact that whites did not reciprocate with the same courtesy.[44] Because he found this practice offensive, but also surely buttressed by a climate of changing race relations, Byas made a decision: "Anybody who took the liberty to call me by my given name, if I didn't know theirs, I was going to find it out and I was going to reciprocate whenever it happened."

The opportunity presented itself while he sat with church members and the bishop of the denomination at the office of a lending institution waiting to see the president. Several people passed by him, saying "Hey Ulysses." Much as he would with members of the black community, Byas responded with "Hey Jimmy," or whoever, much to the chagrin of the blacks who accompanied him. When the president came out of his office and said, "Ulysses, I'll see you in a minute," Byas responded in kind, calling the president by his first name and saying that he could take his time. Aghast, the bishop reportedly said, "Reckon he's going to let us have some money. You are up here calling these folk [by their first names]." The bishop's thinking reflected the mores of the segregated climate in which he had always lived. In the changing climate, however, a courageous and respected professor could challenge previous interaction patterns and initiate the abandonment of old conventions. To the surprise of the bishop, Byas and his colleagues received the money, despite failing to adhere to the racial norms that had previously defined relationships between the races. By having the courage to use the bank employers' first names, Byas demonstrated to other blacks, even leading blacks in the community, that societal norms were changing and that all should embrace a new era. His behavior was so stunning for its period that Byas reports the bishop "preached about" the episode at churches across the conference area.[45]

Byas was also involved in efforts to facilitate integration of the golf course. Several blacks had been inquiring about the quasi-public facility, and they asked Byas to chair the committee to seek an integrated course. The mayor's initial response to the committee's request was "wait," as the president of the bank was concerned about the influence integration could have on the major fund-raising drive in the community. Like many blacks disconcerted by requests to "wait" during the 1960s, the black committee members did not react positively to the president's response. As chair, however, Byas suggested that the mayor actually be given the sixty days requested. Eventually, others agreed. Byas reports that within two days of the sixty-day deadline, the mayor called him asking if he could "get a couple of fellows together so we can tee off." Byas called the other committee members to report: "I want to be the first to tell you that I am going to play golf." Despite having never played golf in his life, Byas joined the group, and golf course in Gainesville admitted its first black players on that day.[46]

The demands of leading a community into new behaviors by intentionally embracing integration sometimes placed the professor at odds with some members of the black community, particularly during a period when splinters were forming in the civil rights movement because of disagreements over the best ways to proceed to achieve equality. In one incident involving civil rights demonstrations in Gainesville, Byas's behavior could be interpreted as resistance to the movement's cause. However, conversation with Byas unravels a more complex explanation for his actions. Civil rights demonstrations erupted in Gainesville, as elsewhere, despite the town's interest in being an All-American City. Byas emphasizes that he was not perturbed by this activity; in fact, he reports that he worked with the demonstrations. However, on one occasion a segment of the black community decided to picket a store where two blacks had already been hired. These community members believed the store had not hired enough blacks. Because the store received a good deal of economic support from the black community, the community wished to send a strong message to the owner of the insufficiency of his response.

When the leader of the group called to ask his opinion, Byas explained that the other stores were not hiring any blacks at all. He questioned why they would picket the store that was at least making an effort to integrate. However, because the professor failed to support their position, some leaders of this protest threatened to picket the school. Byas refers to the particular group as "hotheads," presumably in contrast to the more measured response he and other moderate civil rights advocates traditionally valued. Rising to the direct challenge, Byas replied, "If you come out here and picket the school, you had better not come on school property because you are going to have to answer to me personally, and I am not going to call the police either. I'm going to handle it." Byas is five feet and eight inches tall, and the means through which he intended to handle it is never clarified. Yet his intentional use of the language and intonation of the community conveyed a strong message, easily deconstructed by other members of the community. Students and community purportedly concluded that "you better leave Butler High School and Professor Byas alone. He's with you for picketing downtown for people who won't hire blacks, but he does not support boycotting those who do, and he will not allow you to disrupt the school." Of the situation, Byas explains that "if you straight shoot and you are honest with folk, they may not like you, but they'll respect you."[47]

In these exchanges, Byas provides several forms of support for adults in the black community. Some of his efforts target specific individuals, as with the custodian, police applicants, and individual teachers needing housing; other activities institute systemic structures that could benefit the collective community as well. These include the adult evening school, which could raise the overall educational level of the community, and the subdivision, which initiated a higher standard for black housing in the city. At the same time that he used these mechanisms to broaden the possibilities for black citizens, Byas also modeled the forms of interaction black citizens might assume in a world that allowed them to participate with whites as equal citizens. Although professors have not typically been described in these ways, his behavior is reflective of those of his colleagues in the Association, an agency that had been pushing for integration since its inception.

In sum, the black professor, as exemplified by Byas in this case, played a skillful hand in exchanges with black parents. Although he played the Dr. Jekyll and Mr. Hyde game with superintendents by purposely concealing the intent of many of his actions, he used a different method to reach deliberately into the black community to generate its support for his actions. Byas intentionally employed traditional methods, such as adopting the language of the community and being present in its institutions. However, he also expanded the traditional role by providing programmatic school activities that supported parents' aspirations for their children and that addressed the parents' own needs. By engaging in both of these activities, he would have the full support of parents in building the capacity of the school, and he would be able to create the kind of school he and the faculty believed would best serve black children.

The Limitations of the Professor's Work with Black Parents

Despite his multifaceted efforts to address the needs of the black community, in retrospect, Byas believes he failed in parental involvement. His summation appears odd when compared with the parental activity within his school. According to the school newspaper, the PTA was meeting on the first Wednesday night of each month, and attendance had been "very good." Consistent with his focus on students, during one session Byas invited a speaker to address the parents on the responsibilities of citizenship. At another meeting, the parents were slated to have a panel of presenters who would discuss educational issues with them. Within the school are descriptions of the "grade mothers" who would be responsible for assisting teachers in "any function of the class" and reminding others to attend PTA meetings. By December 1963, Butler High School was also hosting the district PTA meeting. By all accounts, the activities are consistent with those recorded in the historiography of segregated schools and for which parents have been heralded. As Huff Brown has described it, the parents felt part of the school, and the school was working in relationship with the parents, fully understanding that it needed their support to function well.[48]

The explanation for Byas's belief that he failed in this area requires an understanding of his experiences as principal of a desegregated summer school. During the years leading up to full desegregation, he and a white principal rotated being principal of this desegregated summer school. In this capacity, Byas had his first experience being a principal who supervised large numbers of white teachers and students. His performance was reportedly so good that the summer school session he led was deemed to have been the most successful one ever held. Accolades aside, however, the experience provided an important frame of reference through which Byas could contrast his experiences working with black parents and, based on the comparison, his experiences in the black community. He now believes the autonomy black parents gave black schools may have been a mistake. "See, I made a mistake on that score [interaction with parents]. Generally I felt good because they didn't bother me. I called when I needed help and they gave it. They showed up for special events; they backed the school up for disciplinary action we'd take." He points out, however, that this pattern was very different from that of white parents. "Black parents tended to leave the education and the running of the school to the principal and the staff." He notes that "by and large, white parents did not do this." White parents during the desegregated summer school he led called in advance to notify the school if the student was going to be late; black parents did not. In fact, he cannot imagine that black parents would have thought to call. In fact, he says that the minute things white parents called about, "black parents wouldn't pay any attention."

Of more interest than the nature of white parents' involvement verbally at the school was the power Byas noticed that they wielded over school personnel. White parents represented the bankers, lawyers, builders, and other people of influence in the town. Byas notes that he didn't realize the limitations that could be imposed on a school as a result of a powerful parental base. He recalls that during one faculty meeting, as he was talking with teachers about the importance of maintaining standards, a white teacher stood and said that she agreed with him that standards should be maintained. However, she offered an example that would have been an anomaly in the black school. The white teacher explained that she had needed a loan for a car and that the father of one of her students held an influential position that would determine whether she would receive the loan. The parent wanted the child to have an A. The teacher believed the child deserved a C and initially gave him the lower grade. However, in assigning a grade that reflected the actual student performance, the teacher soon found that she was unwelcome in various places in the community, even in the hair salon. "When she tried to stick to it," Byas recalls of her story, "she couldn't even get any rest on the weekend." She said she finally learned that if she just gave him the B that he didn't deserve, "they left [her] alone."

Byas uses the example of this teacher to explain his growing under-standing of the difference power could make in the parental behaviors in the black and white communities. He notes that he never had to be accountable to a community that held some form of financial power over him or whose members might be willing to use their power to influence his personal life. Because the parents of his students were not corporate lawyers or other influential professionals, he did not have to worry that a school decision he made about a child's performance would negatively affect his ability, for example, to buy a home. He explains: "I never had these big shot kids in my class. These big shots wanted their kids to make good grades so they could get in college." The inference here is that a more economically viable black community might have generated differ-ent strategies for the black professor.

Although he does not approve of this type of behavior by white parents, the summer school experience left Byas worried that black parents left too much of the education of their children in the hands of educators. In particular, he worried that black parents would continue to do so as de-segregation occurred, perhaps to the detriment of the black community. If the same level of trust that existed between the black school and the community could not be expected in the integrated school, black parents' traditional style of involvement would not be appropriate for the new en-vironment. Too late, Byas realized that he should have done more to shift the model.[49] Of course, shifting the model could happen only if he stayed at Butler High School.[50]

Conclusion
The Price for Running
Twice as Fast

It takes all the running you can do to stay in one place.
If you want to get somewhere, you have to run twice as fast.
—Ulysses Byas, paraphrasing a favorite quote from
Alice in Wonderland

After eleven years, the ongoing confrontation between the black professor and the white superintendent reached an impasse. The times had changed since Byas first assumed the principalship in Gainesville. As the 1960s drew to a close, the desegregation whites feared and the integration blacks hoped for were converging as school leaders developed plans for a system of schooling that would educate blacks and whites in the same facilities. Amid these conversations, the superintendent approached the professor, confidentially, to let him know that when the black and white schools were integrated in another two years in compliance with the U.S. Department of Health, Education, and Welfare, he was going to increase Byas's salary and recommend that he become an assistant superintendent at the administrative offices. The superintendent mistakenly thought his was a good offer. Instead of firing the professor, as happened in many cases throughout the South, the superintendent was offering Byas a promotion. In fact, he was offering Byas the best salary he would have ever made in his life. However, the superintendent's vision was not broad enough to anticipate Byas's adamant beliefs about justice and integrity in the desegregation process. Therefore, he could not have anticipated Byas's adamant refusal.

"I'm a high school principal," Byas pointedly told his boss. Byas recognized that if he accepted the promotion, he would be placed in a position of meaningless authority. Like other black professors confronted with losing their jobs during this season of desegregation, Byas was being offered an administrative title with little substantive responsibility. By the dictates of whites, a black professor could not be principal of a desegregated high school, even if he was a good principal. "I know I'm the best in this county," Byas continued. "Hell, I am the best in this state."

The white superintendent could not refute Byas's contention. He had recently written the black professor a letter noting that the integrated summer school he had conducted the previous summer was the best one that had been held. He knew that some of Byas's curricular innovations exceeded those at the white school. He knew, furthermore, that the current principal at the white school was someone Byas had helped train. Indeed, when the white principal and Byas had traveled to Florida to observe innovative nongraded high schools, Byas's description of his college-type high school schedule had been so impressive that he had been invited to become a John Hays Fellow; this well-funded fellowship program had allowed the black principal to spend a summer in Bennington, Vermont, reading books and discussing ideas. The white principal had received no such invitation. Still, the dictates of the time discounted the reality of a black professional with superior skills. Whites were conceding to desegregation, but only on their terms. Their terms meant no black high school principals at desegregated schools, not even in Gainesville.

Byas was no fool. He had seen the dismaying efforts at integration thus far in Gainesville, and he was severely displeased. In ways reminiscent of his report to the students at Fort Valley about the way the Disciplinary Committee was behaving toward students, he had already reported to his faculty the race-conscious way black teachers were being selected to teach at the white high school, particularly the focus on the complexion of the teacher's skin. He also knew well the politics of the planning in Georgia through the Georgia Teachers and Education Association (GTEA). Neither black professional organizations institutions, nor black high schools as they had been known, nor black educators were going to be preserved in the new system. Despite having been elected president of the GTEA, he would never succeed to the presidency of the organization. Like other black organizations, the GTEA was being merged into a new organization with whites, the Georgia Association of Educators. His election to the Commission of Secondary Schools at the Association had come to a similar fate. Anticipating the benefits of integration, that group had been dismantled five years earlier. By merely looking at the black representation from northern states at national meetings, Byas could easily discern that the place of leadership, as a general rule, would not be given to blacks in a desegregated world. His choices were to pander to the white educational leaders by accepting the plan of the superintendent, with its personal financial rewards, or to have no part of it. Immediately, but without regret, Byas chose the latter.

"I'm glad to know what you are going to do," Byas responded, his voice rising, "because as soon as I can write you an acceptable letter of resignation, I'm leaving." Furious, he left the superintendent, returned home, and told his wife to start packing because they were "leaving." When she questioned where they were going—the family now included three children—Byas responded that they were not "*going* anywhere." Instead, enunciating carefully, he replied, "We're *leaving*."[1]

His formal letter to the board of education does not reveal his anger about the economic peril created by his decision to leave. Writing on May 15, 1968, he noted that he had two job offers for the next year and requested that he be able to discharge his official duties by the end of June. He wrote that he "shall always be grateful to the Gainesville City Board of Education and the city generally for the many opportunities given me for professional growth." He also expressed his pleasure at the growth of the schools but was careful not to attribute the growth directly to the superintendent. At its conclusion, he cited his obligation to his family as his reason for asking to "be relieved of [his] contractual obligation for the 1968–69 school year."[2]

Byas is direct in pointing out the contradiction between his oral report and the written record. He notes that he wished the public record to reflect a positive stance. His reasoning relates to the public nature of the document and his belief that the official record should not contain the details of the confrontation. Notwithstanding the language of the document, however, his actions capture his blatant refusal to accept the position of a powerless assistant superintendent, and his reported anger was an overt rejection of a system that refused to respect his training, his skills, and his knowledge about education. Although he had ten years as principal in the system and the white man who was to be named principal had no experience as a principal in Gainesville, the desegregated high school would be led by a white man merely because he was white. That Byas's contributions to education could be ignored and he could be displaced because of race was an insult he could not overlook.

For Byas, the story would end well. He would leave this position, resign as incoming president of the GTEA, and assume a position as an assistant to the executive secretary of the organization. In this position, he would publicly decry the decimation of the black teaching profession, including bringing suit against the Gainesville city system for its subsequent treatment of other black educators. With no recommendation from his superintendent, he would also one year later be hired in Tuskegee, Alabama, as the first black superintendent of any of the eighteen segregated southern states. While in Tuskegee he would become a Rockefeller intern, which led to his earning the doctor of education degree at the University of Massachusetts, Amherst, in 1977. His dissertation, reflecting his interest since Fort Valley, would be on adult education; notably, his colleague in the doctoral enterprise would be well-known comedian and actor Bill Cosby. Byas's last position before retirement relocated him from the superintendency in Alabama to the superintendency in Roosevelt, Long Island, where he spent ten years resurrecting a failing school system. Jokingly acknowledging that he had worked professionally "down south and up south," Byas retired to Macon to enjoy the "finishing cantor" of his life. Prior to his departure, however, the school board renamed a school, Ulysses Byas School, in a tribute to his excellence as an educator.

The story of the black professorship would end less well. As many historians have documented, the black high school professor almost completely disappeared in the South after massive desegregation occurred. Professors retired; they were sent to school buildings that contained no children; they were demoted. In one way or another, school boards dismissed most of them. And with their departure was dismantled the system of education on which black communities depended for their uplift. Their story has been masked in public perceptions that they had no story of merit to tell. As Byas explains, "See, people always tried to make us believe that whatever we were doing, even our best, was worse than their worst—which was not true." However, with their firing has occurred a historical blindness that has failed to seek an understanding of the agency of the black professor within the system.

This narrative, of course, fails to delve into the complexity of the diversity of perspective and activity within the principalship. Because it focuses upon providing an in-depth understanding of one principal and the systemic structures that influenced his development, the nuances of difference across black professors are lost. For example, variances in personal commitment, educational training, and geographic region, as well as the complex interrelationships that governed the intersection of these variables, are obfuscated in an account that elevates the complexity of the system and the behavior of one individual within it. However, as Byas's own comments about blacks not being a superior group indicate, professors with less zeal and training existed among them. Moreover, the ways a Dr. Jekyll and Mr. Hyde game might shift if the player were a woman remains an intriguing question but is unanswered. The same is true for understanding the level of graduate training and its relationship to embracing the ideas within the network. One wonders whether, if Byas had failed to go to Columbia and had instead assumed the position offered as a professor at a rural school immediately after college, the singular influence of the network would have been as significant an impetus in creating the professor he became.[3] The presentation of a case focused on one player leaves open for additional probing numerous complexities about the black professor.

The focus on the professional activity of the principal also minimizes other voices that would help inform the leadership he provided. For example, if invited to do so, many students would likely provide fond memories of Fair Street/Butler that parallel descriptions in other books and articles on segregated schools. Indeed, in class reunions and in private letters their praise of the school and their principal is consistent. However, some students might also describe instances where they may have disagreed with the actions of the professor. Any disagreement among the students regarding his actions is not captured here. Another missing voice is that of the teacher. Although teachers' professional activities are included, an account told from the perspective of the professor suggests that the intellectual elite and professors disseminated information *to* teachers rather than that teachers were active agents in creating the educational world described. Fortunately, other scholars, such as Valinda Littlefield, are engaged in documenting the extent to which black teachers were central participants in this professional world. The failure to include their voice in this work does not diminish the significance of their participation. As important, the specific voice of the female educator is missing in this account. Since most of the high school professors and black intellectual elite were male, Byas's perspective on these events is that of a male administrator. The voice of females in general and female professors in particular is not included, in part because gendered differences in the experiences are not typically addressed in the sources.

A final limitation related to perspective is also important to note. The focus chosen for this recounting fails to address the tremendous personal sacrifice necessitated by his leadership in terms of both Byas's time and the added pressures placed on his family. His wife, for example, received a B.A. degree at Bennett College in Greensboro, North Carolina, then a Mus.B. degree (bachelor of music) at Indiana University. She later studied at the Juilliard School in New York City. However, Byas is clear about the benefit he received when his wife decided to remain at home full-time.

He notes that her sacrifice "freed him" to spend as many hours as were needed in his work. "If [he] needed to work two hours after school, sometimes going through every room and seeing what teachers had displayed on the bulletin boards" as a way of assessing teacher performance, he had the freedom to do so. His wife's supervision of the growing family gave him time to read the many journals he received and to "come up with unique solutions to troubling problems in the school without having to worry about getting home late." He emphasizes that sometimes "you've got to have thinking time, where you sit down and look in your own mind's eye and analyze a problem and [think about] what can I do." His wife's willingness to subordinate her professional activities after only two years of teaching in order to support her husband's expanding leadership commitments plays a central, though underexplored, role in his story. Indeed, Byas offers freely that the "blessing" of his wife's caring for the family allowed him to care for the children of other people at school. Moreover, knowing he was the single breadwinner in the family inspired him to perform excellently in his job. "That put an extra burden on me," he reports, "to make sure I did the best job I could so I could advance in the profession." With the four children who would ultimately be born into his household, Byas was clear that he needed an income sufficient to provide for the immediate needs of his home as well as college and other expenses. In this account and others, the ways in which black families sacrificed to allow professors the time to interact with school communities, faculty, professional networks, and superintendents remain buried in the story, as though such sacrifices did not exist and as though they do not help explain why the professor was able to do all that was done.

Nonetheless, several facets of the story of this black professor are worth highlighting. The most central is that of organizational support and development. The historiography of black educators captures teachers primarily as solo agents or as part of a massive organization, such as the teachers' association. Teachers were indeed part of the organizational structures, and they embraced many of the collective values, thus making them their own. However, the historiography omits an understanding of the ways these values were developed among teachers. Teachers did not hold the collective values they did merely because of individual experiences in northern schools of education; nor were these values merely the collective African American ethnic wisdom about teaching children. Rather, the descriptions of black teachers represent an intentional blending of cultural values and teaching expertise, crafted within the school with a professor serving as instructional leader.

As important, professors were not independent agents. Despite their rightful elevation in individual communities as a result of their commitment to the growth and development of the community, professors were part of a larger organizational network that used a common language and embraced similar practices regarding ways to develop impoverished black communities. To imagine the professor as an individual creative agent is too narrow an interpretation. To be sure, the professor could be extraordinarily creative, as is demonstrated in the strategies and ideology Byas utilized in his school in Gainesville. However, Byas's account also demonstrates the layers of mentorship and professional development activity that combined with his personal ingenuity, educational training, and life experiences to produce the school environment. The separation of the principal from continued professional development in the historiography has helped generate the portraits of individual "good" schools, a conclusion that makes a good school an anomaly instead of a component of the larger system of education in which it existed.

The varied layers of professional development are numerous and overlapping. With great seriousness, black educators appear to have embraced all available means to develop themselves so that they could develop children. In their professional world was the best thinking of the black intellectual elite, the black college administration and faculty, and the white graduate schools. Their professional organizations repeated the ideas deemed to be useful in black schools, and they worked collectively to use the organizational structure to demand equality. Whether at a faculty meeting, a regional meeting, or a state meeting, a similar language was used to emphasize agreed-upon principles. These layers, rather than the individual agency of any particular one influence, help explain why the values of individuals in the system are consistent despite differences in region and time.

To be sure, professors' collective intellectual capacity cannot be discounted. As many scholars have noted, black educators represented the largest group of intellectual leaders in the race. They were the talented tenth DuBois described—the would-be doctors and lawyers and politicians who were unable to participate in large numbers in other professions because of restrictions placed upon them. Thus, within the educational conversation were men and women of exemplary intellectual capacity. Their collective ability to create a system of schooling, in this context, must come as no surprise, despite the fact that historiography has never quite imaged them to be that smart. Moreover, they operated within a community ethos that expected them to help others in the race.

In the era in which they lived, these leaders understood well their goals. They lived in a world where the barriers and aspirations were easily visible. They forged collectives that bound them in advancing mutual interests and relied upon the strength of the whole to advance each individual part. Thus, their clearly defined goals result from a sense of urgency that emanated from their segregated circumstances. Without the dire circumstances, sense of urgency these created, and collective desire, the system may not have operated with the same degree of commitment.

Why have we been unable to identify the system of black schooling with its consistency of message, organizational structure, and purpose? The most reasonable response has been the failure of the literature to elevate the role of the professor. Had community voices been more valued in earlier periods, this omission would not have occurred. Since desegregation, black school communities have described the essential role of the professor in the schools they remember. However, by failing to seek an explanation for this standard elevation, the historiography has missed the central component through which the system of black education during segregation functioned. Black college leaders did not interact directly with communities typically; when they appeared in schools, they were invited by the professor. The teacher organizational leadership did not coincidentally address the ideas it did; to the contrary, the leadership that crafted the broad dissemination of ideas across the state was the same leadership most familiar with the problems across the state, the professor. At every marker, whether relationships between parents and school, superintendent and parents, teachers and graduate school, professional ideas and organizations, or professional ideas and schools, the professor appears as the unmarked conductor who helps the system operate.

Some years ago, six former black professors in Georgia reconvened on the second floor of the GTEA headquarters in Atlanta to help provide an understanding of the illusive history of the professor in contemporary scholarship. Sitting around the conference table where they had sat so many decades earlier and "argued with one another all night," they now sought to transmit some understanding of their world to a new generation. They understood their role in the black system of schooling, and they were frank about their disappointment in the desegregated system that occurred. Recounted former principal William Breeding, "We were working together more than they [whites] were and we were ahead of them in a whole lot of ways. We had it together." Byas echoed his point. "People tried to make us believe that whatever we were doing, even our best, was worse than their worst—which was not true." In their concerns about desegregation, they explain that "the first things they did was to [gain] control by getting rid of the black principals. [They understood that] we were the key to all of this." The black professors also frankly contrasted their role with that of their fellow white principals. As Byas notes, the "white principal did not have to assume many of the responsibilities aside from organizing the school that we had to assume in the interests of students."[4] Although the black professor was an administrative leader as well, the professors also played a number of other roles not required of their white colleagues.

The poem that appears in the introduction of this book captures the humility they valued during the period that may have kept the black professor hidden from public view. Although they knew the extent of the requirements of their job, black professors of the era sought no personal accolades for their activity. To the contrary, they valued a leader who people would barely know existed. "And when his work is done, the community will assume that they did it all themselves," or so the poem postulates. One might argue that professors did their jobs very well, for so communities have believed and so historians have written. A peek through the windows into Byas's world, however, reveals just how shallow such a conclusion may have been.

After All Data Are In
Some Notes on Methodology

As did *Their Highest Potential*, this book has relied on historical ethnographic methods. This methodology seeks to delineate a historical period, event, and/or person with attention to time and place but also to infuse meaning into the events through a subaltern lens that elucidates the meaning the period or event held for the person or people involved.[1] The combination of time and perspective is a central tenet of the methodology. The result is intended to be an account that captures the lived world of the participants while also tempering the account to provide context, explore contradictions, and determine the extent to which the story is one that unveils an understanding of a period in history.

Several points are important to convey about the interview data that form the foundation of Dr. Byas's perspective in this text and the juxtaposing of his memories with the document collection. The first is the consistency of his memory over time and with different audiences. This work covers a period of more than ten years, yet his reports of some episodes as given in the first interview parallel, often word for word, his restatement of the events in subsequent interviews. The information given in private interviews likewise parallels that he provides in public lectures, two of which I attended. In each of these public settings, the audience of listeners could easily have contradicted his accounts had the memories been represented incorrectly. However, rather than contradicting his stories, the nods and other verbal affirmations of the audience added validity to the accounts as I originally received them. Moreover, in public meetings with other principals and in private interviews with Emory's doctoral students, Dr. Byas's reported behaviors during the period remain constant. This layering of text has added confidence that his construction of events represent the world as he perceived himself to have experienced it. Although he is more than eighty years old, his memory has remained sharp, and his interviews are almost uniformly internally consistent.

Second, his memories have been consistently confirmed by his documents and other document collections. Some small discrepancies are evident between the verbal report and the paper trail, but typically these differences relate to his attribution of meaning about an event more than his report of the event itself. For example, Dr. Byas might report how much he valued the teachers' meetings, but he does not provide detail on the conferences, except the ones in which he led sessions. A perusal of the documents themselves was necessary to make these linkages. In some cases, his documents and those of others are used to carve an understanding of a period, organization, or event for a reader that exceeds his description. Chapters 3 and 4 are examples of such text. His interviews ascribe importance to the organizations described, but much of the account is derived from documentation rather than his memory, especially since some of the events in the organizations' histories are from periods prior to his participation.

Third, analysis was significantly enhanced by the identification of particular episodes that function as markers in Dr. Byas's life. These markers are events that capture salient moments of influence or explain particular behaviors. In the data analysis, I created a cognitive map of influences on his life as he perceived them, then contrasted this map with a conceptual map of leadership I created using the interviews and documents. Having completed this exercise, I was surprised to discover I had overly emphasized Dr. Byas's professional experiences in the story while minimizing his many descriptions of childhood and college. These analytic tools forced me to restructure the layers of influence and shape an account that did not diminish an aspect of his development that was actually central to his own view of the influences in his life. Chapter 2 is the direct result of the restructuring this exercise mandated.[2]

A central challenge in historical ethnographic work is subduing the temptation to become overly influenced by the lens of the informant. Reflecting upon our journey, I acknowledge Dr. Byas's growth in stature in my eyes over the years of our collaboration. However, while his accounts inspire an understanding of the events and his perspective on the events, his documents provided the corroboration and stabilizing points that crafted the interpretation of the story. Indeed, several of the connections between influential life events in different periods are not ones that Dr. Byas articulated in interviews but are ones generated as a result of the triangulation of repeated talk and document review. The juxtaposition of his verbal account and his documentation is sometimes reflected in the story and other times is masked. Indeed, once the credibility of the account was established, I regularly employed Dr. Byas's often colorful descriptions of events, as his language provides a useful way of introducing his personality and his world to readers who will never meet him in person.

Some boundaries are important to note. In constructing an account of his life as a professor, I have intentionally elevated the Gainesville story over the Douglasville story, despite the fact that he was a professor in both settings. This choice was made, in part, because the Gainesville story provided the most documentary detail. However, I also made the choice for organizational reasons. While stories of his interaction with teachers and with racism in the community in his earlier setting are compelling, the ideas typically recount the same perspectives that emerge full-blown in the Gainesville account. Where necessary, Douglasville events are used to provide the context for a Gainesville account, but I believe the ordering of the story is simplified by omitting a separate Douglasville analysis. Likewise, I have intentionally focused on Dr. Byas's life as a professor while excluding his life as a family member except where it directly influences the school story. Like other black professors of the period, Dr. Byas intentionally separated the compartments of his life, arguing that his family was better protected if it was not involved in, or many times not even knowledgeable about, the details of the challenges of his job. I have respected this historical bifurcation and provided no discussion of his activity beyond the school community.

Throughout this endeavor, Dr. Byas has served as a willing collaborator. His function has been twofold. During initial stages, he served as an elite informant, focusing specifically upon telling stories and supplying documents. When his accounts began to be ones in which I could anticipate the ending, I assumed data saturation and ceased formal interviews. However, in the final stages, his capacity to provide a member checks of the manuscript proved invaluable. He carefully read the first draft of the entire manuscript, offering cogent points that substantially redirected the final year of writing. In particular, he critiqued my lack of understanding of the significance of Fort Valley in his life, my failure to separate the superintendent from the community in explaining events in Gainesville, and my beginning the story of his life several chapters into the book (initially, I ordered the book by unveiling the professional networks over time and then introducing Dr. Byas and his school in the late 1950s). His questions, corrections, and additional observations forced me to reevaluate my interpretation of some of the events, and because of the significance of each idea to the content of the story, I made all necessary adjustments, including a general structural reorganization that changed the time sequence. During his reading of the revised manuscript, Dr. Byas supplied missing details, such as particular names and dates. Except in one account of the navy (which I subsequently modified using the new data he provided), he did not suggest revisions on my interpretations of events in this second check. On his third reading of the manuscript, he expressed appreciation but offered no advice except on the spelling of his wife's name. Because of these detailed readings of the manuscript, I have used a notation system throughout that typically provides links to specific interviews after major stories rather than documenting the source of every individual quote. However, the multiple interviews I had with Dr. Byas and his three readings of the manuscript give me confidence that all quotes accurately capture his perspective on a given subject.

How generalizable is Dr. Byas's story as a professor? Perhaps more than we have historically imagined and less than many would like. Because of the network substantiating his work and because of the reports of black professors throughout the South who behaved in similar ways, I believe the story has some wide applicability to professors in other settings. In particular, I believe the systemic structure was central in delivering a message commonly embraced by myriad professors throughout the South. However, as his later experiences indicate, Dr. Byas is also a man of exceptional intellect and fortitude. These personal attributes likely also made him a bit ahead of some other black professors during the era. If this difference elevates the particulars of his narrative over the activity of other professors such that his story creates an exceptional case, then I would argue the exceptional case also has merit, especially when it uncovers a network of black schooling that has generally failed to capture the historical imagination.

Dr. Byas is adamant that there must come a time when a reasonable man will declare that all data are in. This reasonable woman now so declares. The segregated world Byas inhabited is a complex one, and thus each chapter in this text could form a separate book. Future researchers will unravel the tensions inherent in the story of commonalities I have told. However, while future inquiry will unveil nuances and expanded meanings on the role of the professor, the perceptions provided are not likely to be altered, at least not as they held meaning for this particular professor. For his contributions to a new generation of educational talk, I am grateful; and with this appreciation, we bid the world of the professor good-bye.

Notes

ABBREVIATIONS

GSA Division of Negro Education, Georgia State Archives, Atlanta, Ga.
GTEA Horace Edward Tate Collection of the Georgia Teachers and Education Association, Atlanta, Ga.
SACSR Southern Association of Colleges and Schools Records, Emory University Manuscript, Archives, and Rare Book Library, Atlanta, Ga.
UBP Ulysses Byas Papers, Macon, Ga.

PREFACE

1. Walker, *Their Highest Potential*.

2. A perusal of editions of the *Clarion*, Fair Street High School's newspaper, from December 1957 to March 1968 reveals these activities in abundance. See, for example, "Tigers Win North Georgia Championship Title," "Dramatic Club Float Wins First Place," "Top Tunes Talk," "Homecoming Victory," "Student Council Cabinet," "Keep Smiling," and "Orchids and Onions," *Clarion* 1, no. 2, December 1957, UBP; "Butler's First Homecoming a Success," "Annual Staff Hard at Work," "Coronation Ceremony," and "NHA News," *Clarion* 6, no. 1, December 1962, UBP; "Staff Goes to Press Institute," "Homemakers of Tomorrow," "Tigers Fall under Perry's Pressure in North Georgia Play-Off Game," and "Dance Group Goes to State," *Clarion* 6, no. 2, March 1963, UBP; "Prom Results," "Spring Decorations," "The Seven Lamps of Wisdom to the Senior Class," "E. E. Butler School Band Participates in Band Festival," "Events of the Year (1962–63) at E. E. Butler High School," "Senior Class Play," "Senior Weather Report," "Class Night," "What It Takes to Be Superlative," "What's Next for Teenagers," "Fair Street News," and "Witchy-Witchy," *Clarion* 6, no. 3, May 1963, UBP; "Katz Korner," *Clarion* 7, no. 1, December 1963, UBP; "The Student Council and You," "Southern Regional School Press Institute," "Groups Compete for Awards," "Operation: Beatles vs. Butler," "Radio and News Club Organized (BAM)," and "Ware Breaks School Record," *Clarion* 7, no. 2, March 1964, UBP; "Senior Favorite Tunes," "Activities for the Chorus, Band, and N.H.A.," and "A Perfect Senior Boy or Girl," *Clarion* 7, no. 4, May 1964, UBP; "Butler Tigers Crashed into Record Book," *Clarion* 7, no. 5, December 1964, UBP; "Basketball Teams Hold Banquet," "Senior Play 'Just Ducky,'" "Savannah Band Trip," and "What F.H.A. Has Done for Me," *Clarion* 7, no. 3, May 1966, UBP; "First Parade: History Is Made" and "The New Addition to the Band," *Clarion* 9, no. 1, December 1966, UBP; "First Social Club at Butler High: 'The Esquire Club'" and "Sport Highlights," *Clarion* 10, no. 2, March 1967, UBP; "Hospitality Club

Members Tour Florida" and "Student Council in Action," *Clarion* 10, no. 3, June 1967, UBP; "Crimson Chorus Visits Butler" and "Tigers Have 0-3-3 Season," *Clarion* 10, no. 1, December 1967, UBP.

3. Walker, "Valued Segregated Schools in the South."

4. Report on visit to Dr. Ulysses Byas, Tuesday, March 26, 2002; used by permission of Randall Burkett. I have not used all of the materials described, but only those that inform Byas's years as a high school principal.

5. "Me Speak for Me" is a speech that Byas gave at a meeting of the National Association of Black School Educators; UBP.

6. For examples of revisionist ideas of qualitative research, see Denzin and Lincoln, *SAGE Handbook of Qualitative Research*.

7. *Green v. County School Board of New Kent County* was decided in 1968 by the Supreme Court. As noted by Gary Orfield and Susan Eaton, "this case challenged 'freedom of choice' plans that had been implemented by school districts throughout the South. Such plans gave the students the option of transferring from a black to a white school. . . . In *Green*, the Supreme Court ruled that schools must dismantle segregated dual (or segregated) systems 'root and branch' and that desegregation must be achieved with respect to facilities, staff, faculty, extracurricular activities, and transportation." See Orfield and Eaton, *Dismantling Desegregation*, xxii.

8. Because of his stature, Byas has attracted other biographers and educational leaders who have heralded his career. In *A Victory of Sorts: Desegregation in a Southern Community* (2003), a book based on his dissertation at Georgia State University, Winfred E. Pitts examines school desegregation in Gainesville and includes Byas and his school in the portrait. Another historian, Marilyn Padgett, is examining Byas's years as a superintendent, beginning with the tensions during his first years as superintendent at Tuskegee. In New York, the district where Byas last served as superintendent renamed a school in his honor, and materials about the school have appeared in the popular press. However, none of these portraits has explored his role as a school leader who both orchestrated successful programs in his own setting and simultaneously influenced, and was influenced by, a networked system of black school activity.

9. Although the informants do not make this connection, the practice of black communities calling a principal "professor" likely is linked to the practice in the Northeast of calling teachers "professors."

INTRODUCTION

1. The complete poem was reprinted with permission in the *Herald*, the official organ of the Georgia Teachers and Education Association. See the *Herald* 19, no. 2 (December 1951): 17, GTEA; and the *Herald* 19, no. 3 (February 1952): 22, GTEA. Original from Witter Bynner, trans., *The Way of Life According to Laotzu: An American Version* (New York: Capricorn Books, 1962).

2. The first set of studies on black segregated schools included Adair, *Desegregation*; Hundley, *The Dunbar Story*; Irvine and Irvine, "The Impact of the Desegregation Process on the Education of Black Students"; Faustine Jones, *A Traditional Model of Educational Excellence*; Rodgers, *The Black High School and Its Community*; Sowell, "Black Excellence"; and Sowell, "Patterns of Black Excellence." More recent scholarship emerged in the 1990s. Generally, it has been more widely disseminated and discussed than the earlier studies. See Beauboeuf-Lafontant, "A Movement against and beyond Boundaries"; Cecelski, *Along Freedom Road*; Foster, "Constancy, Connectedness, and Constraints in the Lives of African American Teachers"; Foster, "The Politics of Race"; Foster, *Black Teachers on Teaching*; Jeffries, "The Trickster Figure in African American Teaching"; McCullough-Garrett, "Reclaiming the African American Vision for Teaching"; Morris and Morris, *Creating Caring and Nurturing Educational Environments for African American Children*; Noblit and Dempsey, *The Social Construction of Virtue*; Walker, *Their Highest Potential*; Walker "Caswell County Training School"; and Walker, "African American Teachers in Segregated Schools in the South." These scholarly descriptions are accompanied by a number of locally published histories that span both time periods. See Lenwood G. Davis, *A History of Queen Street High School*; Edwards, Royster, and Bates, *The Education of Black Citizens in Halifax County*; and Tilford-Weathers, *A History of Louisville Central High School*. The work is comprehensively summarized in Walker, "Valued Segregated Schools in the South."

3. Walker, "Valued Segregated Schools in the South."

4. Bracey, "The High School Principalship in South Carolina"; Dean, "Social Studies in the Negro High Schools of Georgia"; Funches, "The Superintendent's Expectations of the Negro High School Principal in Mississippi"; Hatch, "A Study of the Leadership Ability of Negro High School Principals"; Scott, "Professional Functions of Negro Principals in the Public Schools of Florida"; Shaw, "A Study of the Behavior and Beliefs of Public School Principals"; Elizabeth Cooke Smith, "A Study of System-Wide Evaluation in Selected Schools for Negroes in Georgia"; and Thomas, "Some Aspects of Biracial Public Education in Georgia."

5. Jim Anderson has provided a compilation of the dissertations in *The Black Education Professoriate*.

6. Rodgers, *The Black High School and Its Community*; Irvine and Irvine, "The Impact of the Desegregation Process on the Education of Black Students"; Tillman, "African American Principals"; C. Calvin Smith, *Educating the Masses*.

7. In an earlier iteration designed to showcase the principalship in a variety of settings and tentatively titled *Principal Leaders*, these scholars and I intended to provide case overviews of individual principals. Although the story of each principal is now assuming its own individual form, we were all struck by the similarity of the stories during our collaboration. This similarity occurred despite the wide divergence in time and geographic location.

8. Franklin and Meier, *Black Leaders of the Twentieth Century*, xxv; Foner, "Black

Reconstruction Leaders at the Grass Roots." For examples of classic accounts that omit professors as agents, see McNeil, "Charles Hamilton Houston," 228; and Weare, "Charles Clinton Spaulding," 178.

9. Anderson, *The Black Education Professoriate*.

10. See Woyshner, Watras, and Smith Crocco, *Social Education in the Twentieth Century*; and Warren and Patrick, *Civic and Moral Learning in America*.

11. Anderson, *The Black Education Professoriate*.

12. Ibid.

13. For an examination of the Eurocentric culture as it was juxtaposed with black community culture during the Ocean Hill–Brownsville crisis, see Podair, *The Strike That Changed New York*, 52–65.

14. "System of schooling" is here defined as a network of people and organizations who operate with a similar identifiable mission; it is referred to as a "communication network" by Doug McAdam (*Political Process and the Development of Black Insurgency*).

15. Dilworth, "Widening the Circle," 104.

16. Leroy Davis, *A Clashing of the Soul*; Wadelington and Knapp, *Charlotte Hawkins Brown*.

17. Delpit, *Other People's Children*.

18. Tyson, *Blood Done Sign My Name*. The concept of SANKOFA is derived from the Akan people of West Africa. For Sankofa Web reference, see "The Meaning of the Symbolism of the Sankofa Bird," <http://www.duboislc.net/admin/tutorial .html>.

CHAPTER 1

1. *Self-Study of the Gainesville City Schools*, 4, 5, UBP; "Report of Visiting Committee on Re-Evaluation, Fair Street High School," 8, UBP.

2. "Principal's Annual Report—Negro Schools, 1958-1959," 2, Private Collection of School Records, Fair Street–Butler High Schools Alumni Association.

3. Hutchens and Smith, *Hall County, Georgia*, 58, 116, 123.

4. *Self-Study of the Gainesville City Schools*, 4-5, UBP; Sawyer, *Gainesville, 1900–2000*, 46.

5. Byas, interview, February 11, 2000.

6. See the following newspaper articles about the new courses and students' positive response to them: "Twenty-Five Enroll in French Class" and "Students Enroll in Chemistry Class," *Clarion* 1, no. 2, December 1957, UBP.

7. Georgia Conference on Educational Opportunities, *Georgia's Divided Education*, Atlanta, Ga., 1960, UBP; Byas, interview, February 11, 2000.

8. Ashmore, *The Negro and the Schools*.

9. Agnes Stephens, "A Hope Becomes a Reality," *Clarion* 1, no. 2, December 1957, UBP.

10. "Gainesville's School Board, [Report of] the School Expansion Committee," ca. 1959, 31–32, UBP.

11. For enrollment trends, see Ibid., 18. In 1957–58 enrollment was 267, up from 252 the previous the year. It would hold at 265 the following year, then shoot upwards to 345 by 1959–60. Dropout data are available in "Report of Visiting Committee on Re-Evaluation, Fair Street High School," 8, UBP.

12. Georgia Conference on Educational Opportunities, *Georgia's Divided Education*, 3; Pitts, "E. E. Butler High School," 149.

13. Funches, "The Superintendent's Expectations of the Negro High School Principal in Mississippi," 57.

14. Wilson states that Confederate soldiers served as superintendents and were carrying out their religious call. See Wilson, *Baptized in Blood*, 139–45. Kluger provides apt discussion of social science research concerning blacks. See Kluger, *Simple Justice*, 306–7; and Evans, *First Lessons in Georgia History*.

15. In 1970 school boards remained 99 percent white; see *Guide to Developing an Inclusive Integration Plan*, 1, GTEA.

16. Roche, *Restructured Resistance*; O'Brien, *The Politics of Race and Schooling*.

17. Byas explains that the black principals always had to make the superintendents believe they were meeting their low expectations. See, for example, Bays, interviews, January 20, 2000; December 1, 2000; and November 23, 2003.

18. Vontress, "Our Demoralizing Slum Schools," 79.

19. GTEA Principals, group interview, December 1, 2001.

20. Litwack, *Trouble in Mind*.

21. By late October 1949, Governor Herman Talmadge, known for his inflammatory remarks regarding black citizens of Georgia, warned the white citizens of the state that they would have to improve black schools or accept the consequences of failing to do so. Historian Thomas O'Brien credits Talmadge with masterminding the passage of the MFEP by "seiz[ing] on white fear of court-ordered school desegregation to gain support for [the] tax increase" (O'Brien, *The Politics of Race and Schooling*, 67–71). For black schools and the MFEP, see R. L. Cousins, "School Building Program for Negroes, 1952–54, Bi-Annual Report of the Division of Negro Education," GSA.

22. "Recently Adopted Policies of State Board of Education," *Herald* 20, no. 1 (October 1951): 10, GTEA; L. Orene Hall, "Annual Meeting of G.T.E.A. at Albany, Ga., 1952," *Herald* 20, no. 1 (October 1952): 14, GTEA.

23. Dean, "Social Studies in the Negro High Schools," 3.

24. Byas, interviews, November 12, 2004, and December 1, 2000.

25. Byas, interview, November 12, 2004. For examples, see *Herald* 19, no. 2 (December 1951): 4, GTEA; and *Herald* 23, no. 4 (April 1956): 34, GTEA.

26. Ulysses Byas to the School Board, January 30, 1957, UBP; Byas, interview, November 12, 2004.

27. Byas, interview, November 12, 2004.

28. Ibid.

29. Byas, interview, November 21, 2003.

30. Ulysses Byas to the School Board.

31. See "The School Suit in Irwin County," *Atlanta Constitution*, October 24, 1949.

32. Byas, interview, November 12, 2004.

33. Ibid.

34. Byas, interviews, November 12, 2004, and November 21, 2003.

35. Byas, interview, November 12, 2004.

36. I have reported portions of this sequence of events in an earlier article; see Walker and Byas, "The Architects of Black Schooling in the Segregated South."

37. "Matter of Opinion," *Herald* 24, no. 1 (Fall 1957): 15, GTEA.

38. "Report of Visiting Committee on Re-Evaluation, Fair Street High School," 9, 36, UBP.

39. "Public Relations Committee," *Herald* 23, no. 8 (May 1957): 28, GTEA. For national ideas, see *Herald* 34, no. 1 (Fall 1967): 9–13, GTEA, which provides data from the Miller NASSP 1956 bulletin.

40. "Curriculum Survey Conducted by the Fair Street Junior and Senior High School, Gainesville, Ga., 1957–58," 2–3, UBP.

41. Ibid., 3, 20–21, 26–27, UBP.

42. Ibid., 3–4, 14.

43. "The Principal Speaks," *Clarion* 1, no. 2, December 1957, UBP.

44. "Curriculum Survey Conducted by the Fair Street Junior and Senior High School," 14–20, UBP.

45. Ibid., 20–22.

46. Ibid., 32.

47. Byas reports that the survey had been printed in the newspaper's office by an associate. It is possible that the editor had seen the results prior to Byas's formal delivery; however, no evidence is available to indicate prior knowledge. Byas, interview, February 11, 2000.

48. "Fair Street Curriculum Study: Students Rate Poorly in Biological, Physical Sciences," *Gainesville Daily Times*, May 2, 1958, UBP; Sylvan Myer to Paul Anthony, Southern Regional Council, October 1, 1971, UBP.

49. Byas, interview, February 11, 2000; GTEA Principals, group interview, December 1, 2000; Pitts, "E. E. Butler High School," 140.

50. Joel Chandler Harris, the author of the Brer Rabbit tales, was a Georgia native. See Charles C. Jones, *Negro Myths from the Georgia Coast*.

51. Gaines, *Uplifting the Race*, 5; Gaines is extending the work of Hine, "Rape and the Inner Lives of Black Women," 292–97. In reference to the resistance exhibited by blacks, Robin Kelley also suggests the following: "The mask of 'grins and lies' enhanced black working people's invisibility and enabled them to wage

a kind of underground 'guerilla' battle with their employers." Additionally, Kelley draws on James C. Scott's concept of infrapolitics in defining the political history of oppressed people: "The political history of oppressed people cannot be understood *without* reference to infrapolitics [daily confrontations, evasive actions, and stifled thoughts], for these daily acts have a cumulative effect on power relations. While the meaning and effectiveness of various acts differ according to particular circumstances, they do make a difference, whether intended or not"; see Kelley, *Race Rebels*, 7–8.

52. W. F. Crawl, "The Principal and His Image," *Herald* 33, no. 3 (Convention Issue 1967): 25, GTEA.

53. Wilkins, "Freedom Tactics for 18,000,000," 4.

CHAPTER 2

1. Harris, *Defying the Odds*.

2. Sullivan, *Georgia: A State History*, 146, 199; Painter, *Creating Black Americans*, 210. Bartley also overviews the status of all Georgians, noting the depression of economic opportunity that confronted both races; see Bartley, *Creation of Modern Georgia*, 177.

3. Sullivan, *Georgia: A State History*, 143–44; Bond, *Education of the Negro*, 288.

4. As one example of the excitement among blacks in the areas of entertainment and sports, see Painter, *Creating Black Americans*, 214. For information on Georgia citizens with radios, see Pound and Thompson, *Georgia Citizenship*, 276.

5. Byas, interviews, August 10, 2007, and September 5, 1998.

6. Walter W. Felder to Whom It May Concern, 11 January 1990, UBP. Felder was the director of pupil personnel services for Bibb County Public Schools. The text of this letter provides the academic transcript for Byas, along with a list of the teachers for each grade. Of note, the record lists Byas's mother as Mrs. M. Sharpe, a marital title that does not reflect the home status of Byas during his early years.

7. Georgia was the last state to approve free public high schools, and not until 1912 did the state adopt a constitutional amendment supporting public high school education for children of either race. The situation was much more dismal for blacks than for whites. In 1916 only four public high schools were available in the state for blacks, and none of these were in Macon. See Orr, *History of Education in Georgia*, 320; Joiner, Bonner, Shearouse, and Smith, *A History of Public Education in Georgia*, 225; Bartley, *The Creation of Modern Georgia*, 155, 165, 193; "Division of Negro Education Report, 1940–42," 57–58, GSA; and Garrod, Ward, Robinson, and Killkenny, *Souls Looking Back*, 175. It is important to note that white children were also frequently absent from school; Orr reports that both public and private elementary school attendance was less than 56 percent of the total number of children of elementary school age (Orr, *History of Education in Georgia*, 318).

8. Dean, "Social Studies in the Negro High Schools of Georgia," 8.

9. Ibid., 11.

10. Most Byas interviews through the nine-year period are strikingly consistent in their chronology, story focus, and language. His enthusiasm for industrial education, however, only became apparent in later interviews and was often prompted by researchers' questions. Byas, telephone interview, August 30, 2007.

11. This argument of reciprocity between school and community is further explained in Walker, *Their Highest Potential*.

12. Pound and Thompson, *Georgia Citizenship*, 246. Byas's comments on the restrictions in the navy are found in "Veterans Observe Day," <http://www.13wmaz .com/news/new-story.aspx?storyid=45475> (Web editor is Marilyn Peguero).

13. Painter, *Creating Black Americans*, 225, 232; O'Brien, *The Politics of Race and Schooling*, 36; Byas, interview, January 20, 2000.

14. Litwack, *Trouble in Mind*, 96; Hurt, *African American Life in the Rural South*, 97.

15. "Veterans Administration Reports," *Herald* 21, no. 3 (February 1954): 6, GTEA.

16. For a review of college requirements for social studies teachers and Fort Valley in particular, see Dean, "Social Studies in the Negro High Schools of Georgia," 173, 175, 177.

17. Byas, telephone interview, June 5, 2007, and ca. August/September 2007.

18. Byas, telephone interview, June 5, 2007. Byas's first description of Fort Valley is captured in an interview with the author, September 5, 1998. In the subsequent memo check, he elevates the meaning of earlier reported events.

19. Byas, interview, September 5, 1998.

20. During this era, many black teachers were returning to college to receive the degrees that Georgia had mandated during the 1940s as prerequisites for them to maintain their jobs. As importantly, their professional association, GTEA, was also adamant in its belief that black teachers should gain higher levels of education.

21. The Fort Valley story and its significance in Byas's life are captured in detail in Byas, interviews, September 5, 1998, and June 5, 2007.

22. Details on the scholarship program are available in Pirkle, "Study of the State Scholarship Aid Program for Negroes in Georgia." For emergent work on this subject, see Jordan-Taylor, "I Am Not Autherine Lucy!'

23. "Syllabus for Educational Foundations, Education 200Fa," UBP.

24. For his work, Byas received a B– written in blue; however, "wrong paper" written in red makes it difficult to understand the actual evaluation. Education 200Fa, paper submitted by Ulysses Byas, fall semester 1950, UBP.

25. Ibid.

26. Byas recounts the story of Ruth Strang on multiple occasions. See, for example, Byas, interviews, December 1, 2000; June 5, 2007; and September 5, 1998.

27. "Byas: First Year Teaching" Folder, UBP.

28. Ibid.

29. Ibid.

30. GTEA Forty-Third Convention Program, Atlanta, Ga., April 1961, 2, UBP; Hawes Obituary, Monday, January 15, 1996, St. Mary's CME Church, Elberton, Ga., UBP; Byas résumé, UBP.

CHAPTER 3

1. "Division of Negro Education Report, 1958," GSA; Byas, interview, September 5, 1998.

2. "Faculty Evaluation of Fair Street High School, Gainesville, Georgia," UBP.

3. Byas, interviews, September 5, 1998, and January 20, 2000.

4. By 1961 Georgia, with fifty-nine approved black schools, was second only to Florida in total number. Numbers for 1961 are from Geiger, *Proceedings of the Sixty-Sixth Annual Meeting of the Southern Association*, 77–93, UBP. The reports give absolute numbers of schools, and comparisons are made based on these absolute numbers. Without data on the number of schools in each state, no analysis can be made on the proportional representation. The earlier numbers are derived from Geiger, *Proceedings of the Sixty-Sixth Annual Meeting of the Southern Association*. The Evaluative Criteria of 1950 are reflected in Fair Street's faculty evaluation for its continuing approval in 1960. See "Faculty Evaluation of Fair Street High School, Gainesville, Georgia," UBP.

5. Among the other four, Florida ranked first with forty-six schools, followed closely by North Carolina with forty-four and Texas with forty-one.

6. Data on attendance is derived from a compilation of lists available in *Proceedings of the Association of Colleges and Secondary Schools, 1957*, 7–25, UBP.

7. "Minutes of Executive Committee," box 1, SACSR; "Background Paper on SACS," box 15, SACSR; Cozart, *History of the Association of Colleges and Secondary Schools*, 1.

8. Early names of the two associations vary. In minutes of the Southern Association of Colleges and Schools, the black association is referred to as both the Southern Association of Negro Colleges and the Association of Colleges and Secondary Schools for Negroes. According to Cozart's institutional history, the different names in the archival record can be explained by the fact that the Association of Colleges for Negro Youth was a predecessor of the Association of Colleges and Secondary Schools. The reorganization occurred in 1932 and had a "larger base than that provided for the parent body and [was] designed to include secondary as well as collegiate levels of training" (Cozart, *History of the Association of Colleges and Secondary Schools*, 2). Throughout, I refer to them as the "Association," as this is the term by which they most often refer to themselves. Early records also demonstrate the extent to which black educators debated the nature of their relationship to the Southern Association—specifically, whether they should lobby to be an arm of that organization or remain autonomous.

9. J. T. Cater, "What Adjustment or Adaptation, if Any, Should Be Made in the

Application of Standards to Negro Schools?," Association of Colleges and Secondary Schools for Negroes Proceedings (hereafter cited as Association Proceedings), 1935, box 20, SACSR. Jack would later go on to argue that the standards of white colleges should be "rigidly applied" to Negro colleges. In this position, he would be in agreement with his black colleagues, albeit likely for different reasons.

10. Geiger, *Proceedings of the Sixty-Sixth Annual Meeting of the Southern Association*, 7, 145, 175; Cozart, *History of the Association of Colleges and Secondary Schools*, 10.

11. Cater, "What Adjustment or Adaptation," 65–66, Association Proceedings, 1935, box 20, SACSR; "Minutes for 7th Annual Meeting at State Teachers College," Association Proceedings, 1940, 19, box 20, SACSR; "Resolution Adopted by the Commission on Secondary Schools," Association Proceedings, 1940, 38–39, box 20, SACSR.

12. Cozart, *History of the Association of Colleges and Secondary Schools*, 17–18.

13. Ibid., 5–6, 8–9, 21, 25. See also "Report of the Commission on Higher Institutions," Association Proceedings, 1935, 23, box 20, SACSR.

14. Cozart, *History of the Association of Colleges and Secondary Schools*, 6, 8–9.

15. Ibid., 4.

16. Quoted in ibid., 19–20.

17. In *The Black Education Professoriate*, Anderson describes the lack of a black professional organization.

18. "Minutes of Executive Committee," box 1, SACSR; Byas, interview, March 16, 2006.

19. Sixty-Second Annual Meeting of the Southern Association of Colleges and Secondary Schools, box 18, SACSR.

20. Cozart, *History of the Association of Colleges and Secondary Schools*, 2, 58; *Proceedings of the Association of Colleges and Secondary Schools, 1957*, 1–25, UBP; four Virginia Union postcards, one circa 1941 and the others undated, are in the Melford Walker Southern History Archival Collection.

21. I use the term "integrated" rather than "desegregated" in descriptions in which integration is what the black group members sought and expected. Not until later would they realize that their efforts had netted, at best, desegregation. For descriptions of these meetings, see "Report of the Liaison Committee," Association Proceedings, 1953, box 20, SACSR. See also William Kilpatrick, "Education and the World We Live In," *Herald* 7, no. 1 (July 1940): 7–12, GTEA.

22. Association Proceedings, 1952, 26–28, box 20, SACSR; "Report of the Liaison Committee," Association Proceedings, 1953, 37–38, box 20, SACSR.

23. Cozart, *History of the Association of Colleges and Secondary Schools*, 27.

24. Buell Gallagher, "The Secure Community," in *Proceedings of the Association of Colleges and Secondary Schools, 1957*, 56–59, UBP.

25. Anderson, *The Black Education Professoriate*, 30.

26. See "Panel Discussion—Educational Challenges to Member Institutions of

Low Comparative Scores on Standardized Tests" and "Process of Improving Education and Its Product," in *Proceedings of the Association of Colleges and Secondary Schools, 1957*, 81–103, UBP.

27. *Proceedings of the Association of Colleges and Secondary Schools, 1957*, 18, 103–4, UBP. Proctor's transfer to A&T is documented in Gavins, *The Perils and Prospects of Southern Black Leadership*, 166.

28. The link between the Nabrits can be found in the obituaries of both. See Kimetris N. Baltrip, "Samuel Nabrit, 98, Scientist and a Pioneer in Education, Dies," *New York Times*, January 6, 2004; and Eric Pace, "James M. Nabrit Jr. Dies at 97; Led Howard University," *New York Times*, December 30, 1997.

29. Geiger, *Proceedings of the Sixty-Sixth Annual Meeting of the Southern Association*, 161, UBP; *Proceedings of the Association of Colleges and Secondary Schools, 1957*, 33–34, UBP.

30. Oliver Hill, interview. Kluger provides a compelling biography of Mordecai Johnson and his creation of the Howard Law School in *Simple Justice*, 123–26.

31. The advocacy of the Association in 1955 is available in "Resolutions," Association Proceedings, 1955, 34, box 20, SACSR.

32. "Next Steps in Education," Association Proceedings, 1953, 106–9, box 20, SACSR.

33. At a June 21 gathering with the president of both associations, the president of the Southern Association "open[ed] the meeting with the laconic remark, 'Well, it seems the Supreme Court has knocked our projected deadline into a cocked hat.'" His reference was to a previously planned merger deadline of 1960, one likely influenced by the pending *Brown* decision. After this observation, he motioned to "invite members of the Association to meet with respective and appropriate committees of the Southern Association at the national convention in Louisville met with instant and unanimous support" ("President's Message," Association Proceedings, 1954, 23, box 20, SACSR).

34. According to the 1957 Association program, Howard University first received its "approval" rating from the Association in 1934 under Johnson's leadership, joined that year by only seven other of the now sixty college institutions. Only three black colleges received the rating before Howard's approval. Of the 308 high schools who held approved status in 1957, only 10 had preceded Howard in membership. See *Proceedings of the Association of Colleges and Secondary Schools, 1957*, 1–25, UBP; and Mordecai W. Johnson, "Education and the Good Life," in Cozart, *History of the Association of Colleges and Secondary Schools*, 97–99. Cozart omits Howard in his list of founding institutions (see pages 2–6 and the listing of member institutions on pages 160–62.) However, since he lists the instrumental role of O. W. Holmes, dean at Howard during these same years, the records of the 1957 meeting with its dating of Howard's induction are likely more accurate.

35. Quotations in this paragraph and the next two paragraphs from Mordecai W. Johnson, "Achieving World Perspectives by Improving the Quality of Edu-

cation," in *Proceedings of the Association of Colleges and Secondary Schools, 1957,* 103–13, UBP.

36. *Proceedings of the Association of Colleges and Secondary Schools, 1957,* 26, 103, UBP.

37. Speech summarized using Cozart, *History of the Association of Colleges and Secondary Schools,* 19–20. A description of the panel on which this was presented is available in "Critical Problems in the Education of Negroes in the Southern Region," Association Proceedings, 1954, 26, box 20, SACSR.

38. Anderson, *The Black Education Professorate,* 29.

39. Cozart, *History of the Association of Colleges and Secondary Schools,* 103–7.

40. Preston-Grimes, "Teaching Democracy."

41. "Curriculum Offerings in Negro Colleges Contribute to Functional Citizenship," Association Proceedings, 1935, 36–63, box 20, SACSR.

42. "Panel Jury Discussions," Association Proceedings, 1935, 83–88, box 20, SACSR.

43. Ralph J. Bunche, "The Negro's Stake in the World Crisis," Association Proceedings, 1940, 58–84, box 20, SACSR; John Temple Graves, "Not Made to Die," Association Proceedings, 1940, 84, box 20, SACSR. The role of black newspapers during World War I is chronicled in Jordan, *Black Newspapers and America's War for Democracy;* the perspective of black newspapers on World War II and its Double V campaign is described in Savage, *Broadcasting Freedom.*

44. "Report of Commission on Secondary Schools," Association Proceedings, 1935, 26–27, box 20, SACSR; "What Are the Practices among Colleges and Secondary Schools with Reference to Scholarship Aid and Athletic Subsidies?," Association Proceedings, 1935, 68–72, SACSR. See also Association Proceedings, 1935, 73–80, box 20, SACSR.

45. "Report of the Commission on Higher Institutions," Association Proceedings, 1935, 5, box 20, SACSR.

46. Urban, *Gender, Race, and the National Education Association,* 1.

47. "A.T.A. Highlights from the 59th Annual Convention, Miami, Florida," *Herald* 29 (Winter 1962): 11, GTEA.

48. Perry, *History of the American Teachers Association,* 259, 331; Bulletin of the American Teachers Association, May 1954, UBP.

49. "Across the Editor's Desk," *Herald* 21 (February 1954): 8, GTEA.

50. Cozart, *History of the Association of Colleges and Secondary Schools,* 92–153.

51. Perry, *History of the American Teachers Association,* 51–52, 220.

52. Urban, *Gender, Race, and the National Education Association,* 213.

53. Byas, interview, September 5, 1998.

54. Cozart, *History of the Association of Colleges and Secondary Schools,* 6.

55. Horace Mann Bond, "Improving Educational Performance: It Has, It Can, It Must Happen!," in *Proceedings of the Association of Colleges and Secondary Schools, 1957,* 83–89, UBP. Quote from ibid., 88.

56. Byas, interview, March 16, 2006.

57. This discussion omits the white speakers who also attended the Association meetings and some of the administrative details. The goal here is to provide a snapshot of the curriculum that might be expected at an Association meeting.

58. "Minutes of the Thirty-First Annual Meeting of the Association of Colleges and Secondary Schools," in *Proceedings of the Association of Colleges and Secondary Schools, 1964*, 16, UBP; Byas, interview, March 16, 2006.

59. Byas, telephone interview, April 28, 2006.

60. Byas, interview, January 20, 2000.

61. Urban, *Gender, Race, and the National Education Association*, 1.

62. Byas, interview, September 5, 1998.

63. A 1938 required textbook on Georgia history was written by Lawton B. Evans, a white superintendent of schools in Augusta. His vision of race confirms Byas's belief that white superintendents could not be expected to participate in fruitful conversations about racial equality at professional meetings. While describing the increasing educational opportunities for all children in Georgia, including the capacity of the children to have "this little book which you are now reading" for free, Evans fails to even mention black education. Indeed, his discussion of slavery includes the following: "Being well treated, they were free from care, and were therefore happy and devoted to their masters" (Evans, *First Lessons in Georgia History*, 232, 370).

64. Urban, *Gender, Race, and the National Education Association*, 212–15.

65. Byas, interview, January 20, 2000.

66. Byas, interview, September 5, 1998.

CHAPTER 4

1. Gaines, *Uplifting the Race*.

2. Byas, telephone interview, August 19, 2004.

3. "LaGrange Teachers Association," *Herald* 23, no. 3 (February 1956): 37, GTEA.

4. "By-Laws for the School Masters Club of Georgia," UBP.

5. *Proceedings of the Association of Colleges and Secondary Schools, 1957*, 28, UBP; Byas, interview, March 16, 2006; Tate, interview, November 3, 2006.

6. For examples of the men relating national ideas to the local level, see "Region One Classroom Teachers Organize," *Herald* 23, no. 3 (February 1956): 36, GTEA. Names of principals were provided by Byas; however, the list of principals and their affiliation is available in "Report to School Masters Club on Custodial, Clerical, Budgeting and Guidance Services in Nineteen Member Schools," in George Parker, T. N. Hill, and J. C. Reese to Members of the Masters Club, April 25, 1958, UBP. Data on school membership in the Association is available in Cozart, *History of the Association of Colleges and Secondary Schools*, 8.

7. Byas, interview, March 16, 2006.

8. Byas, telephone interview, January 15, 2007.

9. "High School Daily Schedule: Some Reasons Why," "E. E. Butler High School Student Registration," "Daily Schedule of High School Recitations," and "Tabulation Sheet Course Registration," UBP.

10. "Report to the School Master's Club," UBP; *Proceedings of the Association of Colleges and Secondary Schools, 1959*, 11–13, UBP.

11. Walker and Tompkins, "Caring in the Past."

12. Cozart, *History of the Association of Colleges and Secondary Schools*, 20.

13. Byas, interview, March 16, 2006. Byas reports that principals were being forced to meet the criteria already because all schools were being evaluated by the same criteria. However, the principals did not at the time realize that nothing else would be required of them when they became full members.

14. "Strengthen Local Associations: A Guide for GTEA Unit Leaders," 5, GTEA.

15. "Past Presidents of GTEA Make Good College Teachers," *Herald* 23, no. 8 (May 1957): 29, GTEA.

16. "President's Message," *Herald* 20, no. 1 (October 1952): 6, GTEA. Information on the GTEA headquarters can be found in "GTEA Purchases a Home," *Herald* 20, no. 1 (October 1952): 20–21, GTEA.

17. "President's Message: President Homer T. Edwards," *Herald* 17, no. 4 (April 1951): 7, GTEA.

18. "Proposed Structure of Georgia Teachers and Education Association," *Herald* 25, no. 4 (Winter 1958): 32, GTEA; "Past Presidents of GTEA Make Good College Teachers," *Herald* 23, no 8 (May 1957): 29, GTEA; "Board of Directors," *Herald* 23, no. 8 (May 1957): 3, GTEA.

19. Educators who joined the GTEA automatically received its professional journal, the *Herald*. In its articulated purpose, the journal is reported to have the "assigned function . . . to reach every Negro teacher in Georgia, carrying the message to aid in fostering a better educational system for Negroes in Georgia" (*Rising in the Sun*, 49, 54, GTEA).

20. "President's Message," *Herald* 23, no. 7 (Convention Issue 1957): 4, GTEA. Information on the annual program is available in the same volume (4, 8–9).

21. "The 1952 Annual Meeting," *Herald* 19, no. 4 (April 1952): 6, GTEA.

22. Figures for the 1958 Annual Convention are in "State Convention in Retrospect," *Herald* 24, no. 3 (May 1958): 15, GTEA.

23. Flyer, 1961, GTEA. The total membership for 1957 is found in "Picked up from the Field: From the Executive Secretary's Note Book," *Herald* 23, no. 6 (Winter 1956–57): 20, GTEA; "Annual Meeting," *G.T.E.A. Newsletter* 1, no. 1 (August 1962): 6, GTEA.

24. "State Convention Pan-O-Ram," *Herald* 23, no. 8 (May 1957): 6, GTEA.

25. Lewis, *W. E. B. DuBois: Biography of Race*; and Lewis, *W. E. B. DuBois: The Fight for Equality*.

26. Urban, *Black Scholar*.

27. Johnson spoke at the annual GTEA meeting focused on utilizing the Minimum Foundation Program of Education of Georgia to obtain an extended school program. The theme for that year was "Toward Better Education for Georgia Youth." See "Suggested Agenda for Regional GTEA Meetings, 1951–'52," *Herald* 19. no. 2 (December 1951): 20–21, GTEA.

28. The story of Ballard-Hudson has been chronicled by Titus Brown in *Faithful, Firm, and True*.

29. "R. J. Martin Installed as President of ATA," *Herald* 32, no. 1 (Fall 1965): 12, GTEA; "ATA Moves to Atlanta," *Herald* 30, no. 1 (Fall 1963): 24, GTEA. For ATA convention reports, see "Editorial: GTEA to Serve as Host to ATA," *Herald* 23, no. 3 (February 1956): 2, GTEA; and "61st Annual ATA Convention in Atlanta," *Herald* 30, no. 4 (Spring 1964): 29, GTEA. For information on Ira Reid's presence, see "Convention Echoes," *Herald* 27, no. 2 (Spring 1961): 17–21, GTEA.

30. Roche, *Restructured Resistance*, 179.

31. "A New Day in NEA-GTEA Relations," *Herald* 19, no. 1 (October 1951): 8, GTEA. For Emory advertisement, see "1965 Summer at Emory," *Herald* 31, no. 3 (Convention Issue 1965): 38, GTEA; see also "Six Weeks Institute for Teachers," *Herald* 31, no. 3 (Convention Issue 1965): 34, GTEA. For discussion of civil rights legislation, see "We've Got It Started: The Elementary and Secondary Education Act of 1965 Is Only the Beginning," *Herald* 32, no. 1 (Fall 1965): insert, GTEA.

32. "Program: Annual Meeting," *Herald* 23, no. 7 (Convention Issue 1957): 8–9, GTEA.

33. Detail on Opal Dixon Butler is available in "In Memoriam: Mrs. Opal Dixon Butler," *Herald* 27, no. 1 (Convention Issue 1961): 17, GTEA; and "Annual Meeting of G.T.E.A. at Albany, Ga., 1952," *Herald* 20, no. 1 (October 1952): 14, GTEA.

34. Byas, interview, January 20, 2000.

35. Ibid; "Annual Meeting of G.T.E.A. at Albany, Ga., 1952."

36. "Annual Meeting of G.T.E.A. at Albany, Ga., 1952." For teacher of the year information, see "Miss Mattie L. Moon Receives Honor," *Clarion* 1, no. 2, December 1957, UBP.

37. "Our President Speaks: Our Association Faces Another Challenge," *Herald* 32, no. 1 (Fall 1965): 5, GTEA; "Teacher of the Year—1962," *Herald* 28, no. 4 (Spring 1962): 4, GTEA; Laura Johnson, "Dilemma of a Dropout," *Herald* 29, no. 3 (Convention Issue 1963): 18–19, GTEA; "Guidance for the Dropout," *Herald* 30, no. 4 (Spring 1964): 23, GTEA.

38. Byas, interview, January 20, 2000.

39. *Rising in the Sun*, 88, GTEA.

40. "From the President's Desk: President's Message," *Herald* 27, no. 2 (Spring 1961): 4, GTEA; "Convention Echoes," *Herald* 27, no. 2 (Spring 1961): 17, GTEA.

41. "Region Seven," *Herald* 23, no. 8 (May 1957): 20, GTEA; "Notes from the

Field: Regional Teachers Conference, Region IV," *Herald* 23, no. 7 (Convention Issue 1957): 10, GTEA.

42. Earlier that year, Moon had lost the GTEA's state teacher-of-the-year award by only a few points. With her election as director, she became the first female to hold a directorship position in her region. For directorship information, see "Gainesville Teacher's Are Host to Region IV, GT&EA," *Clarion* 6, no. 1, December 1962, UBP. For teacher-of-the-year information, see "Miss Mattie L. Moon Receives Honor," *Clarion* 1, no. 2, December 1957, UBP. *Hall County, Georgia*, by Hutchens and Smith, also lists Mattie Moon as one of the county's distinguished citizens (97).

43. "Notes from the Field: Regional Teachers Conference, Region IV," *Herald* 23, no. 7 (Convention Issue 1957): 10, GTEA.

44. "Regional Meetings," *Herald* 23, no. 4 (April 1956): 31–36, GTEA.

45. "A Suggested Calendar for a Local Association," from "Strengthen Local Associations: A Guide for GTEA Unit Leaders," 24, GTEA; "A Suggestive Program for Regional Meetings G.T.E.A.," *Herald* 16, no. 3 (February 1950): 26, GTEA.

46. "Regional Meetings," *Herald* 23, no. 4 (April 1956): 31–36, GTEA.

47. Regional membership standing is available via chart in *Herald* 24, no. 3 (Convention Issue 1958): 23, GTEA. The chart also demonstrates that Region Three (65 percent) and Region Nine (70 percent) are the regions with the smallest percentage of teachers holding GTEA membership. The *Herald* also reports regional meetings in the following: "Region Seven," *Herald* 23, no. 8 (May 1957): 20, GTEA; "Notes from the Field: Regional Teachers Conference, Region IV," *Herald* 23, no. 7 (Convention Issue 1957): 10, GTEA; "Annual Meeting Region I, GTEA," *Herald* 28, no. 3 (Convention Issue 1962): 20, GTEA.

48. "Regional Meetings," *Herald* 25, no. 4 (Winter 1958): 21–22, GTEA.

49. "Turner County Teachers Association," *Herald* 23, no. 6 (Winter 1956–57): 9, GTEA; "Barrow County," "Madison County," and "Cornelia High School," *Herald* 23, no. 6 (Winter 1956–57): 10, 15, GTEA; "Fulton County Teachers and National Association," *Herald* 23, no. 8 (May 1957): 20, GTEA; "The Decatur County Teachers Assn. Presents," *Herald* 23, no. 7 (Convention Issue 1957): 11, GTEA.

50. "Turner County Teachers Association," *Herald* 23, no. 6 (Winter 1956–57): 9, GTEA.

51. "Suggested Outline for Regional Programs, 1962–1963," GTEA. Other themes over the years included "A Unified Profession Enhances Good Human Relations," Forty-Third Annual Convention Program, Georgia Teachers and Education Association, Atlanta, Ga., April 1961, GTEA; "Annual Meeting of G.T.E.A. at Albany, Ga., 1952," *Herald* 20, no. 1 (October 1952): 14, GTEA.

52. See examples of references to principal leadership in "Our New President Speaks," *Herald* 30, no. 4 (Spring 1964): 4, GTEA; "Principal Retires at Newnan's Central High School" and "Principal W. G. Dixon—Veteran Educator—Retires

after 43½ Years of Meritorious Service," *Herald* 32, no. 1 (Fall 1965): 18–19, GTEA; and James A. Hawes, "Notes from the President's Desk," *Herald* 32, no. 4 (Spring 1966): 5, GTEA.

53. "From the Editor's Desk: Congratulations," *Herald* 19, no. 4 (April 1952): 8, GTEA.

54. In 1964 principals were also noted as continuing their leadership roles, still typically serving as presidents of the GTEA and in other regional and local positions. See "Our New President Speaks," *Herald* 30, no. 4 (Spring 1964): 4, GTEA.

55. For a description of female leadership, see report on the election of Beatrice L. Dominis to head the elementary division of the GTEA in "Notes from the Field: Spalding County," *Herald* 16, no. 3 (February 1950): 31.

56. Byas, interview, January 20, 2000.

57. Ulysses Byas, "Our Georgia Schools," *Herald* 29, no. 2 (Winter 1962): 16–20, GTEA.

58. "Mid-Winter Professional Program," December 11, 1965, UBP.

59. GTEA Principals, group interview, December 1, 2000.

60. While the *Herald* did not report the details of regional and county meetings as regularly as it reported annual meetings, and despite the fact that such reports became increasingly rare after 1960, the journal's coverage was sufficiently consistent across the years to document regional and county meetings as part of the rubric of the GTEA structure and to demonstrate that, in some places, the structure was operative.

61. "Region Six," *Herald* 22, no. 4 (April 1955): 22–23, GTEA; "Principals and Supervisors Meet in Region Four," *Herald* 30, no. 2 (Winter 1963): 15, GTEA.

62. "Region Six," *Herald* 22, no. 4 (April 1955): 22–23, GTEA; "Dekalb County News," *Herald* 22, no. 3 (February 1955): 28–29, GTEA.

63. "Principals' Conference," *Herald* 16, no. 3 (February 1950), 16, 29, GTEA.

64. Ibid., 5, 29, GTEA.

65. "Principals' Council Meets in Buena Vista," *Herald* 22, no. 1 (October 1954): 31, GTEA; "Principals' Conference," *Herald* 16, no. 3 (February 1950): 16, 20, 29, GTEA. The theme of the Fourteenth Annual Principals' Conference was "Public Relations and Educational Statesmanship"; see "Principals' Conference," *Herald* 19, no. 2 (December 1951): 14, GTEA. The theme of the Fifteenth Annual Principals' Conference was "Implementing Today's School Program"; see "Principals' Conference," *Herald* 20, no. 2 (December 1952): 7, 30, GTEA; and "Principals and Jeanes Conference," *Herald* 24, no. 1 (Fall 1957): 21, GTEA.

66. Although Byas was reportedly a leader in various meetings of principals, few records provide detailed descriptions of the activity at those meetings. Even less information is available about the principals' workshops held annually at Atlanta University. However, one letter in Byas's collection, written by two consul-

tants and a coordinator and dated July 20, 1965, thanks him for his participation in a workshop for principals at the university: "We feel certain that there is added knowledge, understanding and interest in . . . [s]cheduling as a direct result of your deliberation." This reference demonstrates the extensiveness of the audience that would learn of the college-type schedule that Byas was then developing with his teachers. See Byas, interview, August 10, 2000.

67. The *Herald* includes a section that describes activities in the schools, and the thematic descriptions often mirror GTEA topics. However, no direct correlation can be found between a principal returning from a state meeting and subsequent changes adopted by the teachers in his or her school. One might infer that the principal was the link; however, this cannot be directly substantiated. For examples of themes on testing and dropouts that appear linked to larger discussions in the GTEA, see "Testing Program," *Herald* 28, no. 4 (Spring 1962): 25–26, GTEA; and "Dilemma of a Dropout," *Herald* 29, no. 3 (Convention Issue 1963): 18–19, GTEA.

68. Byas, interview, February 28, 2002.

CHAPTER 5

1. Because the Hall County public schools consolidated in 1957, rural students were bused to Fair Street. These numbers helped increase enrollment. The class of sixty-two was the last one to graduate from Fair Street. See Hutchens and Smith, *Hall County, Georgia*, 69, 73. Butler graduated from Morehouse College and Meharry Medical School, interned in Kansas City, and began practicing in Gainesville in 1936. See Lovie Smith, "History of Our School," *Clarion* 6, no. 1, December 1962, UBP. For dedication details, see "Dedication" program, E. E. Butler High School, November 24, 1963, UBP.

2. Byas, interview, February 22, 2000.

3. "Gainesville Teachers Are Host to Region IV, GT&EA," *Clarion* 6, no. 1, December 1962, UBP. Butler would also host the Region Four meeting again in December 1966, with the theme "Excellence — an Individual Responsibility." See "Region Four Meets at Butler," *Clarion* 9, no. 1, December 1966, UBP.

4. "President's Message," *Herald* 24, no. 3 (Convention Issue 1958): 4, GTEA. Troup spoke at the Forty-Third Annual Convention; see "Convention Echoes," *Herald* 27, no. 1 (Spring 1961): 17, GTEA. Horace Mann Bond, "Teaching: A Calling to Fulfill," *Herald* 29, no. 3 (Convention Issue 1963): 5–6, GTEA. Evoking Horace Mann, Bond uses a quote that embodies Mann's concepts, but he ignores the ways in which Mann himself did not always hold to his own ideals. Given the historiography of the period, however, Bond's understanding of Mann's complete activities in the area of public schooling may have been limited. Moreover, to hold Mann to his own standards and use them to make an argument would be entirely consistent with the ways in which black educators used the ideas of white edu-

cators, even when the white educators may not have intended their ideas to be used by black educators or applied to black children. For science, see "News-Notes on Education," *Herald* 23, no. 6 (Winter 1956–57): 16, GTEA; "Practical Helps to the Principal for Enriching Elementary Science Instruction" and "Opportunities for Teachers," *Herald* 25, no. 4 (Winter 1958): 13, 22, GTEA; "Lamson-Richardson School Holds First Science Fair" and "Raise Your Sights in Elementary Science," *Herald* 24, no. 3 (May 1958): 7, 11, GTEA; and "The Organization of Local Chapters of the National Institute of Sciences," *Herald* 24, no. 3 (May 1958): 14, GTEA. For articles on reading/language, see "Methods and Materials for Developing Reading in the Content Field," "Majoring in the Essentials," and "Today's Readers," *Herald* 28, no. 2 (Winter 1961): 15, 21, 24, GTEA; "Literacy Education in Georgia," *Herald* 27, no. 2 (Spring 1961): 9, GTEA; "Helping the Slow Learner in English," *Herald* 28, no. 1 (Fall 1961): 5, GTEA; and "Journalism: A Challenge to the High School Student and Teacher," *Herald* 29, no. 2 (Winter 1962): 10, GTEA. Articles pertaining to math include "Modern Mathematics," *Herald* 28, no. 2 (Winter 1961): 27, GTEA; "Traditional and Modern Mathematics," *Herald* 28, no. 1 (Fall 1961): 14, GTEA; and "New Thinking in High School Mathematics," *Herald* 28, no. 3 (Convention Issue 1962): 29, GTEA. Development/guidance articles appear in many forms. See "Needed Integration: Guidance, Curriculum, Instruction, and Administration," *Herald* 28, no. 2 (Winter 1961): 2, GTEA; "Is Your Pupil Vulnerable to Delinquent Behavior?," "The Exceptionality of the Delinquent," "Special Education of the Mentally Retarded," and "Redirecting Adolescent Behavior," *Herald* 28, no. 1 (Fall 1961): 7, 9, 20, GTEA; Convention, 16; "Growing through Human Relations," *Herald* 27, no. 2 (Spring 1961): 5, GTEA; "Foreign Language Teachers Organize," *Herald* 28, no. 1 (Fall 1961): 26, GTEA; "What Constitutes a Functional School Health Program?," *Herald* 29, no. 2 (Winter 1962): 5, GTEA; "Audio Visual Aids in Counseling and Guidance" and "The Parent-Teacher Conference Needs Re-Emphasizing," *Herald* 29, no. 1 (Fall 1962): 14, 17, GTEA; "We Must Move up the Professional Ladder," *Herald* 28, no. 3 (Convention Issue 1962): 5, GTEA; and "What Art Is!" and "Scientific Application through Social Studies Instruction," *Herald* 28, no. 4 (Spring 1962): 7, 10, GTEA.

5. Cozart, *History of the Association of Colleges and Secondary Schools*, 22.

6. "Processes of Improving Education and Its Product," in *Proceedings of the Association of Colleges and Secondary Schools, 1957*, 97, UBP. At the same meeting in 1957, William F. Quillian Jr., president of Randolph-Macon Woman's College in Lynchburg, also directly linked improving the quality of teachers to improving the quality of education. See "A Multiple Approach to Improving the Quality of Education," in *Proceedings of the Association of Colleges and Secondary Schools, 1957*, 116, UBP.

7. At the planning meetings of the new school year, Byas asked faculty members to agree on a weekly meeting date for the year. Although a meeting might not

be held every week, teachers held the designated day as the time for their collective conversation. Except in cases of emergency, which he reports rarely occurred, he did not have "call" faculty meetings, as he believed these impinged upon individual schedules. In fact, Byas believed teachers appreciated his lack of intrusion on their schedule. Byas, interview, February 11, 2000.

8. "The Role of the Principal in Curriculum Development," *Herald* 34, no. 1 (Fall 1967): 9–10, GTEA.

9. Ibid.; GTEA Principals, group interview, December 1, 2000.

10. Byas, interview, February 11, 2000.

11. "Faculty Evaluation of Fair Street High School," UBP.

12. "Fair Street High School's Philosophy of American Secondary Education," ca. 1961, UBP.

13. The five steps were (1) determining what is to be done, (2) selecting what procedures are to be followed, (3) guiding others and/or oneself in following through, (4) evaluating the effectiveness of procedures, and (5) suggesting revisions for later use. Ulysses Byas to All Teachers, 1 September 1965, UBP.

14. *Policy Statements Handbook*, 2, UBP. The *Policy Statements Handbook* also provides some evidence that the collective policy of professional development was iterative. For example, accompanying the statement on teacher lesson plans is a "Check List for Planning and Evaluating a Lesson." This topic builds upon the previous ideas about teacher planning but extends those ideas into the area of evaluation. In the earlier release, evaluation is briefly mentioned under the last bullet point. The checklist, in language consistent with the principal's beliefs, contains information that extends planning to provide precise directives on evaluation. Directed to teachers, the checklist provides twelve questions that, "as you sit at your desk planning a lesson, you may want to ask yourself." The questions cover topics such as whether the lesson is primarily one of "attitudes, skill, concepts, or knowledge" or "a combination of two or more of these." Collectively, they encourage the teacher to delineate the "bull's-eye" point that would be the "teaching target" for that day and to consider whether the aims were specific, "sharp," or "blunt." Teachers are encouraged to be deliberate in their methods, relate the lesson to the students' lives, create a motivational beginning, focus on lesson differentiation that would allow them to meet the needs of both "fast" students and "slow" students, and determine which materials and resources best serve students at different learning levels. In addition to providing a summary for students, the teacher should also be aware of how the current lesson connects with the next one and the role of homework in promoting further expertise. Yet, despite the focus on adequate planning for successful instruction, the memo concludes with a reminder to stay academically flexible. In the final query, the teacher is encouraged to ask: "Am I 'saturated' in this subject so that I can feel free to change the lesson plan if necessary? What do I still need to do to gain background for this lesson (assuming that there is time to do this)?"

15. Fred M. King, "When the Principal Visits the Classroom," *Herald* 28, no. 3 (Convention Issue 1963): 15, GTEA. Curiously, most of the articles in the *Herald* during this period refer to the professor as "principal." This occurred despite the fact that communities still utilized the term "professor." The use of "principal" in the written language likely reflects their identification with professional white associations, where "principal" was the term of choice.

16. "Matter of Opinion," *Herald* 24, no. 1 (Fall 1957): 15, GTEA.

17. W. F. Crawl, "The Principal and His Image," *Herald* 33, no. 3 (Convention Issue 1967): 25, GTEA; "Administration: It Takes Many Hands," *Herald* 28, no. 4 (Spring 1962): 19, GTEA. The latter article also notes the key leadership role of the principal in giving direction to parents and students.

18. Crawl, "The Principal and His Image."

19. Byas first describes his "number one" job in Byas, interview, September 5, 1998.

20. Byas, interviews, February 11, 2000; January 20, 2000; and November 12, 2004.

21. Byas, interview, September 5, 1998.

22. Ibid.

23. "Report of Committee on Testing," *Policy Statements Handbook*, UBP; "General Suggestions for Constructing Objectives Test," *Policy Statements Handbook*, UBP; "Constructing Test Items—Some General Guides," UBP.

24. Byas, interview, February 11, 2000.

25. Appendix B, Annual Meeting, Association of Colleges and Schools, Memphis, Tenn., December 4–5, 1963, UBP.

26. *Policy Statements Handbook*, 7–8, UBP. Block statements added to the document by Byas in his review of the manuscript, November 29, 2007.

27. *Policy Statements Handbook*, 8, UBP; Byas, interview, November 12, 2004.

28. *Policy Statements Handbook*, 7–8, UBP.

29. "How Do You Like Our New Schedule?," *Clarion* 6, no. 1, December 1962, UBP.

30. Angelina Hughey, "Should We Have Study Halls?," *Clarion* 7, no. 1, April 1965, UBP.

31. "How Professional Am I?," *Herald* 29, no. 3 (Convention Issue 1963): 35, GTEA; Sprowles and Smith, *The Principal's Profile*.

32. T. A. Carmichael to Ulysses Byas, 23 October 1959, UBP.

33. Byas, interview, January 20, 2000.

34. For an example, see "The First Course in Chemistry and the Culturally Deprived," *Herald* 33, no. 1 (Fall 1966): 17, GTEA.

35. GTEA Principals, December 1, 2000.

36. "GT&EA Educators Awarded Summer Fellowships," *Herald* 30, no. 4 (Spring 1964): 29, GTEA; "The Principal's Message," *Clarion* 7, no. 5, December 1964, UBP.

37. "Events of the Year (1962–63) at E. E. Butler High School," *Clarion* 6, no. 3, May 1963, UBP.

38. "The President's Message," *Herald* 30, no. 1 (Fall 1963): 4, GTEA.

39. Byas, interviews, November 11, 2004, and November 12, 2004.

40. Timothy U. Ryals, "Tips to the Beginning School Principal," *Herald* 33, no. 1 (Fall 1966): 30, GTEA.

41. "The Role of the Principal in Curriculum Development," *Herald* 34, no. 1 (Fall 1967): 9, GTEA.

42. Byas, interview, November 12, 2004.

43. Byas, interview, February 11, 2000.

44. Byas, interview, November 12, 2004.

45. Byas, interview, February 11, 2000.

46. Handout, undated, from file on Test-Construction: Teacher Made, UBP.

47. Fred King, "When the Principal Visits the Classroom," *Herald* 29, no. 3 (Convention Issue 1963): 15, GTEA.

48. "E. E. Butler High School: Yearly Grades—All Classes by Subject Matter," UBP.

49. Teacher File/Gainesville, UBP.

50. "Principal's Annual Report—Negro Schools, 1958–1959," Fair Street–Butler High School Alumni Association. To preserve the anonymity of this teacher, the dates of the reports utilized are omitted. Douglasville description is from Byas, interviews, November 12, 2004, and October 17, 2005.

51. Byas, interview, November 12, 2004.

52. Byas, interview, February 11, 2000.

53. "Liberty County Training School," *Herald* 17, no. 4 (April 1951): 28, GTEA.

54. "A Mathematician Considers the Current Science Drive with Misgivings," *Herald* 30, no. 1 (Fall 1963): 9, GTEA.

55. Hutchens and Smith, *Hall County, Georgia*, 59; Byas, interview, August 10, 2007.

56. Byas, interview, August 10, 2007.

CHAPTER 6

1. Hutchens and Smith, *Hall County, Georgia*, 59, 79, 80, 88, 90–92.

2. Berry and Blassingame, *Long Memory*, 182; Painter, *Creating Black Americans*, 279; Kelley and Lewis, *To Make Our World Anew*, 203, 215, 236.

3. Fairclough, *A Class of Their Own*, 383.

4. As recounted by T. R. Siddle (1911–2000), among the tales of educated blacks who matriculated successfully in college and then returned home using language different from that of the community is the 1960s joke about the black graduate who tried to explain a math equation to his parents, only to have them correct him: "Pie are not square; pie are round." Clearly, in the mind of the parents, the

child had not only learned little; he had completely rejected the knowledge he had taken with him to college.

5. Byas, interview, January 20, 2000, and February 11, 2000; GTEA Principals, group interview, December 1, 2000.

6. Byas, interview, February 11, 2000.

7. Ibid.

8. Ibid.

9. Byas, interview, November 12, 2004.

10. GTEA Principals, group interview, December 1, 2000.

11. Ibid.

12. Byas, interview, February 11, 2000.

13. Mary Moorehead and Harbin Bernice, "Butler High's First Home Coming a Success," *Clarion* 6, no. 1, December 1962, UBP.

14. Goldfield, *Black, White, and Southern*, 207.

15. Byas, interview, January 20, 2000.

16. 1964 attendance document, UBP; GTEA Principals, group interview, December 1, 2000.

17. Sanford Walker, "Why Don't Fair Street Students Earn Better Grades?," *Clarion* 1, no. 2, December 1957, UBP; Ernestine Williams, "Now, It's Stylish to Study," *Clarion* 1, no. 2, December 1957, UBP; Wanda Smith, "11th Grade A Class News," *Clarion* 1, no. 1, December 1957, UBP; Willie Mae Reed, "National Honor Society Initiation Held at E. E. Butler High," *Clarion* 6, no. 1, December 1962, UBP; Willie Mae Reed, "National Honor Society," *Clarion* 6, no. 1, December 1962, UBP; "Honor Society Member Wins at State Science Fair," *Clarion* 6, no. 2, March 1963, UBP; Bobby Anderson, "Where Do I Go from Here?," *Clarion* 6, no. 3, May 1963, UBP; Lovie Smith, "The Car Causes Drop in Grades," *Clarion* 7, no. 1, December 1963, UBP; Beverly Tombleston, "National Honor Society Initiates New Members," *Clarion* 7, no. 1, December 1963, UBP; Johnny Robertson, "Around the Campus," *Clarion* 7, no. 1, December 1963, UBP; "Importance of School Records," *Clarion* 7, no. 2, March 1964, UBP; "The ABC's for Daily Success," *Clarion* 7, no. 2, March 1964, UBP; and "How to Fail," *Clarion* 7, no. 2, March 1964, UBP.

18. Bernice Harbin, "College Program Night," *Clarion* 6, no. 2, March 1963, UBP; Bernice Harbin, "College Night Program," *Clarion* 7, no. 2, March 1964, UBP.

19. In conclusion, he echoes his capacity to "exchange ideas . . . with principals from other top high schools" and refers students and parents to the thirty-six annual program of the meeting, which could be found in the library. See "The Principal's Message," *Clarion* 7, no. 5, December 1964, UBP.

20. Byas, interview, February 11, 2000.

21. See chart, "E. E. Butler High School National Merit Qualifying Test: Number Correct Answers by Years and Subject," UBP. The seriousness with which Byas approached the SAT and its meaning for black students is also captured in a later

set of book notes. Although it is not known which book he was reading at the time, he summarized the material on page 60 as follows: "The SAT, according to figures compiled from 827 different ETS validity studies conducted between 1964 and 1974, delivers an average accuracy—which statisticians call 'percentage of variance accounted for' or 'percentage of perfect prediction'—of 11.9 percent in the prediction of first year grades."

22. "Fair Street Curriculum Study: Students Rate Poorly in Biological, Physical Sciences," *Daily Times*, May 2, 1958, UBP.

23. Byas, telephone interview, April 28, 2006.

24. Ulysses Byas, "The Principal's Message: The Dropout Nationally," *Clarion* 10, no. 2, March 1967, UBP.

25. Ulysses Byas, "The Principal's Message to the Seniors: Opportunity and You," *Clarion* 8, no. 3, May 1966, UBP.

26. Elmer J. Dean makes this point, although his need for civics training is linked to school dropouts. See Dean, "Social Studies in the Negro High Schools of Georgia," 8.

27. The reluctant social studies teacher was not behaving in ways different from the norm for black social studies teachers in Georgia during the period. See Dean, "Social Studies in the Negro High Schools of Georgia," 195. Perhaps because of their political aspirations and their increasing awareness of the need to attract votes—even black votes—the candidates responded positively to his invitation. Of the thirty-three white candidates seeking office, thirty-two accepted Byas's invitation to speak with the students.

28. In a survey of social studies practices in black Georgia schools during the period, Dean concluded that it would benefit Negro high schools to provide more citizenship experiences in their programs. See Dean, "Social Studies in the Negro High Schools of Georgia," 187–88.

29. "Some Pertinent Issues in Citizenship Education," *Herald* 22, no. 1 (October 1954): 8–9; Cozart, *History of the Association of Colleges and Secondary Schools*; *Rising in the Sun*, GTEA. For information on Georgia's prescriptions for civic education, see Georgia Department of Education, *Georgia Textbook List*. In particular, a 1940 text provides explicit detail on Georgia's expectations for citizenship education. See Pound and Thompson, *Georgia Citizenship*.

30. Byas describes the unsupervised study halls in Byas, interviews, February 11, 2000, and November 12, 2004.

31. Editorials referenced are Ulysses Byas, "From the Principal's Desk: For a Better School," *Clarion* 7, no. 2, March 1964, UBP; and Ulysses Byas, "From the Principal's Desk," *Clarion* 6, no. 2, March 1963, UBP.

32. Ulysses Byas, "The Principal's Message: The Dropout Nationally," *Clarion* 10, no. 2, March 1967, UBP.

33. Painter, *Creating Black Americans*, 278.

34. Byas, interview, February 11, 2000.

35. GTEA Principals, group interview, December 1, 2000; Ulysses Byas, "The Principal's Message," *Clarion* 7, no. 5, December 1964, UBP; "Gainesville City Schools: Adult Class Schedule, Second Semester," UBP.

36. Byas, interview, November 12, 2004.

37. "Contractors Byas and Stephens Announce the Opening of Morningside Hills," UBP; Byas, interview, November 12, 2004.

38. Byas, interview, November 12, 2004.

39. Gerald L. Smith, *A Black Educator in the Segregated South*, 111.

40. Bank note, First Federal Savings and Loan Association of Gainesville, May 2, 1963, UBP.

41. Byas, interview, November 12, 2004.

42. George Whiten to Ulysses Byas, March 6, 1968, UBP; "Constitution and By-Laws of the Citizens Advisory Committee on the Workable Program for Community Improvement" and "Citizens Advisory Committee on the Workable Program: 2/4/68 Minutes of the Standing Committee on Code," UBP.

43. Edwin Butler, "Send-Off Program Held in Honor of Mr. Byas," *Clarion* 7, no. 5, December 1964, UBP; Byas, interview, February 11, 2000.

44. Litwack, *Trouble in Mind*, 35.

45. Byas, interview, February 11, 2000.

46. Byas, interview, July 5, 2007.

47. Byas, interview, November 12, 2004.

48. Mary L. Moorehead, "The P.T.A.," *Clarion* 6, no. 1, December 1962, UBP; "Butler High Hosts Athens District P.T.A. Meeting," *Clarion* 6, no. 2, March 1963, UBP; "Grade Mothers," *Clarion* 6, no. 2, March 1963, UBP; GTEA Principals, group interview, December 1, 2000.

49. Byas, interview, November 12, 2004.

50. Byas, interview, February 11, 2000.

CONCLUSION

1. Byas, interviews, January 20, 2000; February 11, 2000; and August 10, 2007.

2. Ulysses Byas to Board of Education, May 15, 1968, UBP.

3. Many qualitative researchers have written eloquently about the advantages and disadvantages of utilizing a case-study approach to a subject. See, for example, Stake, *The Art of Case Study Research*; Merriam, *Qualitative Research and Case Study Applications*; and Dyson and Genishi, *On the Case*.

4. GTEA Principals, group interview, December 1, 2000; Byas, interview, February 11, 2000; Henry Brown, GTEA Principals, group interview, December 1, 2000; Byas, interview, February 11, 2000.

METHODOLOGY

1. For a historical perspective on the salience of the subaltern lens, see Buras and Apple, "Introduction," 1–9.

2. I am indebted to Miles and Huberman's *Qualitative Data Analysis* for this activity. As a classroom exercise, I decided to complete the assignment given to my students and, through their suggestions, made this important discovery about the story.

Bibliography

Manuscript and Archival Collections

Atlanta, Ga.

Emory University Manuscript, Archives, and Rare Book Library
Southern Association of Colleges and Schools Records

Georgia State Archives
Division of Negro Education

Horace Edward Tate Collection of the Georgia Teachers and
Education Association
Guide to Developing an Inclusive Integration Plan
*Herald: Official Journal of the Georgia Teachers and Educational
Association* (published quarterly)
History Committee and Consultants of Georgia Teachers and
Education Association. *Rising in the Sun: A History of the Georgia
Teachers and Education Association, a Half Century of Progress.*
Atlanta, Ga.: Georgia Teachers and Education Association, 1966.
Strengthening Local Associations: A Guide for GTEA Unit Leaders

Melford Walker Southern History Archival Collection
Virginia Union postcards

Gainesville, Ga.

"Principal's Annual Report—Negro Schools, 1958–1959," Private
Collection of School Records, Fair Street–Butler High
Schools Alumni Association

Macon, Ga.

Ulysses Byas Papers (privately held collection of personal and
professional documents, including letters, school records,
and administrative documents)
Clarion (Fair Street High School newspaper)
Cozart, Leland S., ed. *Achieving an Improved Quality of Education:
Proceedings of the Association of Colleges and Secondary Schools, 1957.*
Concord, N.C.: Association of Colleges and Secondary Schools, 1957.
———. *Improving Educational Performance: Proceedings of the Association
of Colleges and Secondary Schools, 1959.* Concord, N.C.: Association of
Colleges and Secondary Schools, 1959.
———. *Now Is Tomorrow: Proceedings of the Association of Colleges and
Secondary Schools, 1964.* Concord, N.C.: Association of Colleges and
Secondary Schools, 1964.
Geiger, Albert J., ed. *Proceedings of the Sixty-Sixth Annual Meeting of the*

Southern Association of Colleges and Secondary Schools, Miami Beach, Florida, December 1961. Atlanta, Ga.: Southern Association of Colleges and Secondary Schools, 1961.

Policy Statements Handbook

"Report of Visiting Committee on Re-Evaluation, Fair Street High School," 1960

A Self-Study of the Gainesville City Schools, Gainesville, Ga., 1965–66

Interviews by Author

Byas, Ulysses. Interviews, Macon, Ga., September 5, 1998; January 20, 2000; February 11, 2000; February 28, 2002; March 27, 2002; July 2, 2002; November 21, 2003; November 12, 2004; March 16, 2006; August 10, 2007.

———. Telephone interviews, September 2, 2001; November 15, 2001; March 10, 2002; November 14, 2002; November 30, 2002; June 3, 2003; November 21, 2003; August 19, 2004; April 28, 2006; January 15, 2007; June 5, 2007; July 5, 2007; August 30, 2007; ca. August/September 2007; October 30, 2007; June 23, 2007.

GTEA Principals (William Breeden, Henry Brown, Ulysses Byas, Bobby Huff, and Horace Tate). Group interview, Atlanta, Ga., December 1, 2000.

Hill, Oliver. Interview, Richmond, Va., August 31, 2003.

———. Telephone interview, July 19, 2003.

Tate, Virginia. Interview, Atlanta, Ga., November 3, 2006.

Ulysses Byas Lectures and Notes

GTEA Reunion Luncheon, Macon, Ga., November 16, 2001.

Macon, Ga., ca. 2005.

Mt. Zion AME Church, Decatur, Ga., March 14, 2007.

"Reflection on Early Life Story," ca. winter 1998–99.

Sixth Bi-Annual Reunion—Fair Street/Butler High, Georgia Mountain Center, Gainesville, Ga., September 2, 2001.

Books, Articles, Dissertations, and Papers

Adair, Alvis V. *Desegregation: The Illusion of Black Progress.* Lanham, Md.: University of America, 1984.

Allen, James, Hilton Als, John Lewis, and Leon F. Litwack. *Without Sanctuary: Lynching Photography in America.* Santa Fe, N.Mex.: Twin Palms, 2000.

Anderson, James. *The Black Education Professoriate.* SPE Monograph Series. Minneapolis: Society of Professors of Education, 1984.

Ashmore, Harry. *The Negro and the Schools.* Chapel Hill: University of North Carolina Press, 1954.

Bartley, Numan. *The Creation of Modern Georgia.* Athens: University of Georgia Press, 1983.

Beauboeuf-Lafontant, Tamara. "A Movement against and beyond Boundaries: 'Politically Relevant Teaching' among African American Teachers." *Teachers College Record* 100 (1999): 702–23.

Berry, Mary Frances, and John W. Blassingame. *Long Memory: The Black Experience in America*. New York: Oxford University Press, 1982.

Bond, Horace Mann. *The Education of the Negro in the American Social Order*. New York: Prentice-Hall, Inc., 1934.

Bracey, Isaac Cornelious. "The High School Principalship in South Carolina." Ed.D. diss., University of Oklahoma, 1961.

Brittain, M. L., A. H. Foster, John T. Peyton, C. R. McCrory, H. C. Shuptrine, W. J. Nunnally, G. R. Glenn, and T. J. Woofter. *Report of the School Book Investigating Committee*. N.p., 1914.

Brown, Hugh Walter. *A History of the Education of Negroes in North Carolina*. Raleigh, N.C.: Irving Swain Press, Inc., 1961.

Brown, Titus. *Faithful, Firm, and True: African-American Education in the South*. Macon, Ga.: Mercer University Press, 2002.

Buras, Kristen, and Michael Apple. "Introduction." In *The Subaltern Speak: Curriculum, Power, and Educational Struggles*, edited by Michael W. Apple and Kristen L. Buras, 1–39. New York: Routledge, 2006.

Carroll, Thomas G., Kathleen Fulton, Karen Abercrombie, and Irene Yoon. *Fifty Years after* Brown v. Board of Education*: A Two-Tiered Education System*. Washington, D.C.: National Commission on Teaching and America's Future, 2004.

Cecelski, David. *Along Freedom Road: Hyde County, North Carolina, and the Fate of Black Schools in the South*. Chapel Hill: University of North Carolina Press, 1994.

Clark, James Osgood Andrew. "State Uniformity and the Text-Book Question." Address delivered before the Committees on Education of the House and Senate of the State of Georgia, Atlanta, August 26, 1891.

Coley, Richard J. *Growth in School Revisited: Achievement Gains from the Fourth to the Eighth Grade*. Princeton, N.J.: Educational Testing Service, 2003.

Cozart, Leland S. *A History of the Association of Colleges and Secondary Schools, 1934–1965*. Charlotte, N.C.: Heritage Printers, Inc., 1967.

Davis, Lenwood G. *A History of Queen Street High School, 1928–1968*. Kingston, N.Y.: Tri-State Services, 1996.

Davis, Leroy. *A Clashing of the Soul: John Hope and the Dilemma of African American Leadership and Black Higher Education in the Early Twentieth Century*. Athens: University of Georgia Press, 1998.

Dean, Elmer J. "Social Studies in the Negro High Schools of Georgia, 1952." Ed.D. diss., Teachers College, Columbia University, 1955.

Delpit, Lisa D. *Other People's Children: Cultural Conflict in the Classroom*. New York: The New Press, 1993.

Denzin, Norman K., and Yvonna S. Lincoln, eds. *The SAGE Handbook of Qualitative Research*. 3rd ed. Thousand Oaks, Calif.: Sage Publications, 2005.

Dilworth, Paulette Patterson. "Widening the Circle: African American Perspectives on Moral and Civic Learning." In *Civic and Moral Learning in America*, edited by Donald Warren and John J. Patrick. New York: Palgrave Macmillan, 2006.

Dyson, Anne Haas, and Celia Genishi. *On the Case*. New York: Teachers College Press, 2005.

Eaton, Susan E., and Gary Orfield. "Rededication Not Celebration." *College Board Review* 200 (Fall 2003): 29–33.

Edwards, W. C., Preston Royster, and Lazarus Bates. *The Education of Black Citizens in Halifax County, 1866–1969*. Springfield, Va.: Banister Press, 1979.

Evans, Lawton B. *First Lessons in Georgia History*. New York: American Book Company, 1922.

Fairclough, Adam. *A Class of Their Own: Black Teachers in the Segregated South*. Cambridge, Mass.: The Belknap Press of Harvard University Press, 2007.

Foner, Eric. "Black Reconstruction Leaders at the Grass Roots." In *Black Leaders of the Nineteenth Century*, edited by Leon Litwack and August Meier. Urbana: University of Illinois Press, 1988.

Foster, Michele. *Black Teachers on Teaching*. New York: The New Press, 1997.

———. "Constancy, Connectedness, and Constraints in the Lives of African American Teachers." *NWSA Journal* 3, no. 2 (Spring 1991): 233–61.

———. "The Politics of Race: Through the Eyes of African American Teachers." *Journal of Education* 172, no. 3 (1990): 123–41.

Franklin, John Hope, and August Meier, eds. *Blacks Leaders of the Twentieth Century*. Urbana: University of Illinois Press, 1982.

Funches, De Lars. "The Superintendent's Expectations of the Negro High School Principal in Mississippi." Ed.D. diss., University of Oklahoma, 1961.

Gaines, Kevin. *Uplifting the Race: Black Leadership, Politics, and Culture in the Twentieth Century*. Chapel Hill: University of North Carolina Press, 1996.

Garrod, Andrew, Janie Victoria Ward, Tracy L. Robinson, and Robert Kilkenny, eds. *Souls Looking Back: Life Stories of Growing Up Black*. New York: Routledge, 1999.

Gavins, Raymond. *The Perils and Prospects of Southern Black Leadership: Gordon Blaine Hancock, 1884–1970*. Durham: Duke University Press, 1977.

Georgia Department of Education, *Georgia Textbook List for Elementary and High School*. Atlanta: Department of Education, Textbook Division, ca. 1945.

Goldfield, David R. *Black, White, and Southern: Race Relations and Southern Culture, 1940s to the Present*. Baton Rouge, La.: Louisiana State University Press, 1990.

Gordon, Edmund W. "Affirmative Student Development: Closing the

Achievement Gap by Developing Human Capital." *Policy Notes: News from the ETS Policy Information Center* 12, no. 2 (Spring 2004): 1.

Harris, John R. *Defying the Odds*. Brushton, N.Y.: Aspect Books, 1996.

Hatch, Robert Herman. "A Study of the Leadership Ability of Negro High School Principals." Ed.D. diss., Colorado State College, 1964.

Hine, Darlene Clark. "Rape and the Inner Lives of Black Women in the Middle West: Preliminary Thoughts on the Culture of Dissemblance." In *Unequal Sisters: A Multicultural Reader in U.S. Women's History*, edited by Ellen Du Bois and Vicki L. Ruiz, 192–97. New York: Routledge, 1990.

Hundley, Mary Gibson. *The Dunbar Story, 1870–1955*. New York: Vantage Press, 1965.

Hurt, R. Douglas. *African American Life in the Rural South, 1900–1950*. Columbia: University of Missouri Press, 2003.

Hutchens, Linda Rucker, and Ella J. Wilmont Smith. *Hall County, Georgia*. Black America Series. Charleston, S.C.: Arcadia Press, 2004.

Irvine, Russell, and Jackie Irvine. "The Impact of the Desegregation Process on the Education of Black Students: Key Variables." *Journal of Negro Education* 52, no. 4 (Fall 1983): 410–22.

Jeffries, Rhonda. "The Trickster Figure in African American Teaching: Pre- and Post-Desegregation." *Urban Review* 26 (December 1994): 289–304.

Joiner, Oscar H., James C. Bonner, H. S. Shearouse, and T. E. Smith, eds. *A History of Public Education in Georgia, 1734–1976*. Columbia, S.C.: The R. L. Bryan Company, 1979.

Jones, Charles C. *Negro Myths from the Georgia Coast: Told in the Vernacular*. Columbia, S.C.: The State Company, 1952.

Jones, Faustine. *A Traditional Model of Educational Excellence: Dunbar High School of Little Rock, Arkansas*. Washington, D.C.: Howard University Press, 1981.

Jordan, William G. *Black Newspapers and America's War for Democracy, 1914–1920*. Chapel Hill: University of North Carolina Press, 2001.

Jordan-Taylor, Donna. "'I Am Not Autherine Lucy!' Experiences of Black Graduate Students during Jim Crow." Paper presented at the annual meeting of the History of Education Society, Cleveland, Ohio, October 2007.

Kelley, Robin D. G. *Race Rebels: Culture, Politics, and the Black Working Class*. New York: Free Press, 1996.

Kelley, Robin D. G., and Earl Lewis, eds. *To Make Our World Anew*. Vol. 2, *A History of African Americans since 1880*. Oxford: Oxford University Press, 2005.

Kluger, Richard. *Simple Justice: The History of Brown v. Board of Education, the Epochal Supreme Court Decision That Outlawed Segregation, and of Black America's Century-Long Struggle for Equality under Law*. New York: Random House, 1975.

Kober, Nancy. *It Takes More than Testing: Closing the Achievement Gap; A Report of the Center on Education Policy.* Washington, D.C.: Center on Education Policy, 2001.

Lewis, David Levering. *W. E. B. DuBois: Biography of Race, 1868–1919.* New York: H. Holt, 1993.

———. *W. E. B. DuBois: The Fight for Equality and the American Century, 1919–1963.* New York: H. Holt, 2000.

Litwack, Leon. *Trouble in Mind: Black Southerners in the Age of Jim Crow.* New York: Vintage Books, 1998.

McAdam, Doug. *Political Process and the Development of Black Insurgency, 1930–1970.* 2d ed. Chicago: University of Chicago Press, 1999.

McCullough-Garrett, Alice. "Reclaiming the African American Vision for Teaching: Toward an Educational Conversation." *Journal of Negro Education* 62, no. 4 (Autumn 1993): 433–40.

McNeil, Genna Rae. "Charles Hamilton Houston: Social Engineer for Civil Rights." In *Black Leaders of the Twentieth Century*, edited by John Hope Franklin and August Meier, 221–40. Urbana: University of Illinois Press, 1982.

Merriam, Sharan B. *Qualitative Research and Case Study Applications in Education.* San Francisco: Jossey-Bass Publishers, 1998.

Miles, M. B., and A. M. Huberman. Qualitative Data Analysis: An Expanded Sourcebook. 2nd ed. Thousand Oaks, Calif.: Sage, 1999.

Morris, Vivian, and Curtis Morris. *Creating Caring and Nurturing Educational Environments for African American Children.* Westport, Conn.: Bergin and Garvey, 2000.

Noblit, George, and Van Dempsey. *The Social Construction of Virtue: The Moral Life of Schools.* Albany, N.Y.: State University of New York Press, 1996.

O'Brien, Thomas. *The Politics of Race and Schooling: Public Education in Georgia, 1900–1961.* Lanham, Mass.: Lexington Books, 1999.

Orfield, Gary, Daniel Losen, Johanna Wild, and Christopher B. Swanson. *Losing Our Future: How Minority Youth Are Being Left Behind by the Graduate Rate Crisis.* Cambridge, Mass.: The Civil Rights Project at Harvard University, 2004.

Orfield, Gary, Susan E. Eaton, and the Harvard Project on School Desegregation. *Dismantling Desegregation: The Quiet Reversal of* Brown v. Board of Education. New York: The New Press, 1996.

Orr, Dorothy. *A History of Education in Georgia.* Chapel Hill: University of North Carolina Press, 1950.

Painter, Nell Irvin. *Creating Black Americans: African-American History and Its Meanings, 1619 to the Present.* Oxford: Oxford University Press, 2006.

Perry, Thelma. *History of the American Teachers Association.* Washington, D.C.: National Education Association, 1975.

Picott, J. Rupert. *History of the Virginia Teachers Association.* Washington, D.C.: National Education Association, 1975.

Pirkle, William Broughton. "A Study of the State Scholarship Aid Programs for Negroes in Georgia, 1944–1955." Ed.D. diss., Auburn University, 1956.

Pitts, Winfred E. "E. E. Butler High School, Desegregation, and the Gainesville City–Hall County, Georgia, Schools, 1821–1973: A Victory of Sorts." Ph.D. diss., Georgia State University, 1999.

Podair, Jerald. *The Strike That Changed New York*. New Haven: Yale University Press, 2002.

Pound, Merritt B., and Melvin E. Thompson. *Georgia Citizenship*. Richmond: Johnson Publishing Co., 1940.

Preston-Grimes, Patrice. "Teaching Democracy: Civic Education in Georgia's African American Schools, 1930–1954." Ph.D. diss., Emory University, 2005.

Roche, Jeff. *Restructured Resistance: The Sibley Commission and the Politics of Desegregation in Georgia*. Athens: University of Georgia Press, 1998.

Rodgers, Frederick A. *The Black High School and Its Community*. Lexington, Mass.: Lexington Books, 1967.

Savage, Barbara Dianne. *Broadcasting Freedom: Radio, War, and the Politics of Race, 1938–1946*. Chapel Hill: University of North Carolina Press, 1999.

Sawyer, Gordon. *Gainesville, 1900–2000*. Images of America: Georgia. Charleston: Arcadia Press, 1999.

Scott, John Irving Elias. "Professional Functions of Negro Principals in the Public Schools of Florida in Relation to Status." Ph.D. diss., University of Pittsburgh, 1942.

Shaw, William Henry. "A Study of the Behavior and Beliefs of Public School Principals in the Muscogee County School District, Georgia." Ed.D. diss., Auburn University, 1963.

Singham, Mano. "The Achievement Gap: Myths and Reality." *Phi Delta Kappan* 84, no. 8 (April 2003): 586–91.

Smith, C. Calvin. *Educating the Masses: The Unfolding History of Black School Administrators in Arkansas, 1900–2000*. Fayetteville: The University of Arkansas Press, 2003.

Smith, Elizabeth Cooke. "A Study of System-Wide Evaluation in Selected Schools for Negroes in Georgia, 1956–1960." Ed.D. diss., New York University, 1964.

Smith, Gerald L. *A Black Educator in the Segregated South: Kentucky's Rufus B. Atwood*. Lexington: University Press of Kentucky, 1994.

Sowell, Thomas. "Black Excellence: The Case of Dunbar High School." *Public Interest* 35 (Spring 1974): 1–21.

———. "Patterns of Black Excellence." *Public Interest* 43 (Spring 1976): 26–58.

Sprowles, Lee, and Doyne M. Smith. *The Principal's Profile*. N.p., 1963.

Stake, Robert E. *The Art of Case Study Research*. Thousand Oaks, Calif.: Sage Publications, 1995.

Sullivan, Buddy. *Georgia: A State History*. The Making of America Series. Charleston, S.C.: Arcadia Press, 2003.

Thomas, Leland Clovis. "Some Aspects of Biracial Public Education in Georgia, 1900–1954." Ph.D. diss., George Peabody College for Teachers, 1960.

Tilford-Weathers, Thelma Cayne. *A History of Louisville Central High School, 1882–1982*. Louisville Central High School Alumni Association, 1982.

Tillman, Linda. "African American Principals and the Legacy of *Brown*." *Review of Research in Education* 28, no. 1 (January 2004): 101–46.

Tushnet, Mark V. *The NAACP Legal Strategy against Segregated Education, 1925–1950*. Chapel Hill: University of North Carolina Press, 1987.

Tyson, Timothy. *Blood Done Sign My Name: A True Story*. New York: Crown Publishers, 2004.

Urban, Wayne. *Black Scholar: Horace Mann Bond, 1904–1972*. Athens: University of Georgia Press, 1992.

———. *Gender, Race, and the National Education Association: Professionalism and Its Limitations*. New York: RoutledgeFalmer, 2000.

Vontress, Clemmont E. "Our Demoralizing Slum Schools." *Phi Delta Kappan* 45, no. 2 (November 1963): 77–81.

Wadelington, Charles W., and Richard F. Knapp. *Charlotte Hawkins Brown and Palmer Memorial Institute: What One Young African American Woman Could Do*. Chapel Hill: University of North Carolina Press, 1999.

Walker, Vanessa Siddle. "African American Teachers in Segregated Schools in the South, 1940–1969." *American Educational Research Journal* 38 (Winter 2001): 751–80.

———. "Caswell County Training School, 1933–1969: Relationships between Community and School." *Harvard Educational Review* 63 (Summer 1993): 161–82.

———. "Organized Resistance and Black Educators Quest for School Equality." *Teachers College Record* 107, no. 3 (March 2005): 355–88.

———. *Their Highest Potential: An African American School Community in the Segregated South*. Chapel Hill: University of North Carolina Press, 1996.

———. "Valued Segregated Schools in the South, 1935–1969: A Review of Common Themes and Characteristics." *Review of Educational Research* 70, no. 3 (Autumn 2000): 253–85.

Walker, Vanessa Siddle, and Renarta H. Tompkins. "Caring in the Past: The Case of a Southern Segregated African American School." In *Race-ing Moral Formation: African American Perspectives on Care and Justice*, edited by Vanessa Siddle Walker and John R. Snarey. New York: Teachers College Press, 2004.

Walker, Vanessa Siddle, and Ulysses Byas. "The Architects of Black Schooling in the Segregated South: The Case of One Principal Leader." *Journal of Curriculum and Supervision* 19, no. 1 (Fall 2003): 54–72.

Warren, Donald, and John J. Patrick, eds. *Civic and Moral Learning in America.* New York: Palgrave Macmillan, 2006.

Weare, Walter. "Charles Clinton Spaulding: Middle-Class Leadership in the Age of Segregation." In *Black Leaders of the Twentieth Century*, edited by John Hope Franklin and August Meier, 167–90. Urbana: University of Illinois Press, 1982.

West, Earle H., ed. *A Bibliography of Doctoral Research on the Negro, 1933–1966.* University Microfilms (A Xerox Company), 1969.

Wilkins, Roy. "Freedom Tactics for 18,000,000." *New South* 18, no. 2 (February 1964): 3–5.

Wilson, Charles Reagan. *Baptized in Blood: The Religion of the Lost Cause, 1865–1920.* Athens: University of Georgia Press, 1980.

Woyshner, Christine, Joseph Watras, and Margaret Smith Crocco, eds. *Social Education in the Twentieth Century: Curriculum and Context for Citizenship.* New York: Peter Lang, 2004.

Index

78, 82, 114, 123, 252 (n. 24); confrontational spirit, 63–65, 75; culinary expertise, 56–57, 60, 68, 74–75, 176–77; curriculum and, 19, 21, 73, 116, 128, 191, 232, 248 (n. 6); Curriculum Survey, 34–44, 80, 83, 130, 132, 134, 161, 174, 209, 250 (n. 47); democracy and citizenship goals for students, 208–9, 215–19; departure from black schooling, 14–15, 233; desegregated summer school, as principal of, 14, 227–29, 232; desegregation, dealing with, 191–92, 231–33; "Dr. Jekyll and Mr. Hyde" strategy, 11, 24–44, 159; doctor of education degree from University of Massachusetts, Amherst, 234; document collection, x–xi, 241–43, 246 (n. 4); dress, modeling professional, 178–79; as dropout, 52; dropout prevention program, 212–14, 217–18; early leadership skills, 56, 62–64; early life and career, 12, 46, 47, 48–55, 243; early schooling, 51–53, 251 (n. 6); early teaching experience, 65–67; Fair Street High School appointment, 11, 17, 19, 21, 24, 82; first teaching job offer, 67–68, 69; football and, insisting on eligibility with passing average, 205–7; Fort Valley, Disciplinary Committee service, 63–65, 119, 140, 232; Fort Valley State College, suspension from, 64–65, 119, 140; Fort Valley State College experience, 59, 60–68, 71, 78; French language and, 62; Georgia, towns important to, 18; group settings, use of in teaching, 76–77; GTEA, importance of to, xi, 13, 46; GTEA and, 135–58, 159–62, 233; GTEA and, regional Principals and Curriculum Organization service of, 155; GTEA annual Principals' Conference, 155–57, 261–62 (n. 66); GTEA Elementary

and High School Principals' groups and, 152–55; GTEA Resolutions Committee service, 151–52; guidance counselors and, 33–34, 73, 132, 134; higher education, preparation for, 55–59; high school graduation, 118; at Hutchenson Elementary and High School, 22, 25–33, 82, 118; identification card, 121; industrial education and, 53–54, 76, 252 (n. 10); interviews of, ix, 241–42, 244, 252 (n. 10); John Hay Fellowship awarded to, 177, 232; journals subscriptions, 116; later career, 233–34, 246 (n. 8); leadership, as model for teachers, 173–79; leadership style, 163–65, 166, 180–92; learning as lifelong process for, 176–78; lesson planning, 164–65, 264 (nn. 13–14); major influences on, 46; marriage and family, 123, 199, 235–36, 243; "Me Speak for Me," xi, 246 (n. 5); mother's influence, 49, 51–53, 54, 118; parental involvement and, 13–14, 33–34, 77–78, 197–98, 199–200, 204–5, 206–7; parents, limits of work with, 227–29; professional development, 5, 10–11, 13, 16, 83–84, 106–8, 111–17, 124–58; professional educational network of, 12–13, 81, 92–95, 99–106, 124–25, 126–30, 135–58, 244; "professor" terminology, xiii–xiv, 246 (n. 9); reading of book manuscript by, 243–44; registration procedures for classes, 128; religious services and, 198–200; as Rockefeller intern, 234; Roosevelt, Long Island, as superintendent at, 234, 246 (n. 8); school administration, learning, 79–80; school leadership surveys, 173–76; School Masters Club and, 119, 124–35; school newspaper purpose, 209–10; school schedule planning, 128–30,

153; siblings, 48, 53, 123, 221–22; smartness of, 49–50, 52, 56, 61, 119; sponsoring black housing, 221–23; standardized testing, 267–68 (n. 21); teacher commentary on professorial style of, 179–84; teacher dismissal, dealing with, 184, 187–90; teacher evaluation and, 184–90; teacher involvement in decisions by, 29, 35–37, 168–73, 263–64 (n. 7); teacher-made tests, 168–70; teacher professional development and, 162–73, 237; teachers, as part of story of, 235, 236–38; teachers, expectation of multiple certification, 190–91; truancy and, 22–23, 78, 202–3; on unemployment benefit, 57–59; U.S. Navy service, 56–57, 79, 119, 177, 244, 252 (n. 12); unwritten rules and practices, 190–91; vandalism incident and, 203; whites, professional meetings with, 112–17; white superintendent, relationship with, 11, 23–25, 27, 28–33, 34–35, 38–44, 67, 152, 231–33, 249 (n. 17). *See also* E. E. Butler High School; Fair Street High School; Hutchenson Elementary and High School

Caliver, Ambrose, 103
Callison, J. R., 23
Carmichael, T. A., 175–76
Carr, William, 115
Case-study approach, 234–35, 247 (n. 7), 269 (n. 3)
Caswell County High School. *See* Caswell County Training School
Caswell County Training School (CCTS), ix, 98
Cater, J. T., 86
Cedar Hill High School (Cedartown, Ga.), 127
Central High School (Louisville, Ky.), 101
Central University, 93

Cheeks, Grady, 193
City College (New York City), 92
Civil Rights Act (1964), 193
Clarion (newspaper): adult education, 221; features Byas as black representative for Gainesville to All-American Cities, 224; College Night, 211–12, 267 (n. 19); college-type schedule and, 172; Curriculum Survey and, 37; democracy and citizenship goals of, 217–19; group study halls and, 172–73; perfect attendance list in, 209–10; Principal's Message, 213–14, 215; purpose, 207, 209–10; school activities reported in, 245–46 (n. 2); student success, encouraging, 209–12; teacher professional development, 177–78
Clark, Kenneth, 105
Clark Atlanta University. *See* Clark College
Clark College, 144
Clement, Rufus E., 102, 103, 105
Codwell, John E., 95
Columbia University, 27, 98, 120, 128, 140, 197, 198; Byas completing degree at, 76, 82; Byas's experience at, 47, 48, 65, 68–75, 78, 114, 123, 168, 252 (n. 24); historically black colleges and universities and, 70, 71–72; Teachers College, 48, 68–75, 217
Cornelia High School, 150
Cousins, Robert L., 27–28, 157
Cozart, Leland S., 87, 88, 105, 110, 133, 161
Crawl, W. F., 45, 166
Curriculum Survey, at Fair Street High School, 34–44, 83, 130, 134, 174; business education and, 39, 43, 167; completion and presentation, 38–42, 80; guidance counselors and, 33, 40, 132; mass meetings to decide on, 36; newspaper publicity, 41–42, 250 (n. 47); parental involve-

ment in, 37–38, 165; publication, 38; school newspaper, use of to advertise, 37–38, 209; survey methods, 37; teacher work-groups for, 37, 161

Daily Times (Gainesville, Ga.), 42, 250 (n. 47)
Davis, Allison, 8, 100, 101, 105, 141
Davis, John W., 97, 102, 141
Dean, Elmer, 52
Decatur County, 150
Desegregation: black disappointment with results of, xi–xii, 238–39; black educators, opportunities for after, 143, 186; black professors, loss of after, 3, 14–15, 16, 122, 234; black professors and community during, 194, 223–26; Byas attending white professional meetings, 112–17; Byas dealing with, 191–92, 231–33; Byas principal of desegregated summer school, 14, 227–29, 232; civil rights laws and recognition, 193–94; at E. E. Butler High School, 162, 174, 178, 191–92, 208, 217; in Gainesville, Ga., 162, 193–94, 216, 223–25, 231–32, 233, 246 (n. 8); GTEA endorsement of *Brown*, pressures on black teachers, 151–52; increased funding for segregated schools in order to undermine, 25, 133–34, 159, 196, 213, 249 (n. 21); integration vs. desegregation, xi–xii, 231, 254 (n. 21); maintaining, 15; and whites attending GTEA meetings, blacks attending NEA meetings, 142. See also *Brown v. Board of Education*
Dewey, John, 8
Dillard, N. L., ix, 98
Division of Negro Education, Ga., 27–28, 155, 157
Dixon, Marie Hopson, 144
Dixon, Opal, 143
"Dr. Jekyll and Mr. Hyde" strategy, 24–25, 44–46, 134–35, 234, 250–51

(n. 51); used by Association, 84, 134
—used by Byas, 11; development of, 24–26; at Fair Street High School, 33–44, 159; at Hutchenson Elementary and High School, 25–33
Donaldson, Jeff, 220
Douglas County, 17, 32, 168
Douglasville, Ga., 18, 21, 25, 26, 118, 215, 243
Dress code, for black professionals, 178–79
DuBois, W. E. B., 8, 103, 141, 214, 237

East Depot High School (LaGrange, Ga.), 125, 126
Economic Opportunity Act (1964), 193
Educational Testing Service, 93, 95
Edwards, H. T., 127, 137, 170
E. E. Butler High School: adult education at, 220–21; annual homecoming, first, 207; Byas as principal of, ix, xiv, 5, 121, 224; Byas's resignation from, 233; College Board approval for advanced placement program at, 168; College Night, 211–12; college-type schedule, 170–71, 172; custodian at, 221; democracy and citizenship programs, 216–19; democratic study hall, 216–17; desegregation and, 162, 174, 178, 191–92, 208, 217; dress code for black professionals at, 178–79; dropout prevention program, 212–14; establishment, 159, 262 (n. 1); faculty meetings, 162–63, 182–84, 263–64 (n. 7); group study hall, 171–73; gymnasium, 121, 159; lesson planning, 163–65, 264 (nn. 13–14); music on intercom in school tryout, 181–82; parental involvement, 203–7, 227; PTA hosted by, 227; perfect attendance list, 209–10; policy development from faculty meetings, 163, 164–65; *Policy Statements*

in, ix, xiv, 10; Citizens' Advisory
Committee, 223; civil rights demonstrations, 225–26; *Daily Times*,
42, 250 (n. 47); desegregation be-
ginnings, 162, 193–94, 216, 223–25,
231–32, 233, 246 (n. 8); E. E. Butler
Jr., and, 159, 262 (n. 1); as finalist
for fifty-five All-American Cities,
223–24; "Morningside Hills" black
subdivision, 222; white superintendent of, 23–24, 34–35, 41–42
Gallagher, Buell Gordon, 92
Gans, Roma, 120, 140–41, 142
Georgia: "approved" black schools
in, 82–83, 125, 126, 127, 253 (n. 4),
255 (n. 34); Association of Colleges
and Secondary Schools, influence
in, 124, 125–26, 127; black educational community network, 13,
124–25, 135–36; black teachers after
World War II, 68–69, 252 (n. 20);
Byas, towns of important to, 18;
Byas as John Hay Fellowship recipient in, 177; child labor laws,
48; civics education, need for, 215,
268 (nn. 26–29); Great Depression
and, 48, 251 (n. 2); historically black
colleges and universities, 59, 60,
70, 71–72; Minimum Foundation
Education Program, 26, 31, 137, 157,
249 (n. 21), 259 (n. 27); poverty of,
74; professors and religious services, 201–2; racial equality, lack of
in, 115, 257 (n. 63); schools, early
twentieth century, 51–53, 251 (n. 7);
segregated schools of, 17–20, 24,
26, 130–35; Sibley Commission, 152;
white superintendents in, 23–24
Georgia Association of Educators, 232
Georgia Conference on Educational
Opportunities, 20
Georgia Education Association (GEA),
137–38
Georgia Institute of Technology, 143
Georgia's Divided Education (Georgia

Conference on Educational Opportunities), 20
Georgia State Department of Education, 143, 149
Georgia Teachers and Education Association (GTEA): ATA, relationship
with, 142; annual meeting (1957
Macon), 119, 120, 138–46; annual
meeting, overlapped with PTA, 195;
annual meeting, small-group meetings, 143–44; annual meetings,
143, 160–61, 259 (n. 27); annual
Principals' Conference, 155–57;
best black teacher speech at annual
meeting, 144, 147, 260 (n. 42); black
community accommodation for
meetings of, 139; black professors'
role and development in system of,
150–58, 162, 165, 261 (n. 54); Byas,
importance of to, xi, 13, 46; Byas as
assistant to executive secretary of,
233; curriculum and, 147, 155–56;
democratic participation in, 165;
and dress code, for black professionals, 179; Elementary and High
School Principals' groups, 152–55;
endorsement of *Brown* decision,
151–52; gender inequality in, 151,
261 (n. 55); Georgia Education Association (GEA) and, 137–38; guidance counseling discussion, 160;
headquarters, 136–37, 153, 238–39;
integration, approach of and, 232;
intellectual exchange at annual
meetings of, 144–45, 157–58; membership for 1957, 139; Minimum
Foundation Education Program
and, 26, 31, 137, 157, 259 (n. 27);
music and dance at annual meetings of, 145; Principals and Curriculum Organization service, regional,
155; Principals' Workshop, 152, 175;
public relations, 34, 157; regional
directors, 147, 150, 160, 260 (n. 42);
regional meeting, at Butler High

School, 159–61, 262 (n. 3); regional meetings, reflecting annual meetings of, 146–50, 157–58, 260 (n. 51); regional membership, 149, 260 (n. 47); reminiscences of members of, 238–39; Resolutions Committee, 151–52; school policy influence, 158, 262 (n. 67); structure and purpose, 135–38; teachers, encouraging higher degrees for, 252 (n. 20); teachers, high school vs. college, at meetings of, 145; teachers from Butler attending, 178; white attendees at annual meeting, 142–43. See also *Herald*

Gibbs, W. T., 102

GI Bill, 57, 65, 68, 69

Graves, John Temple, 103

Great Depression, 48

Green v. County School Board of New Kent County, xii, 246 (n. 7)

Hall, Orene, 143

Hampton Institute, 93

Handy Craftsman's Creed, 62

Harris, Abram, 103

Harris, John R., 47

Harris, Nelson, 95

Harvard Educational Review, 116, 185

Haverford College, 142

Hawes, James, Jr., 75–76, 79, 81, 82, 113, 137, 190, 199

Herald: advertisements in, as evidence of growing opportunities for black students, 143; "approved" black schools and, 125; black community accommodation for meetings and, 139; circulation, 136; on dress code for black professionals, 179; "Dr. Jekyll and Mr. Hyde" strategy and, 45; on dropouts, 145; on faculty development as professor's role, 162, 165–66; Fair Street High School featured in, 17; famous black educators writing in, 141;

gender inequality and, 151, 261 (n.55); GTEA annual meeting reported in, 144–45; GTEA annual Principals' Conference and, 261 (n. 65); GTEA county school meetings reported in, 149–50; GTEA structure and, 136; Minimum Foundation Education Program and, 26; "President's Message," 138, 160, 262–63 (n. 4); professional development support articles, 153, 154; on professors' role in GTEA system, 33, 151, 162, 165–66, 195, 261 (n. 54), 265 (nn. 15, 17); purpose, 258 (n. 19); regional GTEA reports in, 147–49, 260 (n. 47), 261 (n. 60); school principal leadership issues and, 181; science teaching and, 176, 191; surveys, report about use of, 175; teacher evaluation and, 185; teaching practices articles, 161

Hill, Oliver, 96

Historically black colleges and universities (HBCUs), 59, 60, 70, 71–72

Hollingsworth, Jerry, 178, 191–92

Holmes, O. W., 97, 255 (n. 34)

Hope, John, 10

Houston, Charles Hamilton, 96

Howard University, 9, 93, 95, 96–97, 100, 255 (nn. 30, 34)

How to Study (Science Research Associates and McGraw-Hill), 172

How to Study and How to Be a Better Student (Science Research Associates and McGraw-Hill), 172

Hudson Industrial School, 52–53, 118, 120. *See also* Ballard-Hudson High School

Huff, Bobby, 25

Hughey, Angelina, 173

Hunt, H. A., 60

Hutchenson Elementary and High School, 17, 21; adult education at, 220; "approved" under new name of R. L. Cousins High School, 82;

7–8; black college leaders and, 238; black educators for, graduating from white northern schools, 7–8; black professors being fired as integration approached, 3, 14–15, 16, 231; black professors in, 2–7, 8–10, 15–16, 24–25, 165, 236–38; black teachers' associations, 5–6, 10, 13; budgets, 131–32, 157; civics education in, need for, 7, 215, 268 (nn. 26–29); clerical and janitorial assistance, 130–31; community involvement in, 54, 194–97, 252 (n. 11); community networks in, 8–10, 14; democracy and citizenship goals, 101, 102; "Dr. Jekyll and Mr. Hyde" strategy of black principals in, 24–25; and dress code, for black professionals, 178–79; in Georgia, 17–20, 24, 26; in Georgia, early twentieth century, 51–53, 251 (n. 7); goal of full democracy for black citizens and, 6–7, 8, 10, 12–13; guidance counselors for, 33, 132–33; health and personal hygiene and, 150; historically black colleges and universities, 59, 60, 70, 71–72; increased funding for, in order to undermine integration, 25, 133–34, 159, 196, 213, 249 (n. 21); industrial education, 53, 54; Jeanes teachers and, 143, 155; libraries, 131; Minimum Foundation Education Program and, 26, 31, 137, 157, 249 (n. 21), 259 (n. 27); national agencies for, 104–6; parental involvement, 1, 2, 6, 10, 13–14, 194–203; physical education, 147–48; present attitudes to, 15–16; professional development in, 4, 6, 9, 10, 27, 81, 83, 87, 99–106, 124–25, 157, 166; professors' relationship with black communities, 194–97, 266–67 (n. 4); sanitary facilities, 147; studies on, 1–5, 247 (nn. 2, 4); teacher involve-

ment in decisions, 6, 13; white funding for, 1, 2, 7, 19–20, 45, 86–87; white superintendents and, 23–25, 45, 87, 132, 137, 182, 194, 196. *See also* Association of Colleges and Secondary Schools; Desegregation; Georgia Teachers and Education Association; School Masters Club

Segregated society: black community accommodation for meetings because of, 111, 139; and black teachers after World War II, education scholarships in, 68–69, 252 (n. 22); black veterans after World War II and, 57, 59; black wages and, 52, 57–58; conventions, difficulties faced in attending because of, 138–39; in Gainesville, Ga., 193; golf and, 225; GTEA (black) versus GEA (white), 137–38; hotels and restaurants, 89, 111, 127, 139; Miss Georgia Chick Beauty Pageant, 19; police, 219–20; race riots, 194; retail stores, 226; Southern Association (white) and Association (black), 87–92, 96–97, 227, 255 (n. 33); swimming pools, 18–19, 50, 55; in U.S. Navy, 55, 56–57, 252 (n. 12). *See also* Desegregation

Sharpe, Marie Smith Byas (Byas's mother), 118, 251 (n. 6)

Shaw University, 95

Sibley Commission, 152

Smith-Calhoun, Bettye, 125

Southern Association of Colleges and Schools: "approved" black schools, 81–83, 96, 119, 253 (nn. 4, 5); "approved" black schools, criteria, 84–87, 125–26, 129–30, 133–34, 153, 253–54 (n. 9); Association, briefly integrated with, 90, 254 (n. 21); Association, finally integrated with, 1964, 112, 232; Association, pressure on from, 161; Association, relationship with, 81–92, 106, 253 (n. 8);

Ulysses Byas Elementary School, 122, 234

U.S. Navy, 55, 56–57, 79, 119, 177, 244, 252 (n. 12)

U.S. Office of Education, 84

U.S. Supreme Court: *Brown II*, 97; *Green v. County School Board of New Kent County*, xii, 246 (n. 7). See also *Brown v. Board of Education*

University of Chicago, 73, 93

University of Georgia, 143

University of Massachusetts, Amherst, 234

University of Michigan, 61

Virginia Union University, 90, 95, 97–98, 254 (n. 20)

Vontress, Clemmont, 24–25

Voting Rights Act (1965), 193

Walker Elementary School (Athens, Ga.), 45

Wayne State University, 65

Wesley, Charles H., 103

West Virginia State College, 102

Wilkerson, J. S., 127, 134, 136–37

Wilkins, Roy, 45

World War I, 102, 256 (n. 43)

World War II, 12, 55, 79, 102–3, 119, 256 (n. 43)

Yancey, Sadie, 93

Young, Whitney, 105

DATE DUE